ECONOMICS AND PROPERTY

A Coursebook for Students

of the Built Environme

BY

Danny Myers
B.A. (Econ.) M.Sc. (Arch.)

First Published 1994

ISBN 0 7282 0199 2

Acknowledgements

During the production process of this book several important people have played key roles. I am grateful for their input and hope that they can share some pride in the final product.

Sarah Gilmore and Jill Priday typed the manuscript. Melanie Dunster, who shared my office at the University of the West of England during the two years that this project was developing, read the text and made many valuable observations to improve the clarity. Meanwhile, Ted Masters designed the layout and Pete Rogers crafted the visuals into the necessary computer format; their combined artistic talents have given the book a distinct appearance. And Alex Catalano's copy-editing skills have enhanced the accuracy of the language.

The organisations that gave permission to use their work are mainly listed on page 126, without their journal extracts the whole text would have paled into a poorer existence. The front cover is based on a thermal image produced on a special camera, manufactured by AGEMA:Infra Red Systems, Bedfordshire. Their generosity in supplying the original visual without any financial reward, has helped to keep the fixed costs within the budget. AGEMA's equipment is often used to monitor heat dissipation, which is an area of increasing importance to those concerned with buildings.

Our aim was to produce a text that would match the layout and readability of the comparable introductory books developing within the mainstream of the economics discipline. As the co-author of one of these comparables, *Economics Explained*, the people involved in that project also deserve some acknowledgement for the direction of this text; as do all the colleagues and students that I've met along the way. The list goes on for too long to mention them all by name. I only hope the same cannot be said of the mistakes that may remain within these covers.

Finally it is important to recognise that the whole task of producing the text from the manuscript stage to the book-shop distribution points has been carefully co-ordinated throughout by the team at Estates Gazette, especially Colin Greasby who was responsible for commissioning this title in October 1992.

My thanks genuinely go out to all those named, and if any copyright holder has been over-looked, I apologise and ask you to contact the publisher so that the necessary arrangements can be made.

The author and publisher gratefully acknowledge permission to publish material in chapters 1, 7 and 8 which first appeared on pages 3/4, 10, 18/19, 316–326 and 335/6 of *Economics Explained* (Collins Educational 1991, Second Edition) by Peter Maunder, Danny Myers, Nancy Wall and Roger Leroy Miller.

Designed by: Ted Masters
Typeset by: Barbers Ltd, Wrotham Kent
Printed by: Cradley Print Ltd, Warley, West Midlands

Contents

Tutorial Readings iv

Letter to the Reader v

CHAPTER 1:   An introduction to economics 1

CHAPTER 2:   Economic systems for resource allocation 9

CHAPTER 3:   The market mechanism 17

CHAPTER 4:   The theory of demand 27

CHAPTER 5:   The theory of supply 33

CHAPTER 6:   Elasticity of demand and supply 39

CHAPTER 7:   Costs of the firm: property construction, development
                          and consultancy 49

CHAPTER 8:   Theory of the firm (part 2): property construction, development
                          and consultancy 61

CHAPTER 9:   Market failures and government remedies 71

CHAPTER 10:   Managing the macroeconomy 83

CHAPTER 11:   The circular flow of income: its measurement and manipulation 89

CHAPTER 12:   From demand-side to supply-side 95

CHAPTER 13:   Inflation and expectations 101

CHAPTER 14:   Money, financial institutions and interest rates 109

CHAPTER 15:   The public-private sector debate 121

Dictionary: 135

Answers: 145

Index: 149

Tutorial Readings

Chapter 1   The built environment: the economy's shadow 6
And in the beginning there was the wealth of nations 7
The advert 8

Chapter 2   An interview with the leader of the opposition, prior to the 1992 general election 13
Wall comes tumbling down 15
Is the housing market working? 15
Architects need economic awareness 16

Chapter 3   The international property market and exchange rate mechanism 22
Transactions in the property market 24

Chapter 4   Some determinants of effective demand for property 30
Business parks: what you get is what you want? 31

Chapter 5   Finding a definition of market value for property 36
The construction industry and its new contracts 38

Chapter 6   What determines land values 46
Introducing the property cycle by bringing together elasticities 47

Chapter 7   Graveyard management 57
The costs of sick building syndrome 58
Design and build 59

Chapter 8   An alternative theory of the firm 67
Profit maximising and the price developers pay for land 68
The cement cartel has cracked up 69
34,000 pubs and what have you got? 70

Chapter 9   Professional deregulation: ARCUK — R.I.P. 79
Planning gain 79
The failing market for rented housing 80
Commercial property: cycles and leases 81

Chapter 10 The 1993 budget 86
UBR - for those not in business? 87
The problems of policy and forecasting 88

Chapter 11 Housing equity withdrawal 93
The multiplier in reverse 94
Chaos theory 94

Chapter 12 The housing market: an intermediate macroeconomic target 99
Commercial property and the construction sector 100

Chapter 13 Core inflation 106
The 'upward only' rent review clause 107
Inflation and some effects on property 108

Chapter 14 Deregulation of financial intermediaries 115
Negative equity 1988 to 19?? 116
Aspects of property finance 116
Discounted cash flow (DCF) 117
The relationship between mortgage rates and other rates in the spectrum 118
A pension fund case study: the Church Commissioners 119

Chapter 15 Designing away problems in inner city estates 126
Government housing initiatives 127
Market housing initiatives 128
A case for housing tenure reform 128
Research into occupier's requirements: the customer is king 129
Building regulations in a deregulated Britain? 129
Funding infrastructure in the 1990s 130
A letter against the privatisation of BRE 130
Problems of valuation and privatisation 131
Research and development or science fiction? 132
Demographic data 132
Changes of law: a public or private sector responsibility? 133

Estates Gazette
London, 1994

Dear Reader

<u>Ref: Guide to using this book</u>

This book has been specifically designed for students studying Economics as part of an undergraduate programme relating to Surveying, Construction, Housing, Planning, Architecture or some similar specialism leading to a profession within the built environment.

To maximise the effective use of the text it would be beneficial if you recognised right at the outset the main learning strategies that it has been designed around.

Firstly, each chapter has summaries every few pages to help clarify the main concepts that have been covered. These <u>Chapter Summaries</u> are numbered and cross-referenced to form another learning strategy of the text, namely: <u>Chapter Summaries to Review</u>. Each new chapter commences with a list of these to encourage students to look back to the relevant sections already covered and to generally highlight the integrated nature of the subject matter.

Thirdly, technical terms relating to property and economics are <u>highlighted in bold the first time they effectively appear in the text</u>. Subsequently, these essential terms, along with those shown in the headings, are gathered at the back of the book with brief definitions to form a <u>basic dictionary of economics and property</u>. (Those concepts that are central to the explanation are also <u>given detailed definitions within the main text</u> and these are identified in colour.)

Towards the latter half of each chapter two further important features occur. The sections entitled <u>Tutorial Preparation</u> are intended to encourage students to consolidate the economic content of each chapter and begin to appreciate its relevance to the built environment. These preparatory exercises either direct students towards library research or involve short practical exercises. (Where <u>definite answers</u> exist to these tasks they have been gathered right at the back of the book, just before the index.) The <u>Tutorial Readings</u> are even more applied, since they involve carefully selected extracts from the specialised professional journals and newspapers that you may one day subscribe to. These are concluded with sets of questions to prompt analysis and discussion. The Tutorial Preparation and Tutorial Reading sections that conclude each chapter could either form the focus of a tutor led seminar, or provide a package of open learning materials for students involved in a distant learning system.

Together these design features should help you master the subject quickly and pass the related exam. Our main aim, however, has been to enable the learning process to be an enjoyable and rewarding experience. We hope we have succeeded .

Good luck with your course

Danny Myers

1

An introduction to economics

Most students reading this book will eventually be involved in one stage or other of a building's life cycle, as outlined very briefly in figure 1.1. Some may be studying for jobs requiring an understanding of all 5 stages, while many others will find themselves concerned with just one specific stage, eg maintaining or refurbishing the finished product.

Figure 1.1   The stages of a building's life cycle

Five stages of a building's development	Examples of activities involved
● ACQUISITION	1 Negotiating price of land 2 Paying fees to solicitors etc 3 Organising funding for land
● DESIGN & CONSTRUCTION	4 Estimating building costs 5 Liaising with architects, quantity surveyors, engineers 6 Funding building costs
● MARKETING	7 Organising advertising 8 Liaising with letting agents 9 Sale/rent of completed building
● REPAIR & MAINTENANCE	10 Monitoring energy usage 11 Facilities management 12 May include refurbishment at some later date
● REDEVELOPMENT	13 May necessitate demolition 14 Negotiating new planning permission 15 Satisfying new Building Regulations

Underlying the building process, from conception to demolition, is a lot of economics (about 150 pages worth). Economics should not be regarded as a discipline solely related to the study of costs. The subject matter is far broader, and as this text will demonstrate, economics affects the work of all professions within the built environment.

Scarcity: The Central Problem

Economics is all about the allocation of scarce resources which have alternative uses. This is far more complex than it first appears. Many of the world's resources (factors of productions) are finite, yet people have infinite wants. We are, therefore, faced with a two-pronged problem: at any point in time there is a fixed stock of resources, set against an insatiable amount of wants. This problem is formally referred to as **scarcity**. In an attempt to reconcile this problem, economists highlight that people must make careful choices—choices about what is made, how it is made, and for whom it is made. Indeed, at its very simplest level economics is 'the science of choice'.

Resources (or Factors of Production) Are Scarce

Resources can be defined as the inputs used in the production of those things that we desire. When resources are productive, they are typically called factors of production. Indeed, some economists use the terms resources and **factors of production** synonymously. The total quantity, or stock, of resources that an economy has determines what that economy can produce. Every economy has, in varying quantities, vast amounts of different resources, or factors of production. Factors of production can be classified in many ways. One common scheme of classification includes natural, human and manufactured resources.

Natural Resources – Land and Mineral Deposits

Basically, **land** (with its inherent mineral deposits) is the natural resource we think of most often. Some land can grow very large amounts of crops without any addition of fertilizer; other land is incapable of growing anything in its natural state. Today, some economists contend that natural resources are often the least important factors of production in an economy. They believe that what is more important is the transformation of existing resources into what is truly usable by man, and that transformation requires the other types of resources—labour and capital. This point becomes understandable if we do not simply think of land as the only natural resource. The resources of the oceans and polar ice-caps are attracting increasing interest. Thus natural resources include the world's water, climate and vegetation.

Human Resources – Labour

In order to produce the things we desire, a human resource must be used. That human resource consists of the productive contributions of **labour** made by individuals who work, for example, coal miners, ballet dancers, and construction workers. The contribution of labour to the production process can be increased. Whenever potential labourers obtain schooling and training, and whenever actual labourers obtain new skills, labour's contribution to productive output will increase. When there is such an improvement to human resources we can say that there has been an increase of **human capital**.

Manufactured Resources – Capital

When labour is applied to land to grow wheat or build a house, for example, something else is used. It may be a plough, tractor or cement mixer. That is to say, land and labour are combined with manufactured resources in order to produce the things we desire. These manufactured resources are called **capital** which consists of machines and tools.

1

Another Human Resource – Entrepreneurship

There is, in effect, a fourth type of input used in production. It is a special type of human resource; it consists of entrepreneurial ability, or **entrepreneurship**. Entrepreneurship is associated with the founding of new businesses, or the introduction of new products and new techniques. But it means more than that. It also encompasses taking risks (possibly losing large sums of wealth on new ventures), inventing new methods of making existing goods and generally experimenting with any type of new thinking that could lead to a monetary benefit.

Without entrepreneurship, businesses would find it difficult to survive. Clearly, entrepreneurship as a human resource is scarce: not everyone is willing to take risks or has the ability to make successful business decisions.

We see the classification of resources in figure 1.2.

Figure 1.2   Resource classification

We can arbitrarily classify resources or factors of production into those that are natural, human and manufactured. We have denoted specific names within those three classifications.

Natural resources	Human resources	Manufactured resources
Land	**Labour and entrepreneurship**	**Capital**

Scarce resources produce what are called economic goods—the subject of our study throughout this book.

Economic Goods

Any good (or service) produced from scarce resources is also scarce and is called an economic good. Because economic goods are scarce, we constantly face decisions about how best to use them. After all, the desired quantity of an economic good, by definition, exceeds the amount that is directly available from nature at a zero or free price.

However, not all goods are economic; *some* are free.

Free Goods

There are, of course, some things that are free. We call them **free goods**, as opposed to economic goods. Not many are left. Economics textbooks used to call air a free good but that is really no longer true because, in many of the world's cities, pollution makes air unpleasant to breathe. In many mountain areas, clean air is still a free good (once you are there); you can have as much as you want at a zero or free price and so can anybody else who bothers to hike up to where you are. There is no scarcity involved. Who is interested in free goods then? Certainly not most economists. Perhaps physicists, hydrologists, biologists and chemists are interested in free air and water, but the economist steps in only when the problem of scarcity arises and people become concerned about how to use the scarce resource. We have seen throughout our history that as population and production increase, many 'free' goods become 'economic' goods, such as land for mining, water and air for industrial uses, and water for hydroelectric power. To the native American Indians, tobacco leaves were a free good: the Indians could have all that they wanted. After Sir Walter Raleigh, however, tobacco leaves became (and remain) an economic good.

Choice

Scarcity forces us to choose. You have to choose whether to carry on at school or go to work. If you take a job then you must give up taking unemployment pay. You have to choose between going out on a date or studying. Government policy-makers have to choose between using resources to produce military goods or say, more educational services. In fact, the concept of choice forms the basis of our formal definition of **economics.**

Economics is the social science studying human behaviour and, in particular, the way in which individuals and societies choose among the alternative uses of limited resources to satisfy unlimited wants.

As we see throughout our study of economics, the choices we make affect not only how we live today, but how we will live in the future. Moreover, the choices that we can make are constrained not only by scarcity but also by political, legal, traditional and moral forces. In other words, there are many non-economic forces that influence our decision-making processes. In this text, however, we will concentrate on how economic forces affect our choices–especially those choices that affect the built environment.

Chapter Summary 1.1

- **Economics is a broad subject impinging on many stages of a building's life cycle.**

- **Scarcity is a two-sided concept with competing wants on one side set against limited resources on the other.**

- **We use scarce resources, such as land, capital and entrepreneurship, to produce economic goods.**

- **Economic goods are those that are desired but are not directly obtainable from nature to the extent demanded or desired.**

- **Scarcity requires us to choose and economics is the study of how we make those choices.**

Scarcity and Opportunity Cost

Analytically it is necessary to consider carefully the definition of scarcity: every individual has competing wants but cannot satisfy all of them given limited resources. Therefore, a choice must be made. When that choice is made something that is also desired has to be foregone. In other words, in a world of scarcity, every want that ends up being satisfied results in some other want, or wants, remaining unsatisfied.

Choosing one thing therefore, inevitably implies that another possible opportunity has been missed, lost or foregone. To highlight this dilemma economists refer to the concept of **opportunity cost.**

Let us assume that of all the other things you could have done instead of reading this book, the thing you *most* wanted to do, but did not do, was to watch television. If that is the case, then watching television is the opportunity cost of reading this book. Opportunity cost is defined as the highest valued alternative that had to be sacrificed for the option that was chosen. Opportunity cost is a powerful concept that allows us to place a value on the resources that are used to produce something.

The Trade-offs Facing you

Whatever you do, you are trading off one use of a resource for one or more alternative uses. The value of these **trade-offs** is represented by the opportunity cost just discussed. Let us examine the opportunity cost of reading this book. Assume that you have a maximum of four hours per week to spend studying just two topics—economics and construction technology. The more you study economics, the higher will be your expected grade; the more you study construction technology, the higher will be your expected grade in that subject. There is a trade-off, then, between spending one more hour reading this book and spending that hour studying construction technology. This can be illustrated in a graph that shows the trade-off involved.

Graphical Analysis

In figure 1.3 we have put the expected grade in construction technology on the vertical axis and the expected grade in economics on the horizontal axis. In this simplified world, if you spend all your time on economics, you will get a B in the course but you will fail construction technology. On the other hand, if you spend all your time on construction technology you will get a B in that subject and you will fail economics. The trade-off is a special case: one to one. A one-to-one trade-off means that in this case the opportunity cost of receiving one grade higher in economics (for example, improving from a D to a C) is one grade lower in construction technology (falling from a D to an E in our example).

Production Possibility Curve

The diagram in figure 1.3 shows the relationship between the possible results that can be produced in each of two activities, depending on how much time you choose to put into each activity. Economists call this kind of diagram a **production possibility curve.***

If you consider that what you are producing is a grade when you study economics and construction technology then figure 1.3 can be related to the production possibilities that you face. The line that goes from B on one axis to the B on the other therefore becomes a production possibility curve. It is defined as all possible combinations of the maximum amount of any two goods or services that can be produced from a fixed amount of resources. In the example, your study time is limited to four hours per week. The two possible outputs are grades in construction technology and grades in economics. The particular production possibility curve presented in figure 1.3 is a graphic representation of the opportunity cost of studying one more hour in one subject. It is a *straight-line production possibility curve*, which is a special case. (The more general case will be discussed next.)

Society's Choice

The straight-line production possibility curve in figure 1.3 can be generalised to demonstrate the related concepts of scarcity, choice and trade-offs facing an entire nation. You may have already heard the phrase, 'guns or butter'. Implicit in that phrase is that at any point in time a nation can either have more military

---

*Other terms used for production possibility curves are: production possibility frontier, production possibility boundary, production possibilities curve and transformation curve.

Figure 1.3 Production possibility curve for grades in construction technology and economics

On the vertical axis, we measure the expected grade in construction technology, on the horizontal axis, the expected grade in economics. We assume that there are only 4 hours in total time that can be spent per week on studying. If all 4 hours are spent on economics, a B is received in economics and an F in construction technology. If all 4 hours are spent on construction technology, a B is received in that subject and an F in economics. There is a one-to-one trade-off. If the student is at point x, equal time (2 hours a week) is spent on both courses and equal grades of D will be received. If a higher grade in economics is desired, the student may go to point y where 1 hour is spent on construction technology and 3 hours on economics and receive a C in economics, but an E in construction technology.

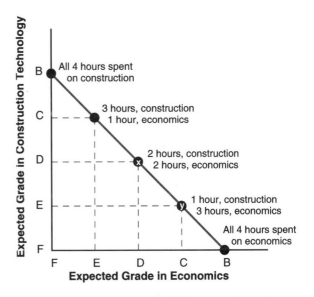

goods (guns) or civilian goods (butter) but it cannot achieve producing more of both—given the existing level of resources. Let us develop this type of explanation by considering the construction of a building on a parcel of land in Hyde Park, London. We shall assume that there are only two types of building that may be viable from a planning context. In figure 1.4 (panel a) is a hypothetical numerical table of trade-offs expressed in terms of square feet allocated to car parking or retail facilities. If no car parking facilities are provided, the whole building may be dedicated to retail outlets. On the other hand, no resources may be allocated to the retail sector and the whole building may be used as car park. In between there are various possible combinations. These combinations are plotted as points A, B, C, D and E in figure 1.4 (panel b). If these points are connected, a production possibility curve is created demonstrating the trade-off between the production of either a car park or retail area. These trade-offs occur on the production possibility curve.

Assumptions Underlying the Production Possibility Curve

There are a number of assumptions underlying this particular curve. Firstly, we are referring to one particular plot of land (production possibility curves always refer to a given set of resources). Secondly, we assume that the state of technology does not change. Therefore, no earth-shaking invention could significantly reduce the cost of

Figure 1.4   A trade-off between car parking and retail units on a parcel of land

Production is measured in square feet. We look at five combinations from A to E. The first one, A, involves the production of no retail space, which allows us—using all of our resources—to produce 48,000 sq ft of car parking space. At the other extreme, combination E, no car parking facilities are produced, therefore using resources to their maximum, 40,000 sq ft of shops can be built. These combinations are given in panel (a). The combinations A to E are plotted on the graph in panel (b). Connecting the points A to E with a smooth line gives a production possibility curve for car parking and retail outlets.

Panel (a)

Combination	Car Parking (square feet)	Retail Units (square feet)
A	48000	0
B	38000	14000
C	32000	24000
D	16000	36000
E	0	40000

Panel (b)

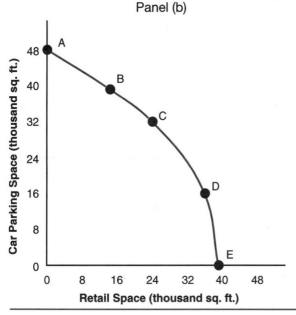

Figure 1.5   Shifting production possibility curve

In panel (a), we see that improved productivity will shift the entire production possibility curve outwards over time. In panel (b), a reduced amount of labour available to the economy will shift the entire production possibility curve inwards over time.

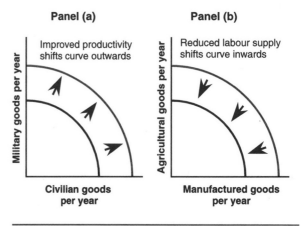

Why the Production Productivity Curve is Bowed Outward

In the example in figure 1.3, the trade-off between a grade in construction technology and a grade in economics was one to one. The trade-off ratio was fixed. That is to say, the production possibility curve is a straight line which, as we pointed out before, is a special case. Figure 1.4 is the more general case, showing a bowed production possibility curve. This highlights that some resources are better suited to the production of some things than they are for other things. In other words, resources are not as a rule equally adaptable to alternative uses. Consequently we do not experience a constant opportunity cost ratio, as we suggested between economics and construction technology. Indeed, the general rule is entirely the opposite: as society takes more and more resources and applies them to the production of any specific item the opportunity cost for each additional unit produced increases at an increasing rate. This rule is formally referred to as the **law of increasing opportunity costs.**

For example, in the discussion illustrated in figure 1.4, we need to appreciate that having just a few parking spaces on the roof would be more than proportionately resource intensive, since ramps would have to be provided throughout the building for entry and exit. Car parking spaces and retail outlets cannot, therefore, be traded one for one. This feature recurs in many decision-making scenarios, since all resources have different qualities. Thus concentrating more and more on one type of good or service often necessitates the use of less efficient resources for that purpose. As a rule of thumb, therefore, the more highly specialised resources are, the more bowed society's production possibility curve will be.

Scarcity Revisited

We have emphasised that productive resources are limited. Thus we must make choices about how we use them. We have to decide how much of which goods we will produce with our resources. For our purposes here, there will be only two choices: those goods that we consume directly, called **consumer goods**—food, clothes, cars—and those that we consume indirectly, called **capital goods**—machines, buildings and equipment. Everyone acts as a consumer in using consumer goods. On the other hand, capital goods, such as lathes, factories and engines are used to make the consumer goods to which we have just referred.

one or other of the building's uses (production possibility curves are always constructed on the assumption that factors remain constant). Indeed, if any of the factors of production changed in quality or quantity, then the production possibility curve will shift. Any improvement in technology will move the whole curve outwards to the right as shown in figure 1.5 (panel a) where we present a trade–off between military and civilian goods. Any significant reduction in the labour force, all other things held constant, will shift the entire production possibility curve inwards to the left as in Figure 1.5 (panel b) where we present a trade–off between agricultural or manufactured goods. The important point to notice from these varied examples is that production possibility curves can be used to illustrate the trade-offs that occur when considering the use of *any* set of resources. The resources will always be scarce in relation to the amount of wants they may satisfy. Consequently choices will have to be made.

Ideally the aim is to operate on the production possibility curve. Achieving combinations that lie inside the curve means that the resources concerned are not being fully utilised. This could be due to unemployment. Points beyond the production possibility frontier are impossible to achieve during the present time – period and are targets for the future. This could be achieved by improving technology.

Whenever we use productive resources to make capital goods, we are implicitly forgoing current consumption. We are waiting for some time in the future to consume the fruits that will be reaped from the use of capital goods. Indeed, if we were to produce only consumer goods now and no capital goods, then our capacity to produce consumer goods in the future would suffer. Here we see a trade-off, one which lends itself to the sort of graphical analysis that we have used already in this chapter.

Chapter Summary 1.2

- In a world of scarcity, satisfaction of one want necessarily means the non–satisfaction of other possible wants.

- Any use of a resource involves an opportunity cost because an alternative use, by necessity, was sacrificed (foregone).

- Trade-offs are represented graphically by a production possibility curve showing the maximum output combinations obtainable over a one-year period from a given set of resources.

- Points outside the production possibility curve are unattainable; points inside represent an inefficient use or under–utilisation of available resources.

- Since many resources are better suited for certain productive tasks than for others, society's production possibility curve is bowed outwards reflecting the law of increasing opportunity cost.

- Consumer goods are used directly by consumers.

- Capital goods are the means by which consumer goods are produced and are not directly used by consumers.

Microeconomics versus Macroeconomics

Economics is typically divided into two types of analysis: **microeconomics** and **macroeconomics**. Consider the definitions of the two terms.
Microeconomics is the study of individual decision–making by households and firms. Macroeconomics is the study of economy-wide phenomena resulting from group decision-making in all markets. As such, it deals with the economy as a whole.

The best way to understand the distinction between microeconomics and macroeconomics is to consider some examples. Microeconomic analysis would tackle the effects of changes in the price of petrol relative to other energy sources. It would be involved in the examination of the effects of new taxes on a specific type of property. If rent controls were reinstituted in the UK, how individual tenants and landlords would react to such controls would be in the realm of microeconomics. The raising of wages by an effective union strike would be analysed using the tools of microeconomics.

On the other hand, questions relating to the rate of inflation, the amount of national unemployment, the growth of production in the whole economy and numerous other economy-wide subjects all fall into the realm of macroeconomic analysis. In other words, macroeconomics deals with so-called *aggregates* or totals, such as total output in an economy. It is a study, therefore, of aggregate behaviour rather than individual behaviour.

You should be aware, however, of the blending together of microeconomics and macroeconomics in modern economic theory. Modern economists are increasingly using microeconomic analysis—the study of

decision-making by individuals and by firms—as the basis of macroeconomic analysis. They do this because, even though aggregates are being examined in macroeconomic analysis, the groups are made up of individual households and firms. Consider an example: some (macro) economists believe that reducing income tax rates will lead to greater total output. Why? Because, using microeconomic analysis, they predict that individuals will respond to lower income tax rates by working longer, taking fewer holidays and taking on second jobs. The task is then to establish whether empirical evidence supports these predictions.

Positive versus Normative Economics—What is versus What Ought To Be

Economics is a social science; it uses *positive* analysis. This is a scientific term that relates to the value-free nature of the inquiry; no subject or 'gut' feelings enter into the analysis. Positive analysis relates to basic statements, such as *if A, then B*. For example, if the price of petrol goes up relative to all other prices, then the amount that people will buy will fall. That is a positive economic statement. It is a statement of *what is*. It is not a statement of anyone's value-judgement or subjective feelings. 'Hard' sciences, such as physics and chemistry, are considered to be virtually value-free. After all, how can someone's values enter into a theory of molecular behaviour? But economists face a different problem. They deal with the behaviour of individuals, not molecules. Thus, it is more difficult to stick to what we consider to be value-free or **positive economics** without reference to our feelings.

When our values come into the analysis, we enter the realm of **normative economics**, or normative analysis, which is defined as analysis containing whether explicitly or implicitly, someone's values. A positive economic statement is: 'If the price of books goes up, people will buy less'. If we add to that analysis the statement 'and therefore we *should* not allow the price to go up', we have entered the realm of normative economics; we have expressed a personal opinion or value-judgement. In fact, any time you see the word *should*, you will know that values are entering into the discussion.

The world of value-judgements is the world in which individuals' preferences are at issue. Each of us desires for different things: we have different values. When we express a value-judgement, we are simply saying that we prefer, like, or desire. Since individual values are quite diverse, we expect—and indeed observe—people expressing widely varying value-judgements about how the world should or ought to be.

A Warning

It is easy to define positive economics. It is quite another matter to catch all unlabelled normative statements in a textbook like this one, even though an author goes over the manuscript many times before it is printed. Therefore, do not get the impression that a textbook author will be able to keep personal values out of the book. They will slip through. In fact, the choice itself of which topics to include in an introductory textbook involves normative economics. There is no value-free or objective way to decide which ones to use. The author's 'gut feelings' ultimately make a difference when choices have to be made. From your own personal standpoint, what you might hope to do is to be able to recognise *when* you are engaging in normative as opposed to positive economic analysis. Reading this text should equip you for that task.

- Microeconomics involves the study of *individual* decision–making.

- Macroeconomics involves the study of *aggregates*.

- Modern economic theory often involves blending these two branches together.

- Positive economics indicates what *is*, whereas normative economics tells us what *ought* to be.

Tutorial Preparation

1 Begin a glossary of terms, by attempting to define in your own words the concepts shown in bold print in chapter 1.

2 Look up various definitions of economics and/or try and phrase your own definition.

3 Try and identify in your own words the relevance of economics to your particular course specialism.

Tutorial Reading

The Built Environment: The Economy's Shadow

The most powerful image of a booming economy is a building site, bustling with cranes and hard hats. The strongest symbol of a slump is an empty office block, plastered with 'to let' signs. The property business cycle seems to exaggerate what is happening to jobs, incomes and prices in the economy generally.

As cynical investment analysts have remarked, if you can see more than 12 cranes from your office window you are probably witnessing the start of the next recession.

When new buildings find no tenants, the consequences multiply. Not only do construction workers loose their jobs, nor is it just that there is a fall in demand for cement, bricks, steel and glass.

The ramifications quickly involve the rest of the economy. To take one example: during the 1980's bankers rushed into property to finance lending. In Britain alone, bank lending to property companies rose from less than £7bn in 1985 to almost £40bn in 1989. But eventually the bubble burst. By 1992 record numbers of bankruptcies existed in the industry.

While the buildings were going up, they were a marvel. Completed, they were a nightmare. Empty factories and offices produce no income; bank interest goes unpaid; the banks themselves begin to suffer.

Once property assets loose value, banks have to rein in their lending to everybody, not just to those cursed property men. Tighter credit tips economies into recession—nobody expands into new offices and factories. So the burst bubble in the property sector floods the other sectors of the economy.

Economies are, therefore, first boosted by construction, then damned by it. Consequently many economists believe the construction and property sectors provide good advance warning of future trends for the general economy.

Source: Adapted and extended from: 'Growth's dead weight' *The Economist* 15 June 1991.

Questions

1 What is the opportunity cost of the empty factories and offices?

2 Using some of the goods mentioned in the article, give examples of capital goods.

3 Why would a trade–off graph between office development and agricultural development not produce a straight line?

4 a) Using a production possibility curve explain the trade-off between different types of building (eg housing and offices)

b) How may this specific curve be shifted outwards to the right?

5 Why do the general business cycle and the construction industry cycle not move simultaneously?

6 State four ways that the construction and property sectors could be regarded as central to an economy.

7 State three ways that you anticipate the study of economics will benefit your future professional career.

8 What do you understand by the title given to this first tutorial reading?

Tutorial Reading

And in the Beginning There was the Wealth of Nations

Government expenditure depends on the wealth generated by the community that it represents. For example, we can not afford more hospitals, more social housing provision and more education until the community has generated the wealth to pay for them. Underlying this type of comment is the notion that there are separate 'wealth-producing' and 'wealth-consuming' sectors in every economy.

The wealth-producing sector, however, is difficult to define. One definition springs from an ancient idea (*mercantilism*) that wealth is what we earn from overseas and so is generated by exporting industries. Conversely, of course, importing is wealth-consuming. This is a clear distinction but an erroneous one. It suggests that a country

so well endowed that it is self-sufficient can generate no wealth!

Later on, wealth production came to be associated with industrial production and this is the view which is still widely held today. In this case, the 'wealth-producing sector' is taken to mean a rough amalgam of manufacturing, mining and agriculture. What they have in common is that they produce material goods and sell them on the open market.

The service sector of the economy is not so easily classified. It clearly produces no material goods, at least not directly, and so must be part of the wealth-consuming sector. But parts of the service sector are widely regarded as wealth-producing (eg the Stock Exchange and banks). This is probably because these services support the

manufacturing sector and so are indirectly productive.

This apparent distinction between wealth-producing and wealth-consuming leads to the idea that wealth producers have a priority status in society, since their activities seem to be a pre-condition for wealth consumption to occur. For example, we cannot provide more social housing until we have produced (and sold) more motor cars.

The implications of this view are wide and significant, and need careful consideration—especially if we are to understand the role that economists play in society today.

Source: Adapted from 'The wealth-producing sector' *The Economic Review* April 1992

Questions

1 The views expressed in the extract may be mistaken. To consider them carefully state your opinion of the following two questions.

a) Would the production of council housing be considered as wealth-consuming or wealth-producing?

b) Would the production of government-subsidised office units be considered as wealth-consuming or wealth-producing?

2 Using the concept of opportunity cost, consider activities that are wealth-consuming or wealth-producing, and discuss which are more important to an economy.

3 Using a production possibility curve, explain why it may be important for an economy to aim at shifting the curve to the right.

4 How may your degree specialism be regarded as important to the whole economy?

5 What relevance does the title of this reading have for the history of economics? (Hint: Adam Smith)

6 a) In today's terms, how would you define economics?

b) Can you identify any connections between the definition you have stated and the seemingly conflicting goals of wealth-consuming and wealth-producing activities?

Tutorial Reading

The Advert

Some insight into your future career can be gleaned by studying the job pages. For example, consider the following advertisement taken from *Estates Gazette* in April 1992 and answer the following questions.

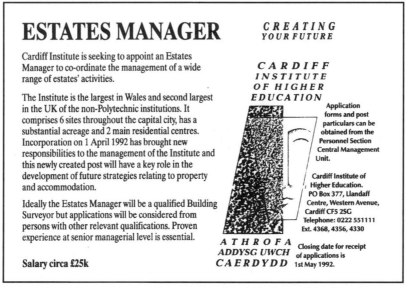

ESTATES MANAGER

CREATING YOUR FUTURE

CARDIFF INSTITUTE OF HIGHER EDUCATION

Cardiff Institute is seeking to appoint an Estates Manager to co-ordinate the management of a wide range of estates' activities.

The Institute is the largest in Wales and second largest in the UK of the non-Polytechnic institutions. It comprises 6 sites throughout the capital city, has a substantial acreage and 2 main residential centres. Incorporation on 1 April 1992 has brought new responsibilities to the management of the Institute and this newly created post will have a key role in the development of future strategies relating to property and accommodation.

Ideally the Estates Manager will be a qualified Building Surveyor but applications will be considered from persons with other relevant qualifications. Proven experience at senior managerial level is essential.

Salary circa £25k

Application forms and post particulars can be obtained from the Personnel Section Central Management Unit.

Cardiff Institute of Higher Education. PO Box 377, Llandaff Centre, Western Avenue, Cardiff CF5 2SG Telephone: 0222 551111 Ext. 4368, 4356, 4330

ATHROFA ADDYSG UWCH CAERDYDD

Closing date for receipt of applications is 1st May 1992.

Source: *Estates Gazette* Reproduced by permission of Cardiff Institute of Higher Education

Questions

1   State some reasons why this estate manager should ideally be a qualified building surveyor.

2   What would the 'other relevant qualifications' suggested in the final paragraph possibly entail?

3   How may a study of economics help prepare someone for this type of work?

4   How much would the estate manager be paid if the advert appeared today?

2 Economic systems for resource allocation

Chapter Summaries to Review

- *Scarcity (1.1)*
- *Scarce Resources (1.1)*
- *Trade-offs (1.2)*
- *Production Possibility Curve (1.2)*

Because we live in a world of scarcity, we have to make decisions about how resources should be allocated. To take a surrealistic example, when you open your front door in the early morning, there are not millions and millions of full milk bottles covering the neighbour's lawn. Neither is there no milk. There is just enough bottled milk to meet the demands: say, the two pints your neighbour ordered. This represents an effective allocation of resources. What this chapter will explain is: how does this fine tuning of agricultural resources occur, given the multitude of other products that also need to be decided upon?

The problems of **resource allocation** are solved by the **economic system** at work in a nation. Resource allocation involves answering the three questions of *what, how and for whom* goods and services will be produced. That is economists study: who gets what, (when) and how? The answers they discover vary around the world, according to the economic system employed.

Economic Systems: Two Extremes

In general terms we can envisage the nations of the world tending towards one of two basic economic model systems. Each of these **models** brings together producers and consumers in different ways and each needs to be appreciated in order to understand how the universal questions about resource allocation are resolved.

In figure 2.1 we begin our presentation of the economic systems of the world by introducing two extremes: the **free market model** and the **centrally planned model** (along with two exemplar nations).

Figure 2.1 A spectrum of economic systems

On the extreme right-hand side of the diagram is the free market model, and on the extreme left-hand side, the centrally planned model. Albania is a country whose system closely resembles the centrally planned model. On the other extreme is Hong Kong, which comes close to the free market model. In between are the mixed economies of the remaining nations of the world.

The Free Market Model

The free market system is typically characterised by limited government involvement in the economy, coupled with private ownership of the means of production. In other words, individuals pursue their own self-interests without government constraints: the system is decentralised.

An important feature of this system is therefore **free enterprise**. This exists when private individuals are allowed to obtain resources to organise those resources and to sell the resulting product in any way they choose. In other words, neither the government nor other producers can put up obstacles or restrictions to block a business person's choice in the matter of purchasing inputs and selling outputs.

Additionally, all members of the economy are free to choose what to do. Workers may enter any line of work for which they are qualified, and consumers buy the goods and services that they feel are best for them. The ultimate voter in the capitalist system is the consumer, who votes with pounds and decides which product 'candidates' will survive. That is, there is **consumer sovereignty** in that the final purchaser of products and services determines what is produced.

Another central feature of the free market economy is the **price mechanism**. Prices are used to signal the value of individual resources, acting as a kind of 'guidepost' which resource owners (producers and consumers) refer to when they make choices. The flow-chart in figure 2.2 introduces how the price mechanism works. For example, when supply exceeds demand a price change occurs which brings the producers and consumers into harmony. This is precisely what happens during the January sales: the price of stock that has not been previously sold is reduced, to the point where demand is sufficient to clear the market. Conversely, when demand exceeds supply, the price of the good in question will rise until the market is in balance. This may be seen at a property auction where, to begin with, several buyers compete for a specific property: together they bid the price up, until finally there is only one interested party prepared to pay the purchase price to the **vendor**.

Prices can thus be seen to generate signals in all markets (including factor markets): they provide information, they affect incentives, they enable buyers and sellers to express opinions. And, providing that prices are allowed to change freely, they will ultimately bring an economy into balance, where there is neither excess demand nor excess supply.

Figure 2.2   A flow-chart showing the price mechanism at work

Price movements co-ordinate the decision-making processes of consumers and producers. When supply exceeds demand, the price of a product will need to fall for the market to clear. Conversely, if demands exceeds supply the price of the product will rise. For the price mechanism to function in all markets, it is important that resources are owned privately and can move freely between competing uses.

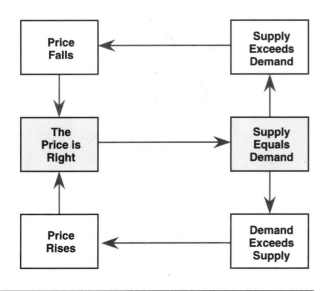

It may be self-evident by now that other terms used to describe the free market economy are 'market' or 'capitalist' economy.

Summary: What? How? For Whom?

What. In a free market economy, the consumers ultimately determine what will be produced by their pattern of spending (their voting in the market-place). As far as producers are concerned, their motivation as to what goods are produced is determined by the search for profits.

How. Since resources can substitute for one another in the production process, the free market system must decide how to produce a commodity once society votes for it. Producers will be guided (by the discipline of the market-place) to combine resources in the cheapest way possible for a particular standard or quality. Those firms that combine resources in the most efficient manner will earn the highest profits and force losses on their competitors. Competitors will be driven out of business or forced to combine resources in the same way as the profit makers.

For Whom. The 'for whom' question is concerned with the distribution of goods after production. How is the pie divided? In a free market economy, production and distribution are closely linked because incomes are generated as goods are produced. People get paid according to their productivity; that is, a person's income reflects the value that society places on that person's resources. Since income largely determines one's share of the output 'pie', what people get out of the free market economy is based on what they put into it. The only exceptions to this rule are the recipients of state benefits, such as the handicapped and elderly, who are not capable of contributing to the productive process.

The Centrally Planned Model

A centrally planned system (also referred to as a 'command economy') is typically characterised by a dominant government sector, coupled with the common ownership of resources. In other words, there is a central planning authority that takes the place of the price mechanism in allocating resources. The precise nature of a central planning authority depends upon the political system in the economy concerned. Indeed it is worth noting that the terms 'socialist' or 'communist' properly refer to political systems and not economic systems. In fact, a right-wing dictatorship could operate a centrally planned economic system as effectively as a left-wing commune.

The common motivation for having a centrally planned system is the conviction that government commands are more likely to produce the 'right' mix of output, while the market mechanism may seem to operate in favour of the rich. Central planning creates the opportunity to direct resources to the society's most pressing needs, without the distraction of conspicuous consumption. As J. K. Galbraith, a respected American economist, once observed: one of the few saving graces of the disintegrating communist economies is that nearly everyone has some kind of home, whereas many capitalist economies have not yet resolved the problem of providing affordable housing for the poor.

The flow-diagram in figure 2.3 outlines what a centrally planned system might involve. The three-stage process shown is a simplification of a bureaucratic reality. For instance, at stage one, various planning committees will exist to consider specific economic sectors and/or geographic areas. Similarly (at stage two), the production targets and wages would not necessarily arise as direct commands but will be 'negotiated' with factory officials, workers, management and others involved in the chain of production. Finally, by stage three, the plans may have become fraught with many difficulties, to the extent that there may be shortages and/or surpluses.

Today, the difficulties of formulating and implementing central plans have made many of those involved in government-orientated systems look with envy to the efficiency of the market mechanism. This will be dealt with in the subsequent section on mixed economies; but you must first understand the centrally planned system in case it appears in one guise or another during your professional career.

Figure 2.3   A flow-diagram showing the general principles of a centrally planned (model) economy

For such a system to work, the resources need to be centrally owned and controlled.

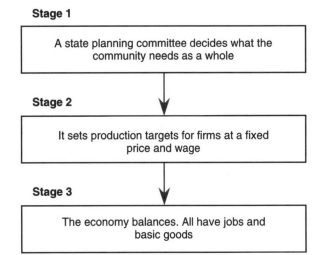

Stage 1

| A state planning committee decides what the community needs as a whole |

Stage 2

| It sets production targets for firms at a fixed price and wage |

Stage 3

| The economy balances. All have jobs and basic goods |

Summary: What? How? For whom?

What. In a centrally planned economy the collective preference and wisdom of the central planners ultimately determine what is produced.
How. The central planners decide on the methods of production. This means that they need to know how many resources to allocate to each industry, many of which inter-relate.
For whom. The forces that determine the relative rewards people get from producing are set by the central planners rather than the market. Thus market forces are not all-important in determining factor rewards. There may be more opportunity to achieve some kind of equality.

Chapter Summary 2.2

- The centrally planned (model) economy relies on government commands rather than decentralised markets. It is also referred to as a command economy.

- The political character of a centrally planned economy is indeterminate.

- The key attributes of a centrally planned (model) economy are: (1) the government owns and controls most of the resources; (2) production targets are identified by a planning committee; (3) the rewards for producing are usually set by the state rather than the market; (4) there is a desire to achieve the 'right' mix of output.

- In any centrally planned system there are problems co-ordinating the different sectors.

- The difficulties of formulating and implementing the central plans have caused many command economies to take an interest in the market mechanism.

The Mixed Economy

The two economic systems already introduced in this chapter do not exist in a pure form. The economic models used are simplified representations of the real world. In practice, most economic systems are far more complex; countries are neither purely free-market in their orientation nor purely planned. In the complex setting of everyday life, all nations have a **mixed economy**. Economists do not, therefore, end up studying systems where activities of consumers and producers interact freely through a market or simply according to government plans. Economists study systems which contain mixtures of private decision-making and central organisation; the private decisions (being made in response to market forces) exist alongside the centralised controls of state legislation and economic plans.

One way of comparing the range of economic systems that exist in the world is to consider them located on a spectrum such as that in figure 2.1. We reserve this actual exercise for tutorial preparation but clearly all economies of the real world are mixed economies; some may come close to one or other of the economic models, but no nation will fit precisely into the pure planned or pure free market category. Reserving the spectrum exercise provides educational value, it also excuses us from presenting out of date information. During the last two decades there has been considerable movement along the spectrum. For example, under the influence of **perestroika**, economies of the Eastern Bloc are shifting slowly away from the pure centrally planned model, while many European economies (particularly Britain) are shifting towards the free market model under the influence of privatisation and **deregulation**.

Economies shifting in this way reflect changes in national aspirations and culture. Indeed, the transition of command economies during the 1990s has attracted considerable news coverage. Russia and China, for instance, have both tried to harness some of the efficiency of the market mechanism in an attempt to raise the standard of living of the Russian and Chinese people. Consequently, the government's role in these nations has been reduced during recent years.

These changes to the economic system have not gone unchallenged. For example, the Soviet Congress gave Gorbachov only 59 percent of its votes in 1990, even though he was the sole candidate for president. In East Germany, only 48 percent of the voters chose the coalition that advocated radical reform and union with West Germany. China rejected restructuring if it meant destroying the socialist principles upon which the country was built.

Similarly, in the UK the public-private sector mixture has varied over time because of the differing philosophies that the main political parties have towards state intervention. The desirability of less or more public ownership of industry has long been at the heart of the political divide between the Labour and Conservative parties. The Labour Party has generally aspired to an extension of the public sector in the pursuit of socialist ideals. The Conservative Party has broadly opposed this and, indeed, tried to reduce the influence of the state in favour of market-orientated efficiency.

Chapter Summary 2.3

- In reality all economies are mixed economies, since elements of private markets and state coexist in all nations.

- It is the 'degree' of market orientation or of state intervention that distinguishes one economic system from another.

- Economies of the world are in a state of flux and political views will continue to bring change.

Equity versus Efficiency

Much of the opposition to market reforms relates to the issue of social justice. There are certainly many inequalities spawned by the market mechanism. For example, those with the greatest wealth have most 'votes' about what is produced, while those with no incomes, if left to fend for themselves, get nothing.

On the other hand, the market mechanism does provide an elaborate system of communication between producers and consumers that effectively signals 'what' to produce and 'how'.

The concepts of **equity** and **efficiency** relate to these two features of market-driven economies and will enable us to consider one final time the recurring resource allocation questions of 'what', 'how' and 'for whom'.

Efficiency

In economics, efficiency is mainly concerned with resolving the questions of 'what' to produce and 'how'. The concept is accordingly often divided into two parts—**productive efficiency** and **allocative efficiency**, both of which are satisfied in a pure free market economy.

Productive Efficiency

Productive efficiency means using production techniques that do not waste inputs. In other words, we can assume that within the market economy businesses will never waste inputs: they will not use 10 units of capital, 10 units of labour, and 10 units of land when they could produce the same amount of output with only 8 units of capital, 7 units of labour and 9 units of land. Productive efficiency therefore refers to output that is produced at the lowest possible cost. It depends upon managers responding 'correctly' to the various input prices facing them. The more expensive the inputs, the more incentive managers have to economise using them. The market signals, therefore, 'how' production should technically occur.

Allocative Efficiency

This concept relates to maximising the total value (sometimes called utility) of our available resources. That means that resources are moved to their highest-valued uses, as evidenced by consumers' willingness to pay for the final products. The process of demand and supply guides resources to their most efficient uses. Individuals as business people seeking their own self-interest end up—consciously or unconsciously—generating maximum economic value for society. 'What' is produced, therefore, should involve no welfare losses; the utility of all groups in society should have been considered.

Equity

Equity does not, in its economic sense, simply mean 'equality'. In our context, equity relates to 'fairness' and 'social justice'. From an economist's point of view, therefore, discussions of equity become closely related to considerations of income and wealth distribution: the 'for whom' question.

Equity may also be broken down into two parts—**horizontal equity** and **vertical equity**—both of which depend upon government intervention.

Horizontal Equity

This concept involves government policy aimed at treating people identically. For example, a government system of horizontal equity would support equal opportunities between people of identical qualifications and experience, regardless of race or gender.

Vertical Equity

This concept is more contentious, since it is concerned with being 'fair' by providing different government support to different categories of people. Vertical equity, therefore, is about reducing the gap between the 'haves' and the 'have-nots'. This basically involves taxing the rich to pay for the poor.

It is clear from the explanations above that equity and efficiency are not comfortable bed–partners. In fact, they may be as distant as the two economic models we began with. This is shown in figure 2.4 where we employ a similar spectrum to that of figure 2.1, but this time in the extreme left-hand box we have located the concept of equity and in the extreme right-hand box, the concept of efficiency.

Figure 2.4   A spectrum showing the trade-off between equity and efficiency

Following the format of figure 2.1 we now show on the extreme right-hand side of the diagram the concept of efficiency, and on the extreme left-hand side is the concept of equity. Ghosting through are the original economic systems that were located in the boxes; these help to explain why the qualities of equity and efficiency experience a trade-off relationship.

The implication is that to foster efficiency, free market behaviour should be encouraged, and conversely, to achieve equity requires more government intervention. It is the trade-off between these two qualities that, to some extent, accounts for the changes that nations are experiencing with their economic systems. The equity–efficiency trade-off certainly explains why all nations have mixed economies.

We shall review the qualities of 'efficiency' and 'equity' again in the final chapter. By then, you should have a more sophisticated understanding of economics and its policy applications in the UK. You will also have developed professional values which will enable you to recognise that economists are more confident in making recommendations about efficiency than equity. Social, political and philosophical attitudes will also impinge upon your future careers and the decisions you make.

Chapter Summary 2.4

- There are two concepts of efficiency: (1) productive efficiency—when inputs are not wasted; and (2) allocative efficiency—when resources are employed in their highest-valued uses.

- There are two concepts of equity (or fairness): (1) horizontal equity—the equal treatment of equals; and (2) vertical equity—the unequal treatment of unequals.

- A market system encourages efficiency and a government system promotes equity.

Tutorial Preparation

1 Define in your own words the following three types of economic system:

    a. A pure free market economy

    b. A mixed economy

    c. A planned economy

2 a. From page 9 copy the figure 2.1 (entitled: A spectrum of economic systems) and try to locate the following countries on the spectrum: UK, USA, Russia, Japan, France, East Germany, China, Singapore and Australia.

    b. Compare your spectrum with those of other students. Resolve any disagreements by studying recent newspaper articles. Agree on an up-to-date spectrum, adding any other countries that you are knowledgeable about.

    c. One of the problems with the spectrum as presented in figure 2.1 is that it has no scale. Design a scale that could be used to locate each nation more accurately.

3 Using a production possibility curve, describe the trade-off that exists between equity and efficiency.

4 Make some notes based on official documents of government housing policy. For example, Conservative policy documents such as: the 1987 White Paper *Housing: The Government's Proposals* (CM 214), *Choice for All in Housing*, published 1990; or Labour policy documents, such as: *A Welcome Home*, published 1991, *Building a Better Britain*, published 1992.

If you cannot find any of these, read magazine commentaries, such as the review of the election manifestos in *Building*, 17 March 1992. If these sources fail, many of the books on housing have a chapter on government policy. (The first tutorial reading of this chapter will help consolidate this note-taking exercise.)

Tutorial Reading

An Interview with the Leader of the Opposition, Prior to the 1992 General Election

What is your view of the Conservative government's housing record?

I know how important it is for people to be able to own their own home. I constantly see young people in my constituency in despair because they have no hope of finding a house they can afford.

I see young people on the streets of our cities without shelter of any kind. Those people are homeless because for 13 years Conservative governments have had no policies to house them. Now it is a time for a change.

You are promising a boost to housebuilding, funded by council house sales receipts. Does this mean your programme will be organised by local councils?

It is right that money [from capital receipts] should be used to build new homes. In fact, it is essential. In the 1980s Britain built almost 1 million fewer homes than in any peacetime decade since the First World War.

We will begin a phased release of capital receipts through the local authorities' own housing investment programmes. When our national housing bank is established we will encourage local authorities that are rich in receipts, but have relatively low housing needs, to lend to the bank, which in turn will be able to lend on to other local authorities, housing associations or other builders of low-cost homes for rent.

What role do you see for volume housebuilders in this programme?

We have made it clear in our document *A Welcome Home* that, as well as providing new homes for sale, the housebuilding industry must be contracted to provide most of the new homes for rent.

What checks would be put in place to stop a repetition of the design disasters of the 1960s?

We want to build up our housing programme at a steady but sure rate so that building supplies and skills can keep pace.

We will have new designs tested by our [proposed] National Design and Technology Centre to ensure that innovatory techniques which appear to offer quick and easy solutions in the short term do not conceal disadvantages in the longer term.

How will the proposed housing bank work?

It will be charged with bringing private finance into public housing. It will be a public limited company, set up outside of government. It will borrow from the international capital markets, and lend to social and responsible private landlords and to housebuilders building for rent or low-cost home ownership.

It will be of special use to housing associations that suffer much higher rates of interest than councils under the current system. A specialist bank can better assess risk. There are similar institutions in Australasia, France and Sweden . . . .

What is the Labour view on the use of architectural competitions for major public buildings?

We want to see standards of design for public buildings improve. This is already happening in a number of Labour authorities and imaginative proposals for London have been set out in the recently published book, *A New London*, commissioned by the Labour Party from the architect Sir Richard Rogers.

We propose that the design of all public buildings costing more than £3 million should be decided by competition. We will implement a series of initiatives to encourage higher standards of design in public and private buildings, promote the work of younger architects, and to seek to restore values of civic pride to the public works of our towns and cities....

What can the industry expect from a Labour government that it won't get from the Tories?

I think we would need a special issue of your journal to outline this. In short, we will phase the release of capital receipts—which everyone in the industry wants. We will invest in infrastructure and start to repair our schools and hospitals. We will move towards a regime of stable interest rates.

We will enable better long-term planning of public projects, to allow the industry to gear up for expansion. We have a real commitment to training the workforce.

Finally, and perhaps most importantly, we will foster a new spirit of partnership between government and industry. We will listen to industry's needs to the benefit of the economy and the community.

Source: Adapted from (pp 24-25) 'Can Labour build a better Britain' *Building* 27 March 1992

Questions

1   What kind of problems have presented themselves that relate to the buildings of the 1960s?

2   What government-funded organisation currently does the work of the proposed National Design and Technology Centre?

3   Name the government minister (spokesperson), and the opposition party equivalent, presently responsible for housing and construction.

4   What issues make up the Conservative Party housing policy at present? (See tutorial preparation number 4 for references.)

5   Give three examples to illustrate how during a Labour administration the government would become involved in the property market?

6   Discuss how the concepts of equity and efficiency relate to the housing policy of the Labour Party and the Conservative Party.

Tutorial reading

Wall Comes Tumbling Down

The dismantling of the Berlin Wall in November 1989 provided a stark comparison of economic systems. Millions of East Germans flocked to West Berlin to buy goods that were not available in the East. Electronic toys, radios, cosmetics and chocolates were at the top of the shopping list. The East Germans had to pay high prices, but at least they had the chance to buy the goods they desired.

West Berliners went on a shopping spree as well, as the price of necessities had been kept low by the East German government. So West Berliners rushed into East Berlin to buy boots, sausages, women's lingerie and children's clothes. So much merchandise was being carted off to West Germany that the East German government had to halt sales to foreigners and impose border controls to slow the outflow of available goods.

When the Berlin Wall fell, consumers on both sides got a clear view of the differences between market- and command-orientated economies. The central economic questions however, remained the same on both sides of the Berlin Wall.

Source: Adapted from (p 31) *The Economy Today* by B Schiller, McGraw Hill 1991.

Questions

1 Describe the economic systems employed in East and West Berlin before the wall fell.

2 State at least three effects that the dismantling of the Berlin Wall would have on the East German property market.

3 Give one property-related example that represents the change of economic systems in East Germany since November 1989.

4 Consider Galbraith's statement on p 10 in the light of the developments in East and West Berlin.

5 What are the central economic questions that have remained the same on both sides of the wall?

Tutorial reading

Is the Housing Market Working?

. . . The housing crisis has been grinding on since autumn 1988. Time passes and still no one dares to make an objective statement about the outcome.... For every statement advanced in favour of recovery, there is a measured step back.

No sooner does one property writer announce that the important lost jump-leads of the housing market, the first-time buyers, have finally been found; than another confesses that nearly 500,000 households are bankrupt because they have mortgage debts greater than the value of the houses and their indemnity insurance policies will fall short.

No sooner do we learn housing starts for the first quarter of the year were unusually high at 42,000 units, than we are reminded that some 100,000 existing houses have been repossessed...

The housing market is not big business, it is not even a big institution like the church or the army. Its moneylenders may be bigger than the banks, but the operational units in the housing market are the money borrowers, the millions of individual households.

The housing market is not under central control: it is more like an enormous band of bandits that assembles as if by magic in anticipation of booty and dissolves just as magically when someone gets a bloody nose. Unlike the firms quoted on the stock market, every unit of the 17 million owner-occupied housing market is autonomous, with all the rapid decision-making and freedom of action that entails.

It is because this flexibility and diversity is not understood that the housing crisis has seemed like a defeat. A defeat it has been but not for home-owners.

Source: Adapted from (p24) 'Brigands sit tight on their housing hoards' *Building 22 May 1992*

Questions

1 What economic system is being outlined?

2 a) Calculate 500,000 as a percentage of 17 million.

   b) What significance does this percentage represent?

3 'Every unit in the housing market is autonomous'. Explain and discuss this statement.

4 Is the housing market equitable?

5 Who, if anyone, has been defeated by the housing crisis?

Tutorial Reading

Architects Need Economic Awareness

Perhaps the worst mistake made by the British architectural profession in this century has been to tolerate the delegation of responsibility for estimating building costs. To claim to advise clients on their interests without reference to costs is a fantasy. Fortunately, information technology is coming to the rescue. It is an integrating force and has the potential to bring cost data back where it belongs—in the designer's consciousness.

Architects have always been deeply involved in urban design. They have been conspicuously successful in turning their attention to the conservation, repair and rehabilitation of the fabric of existing buildings. An even greater opportunity lies in extending these hard-won technical skills to planning and replanning the use of cities, and of the entire existing building stock.

Architects are also the obvious source of advice to clients on the **procurement** of architectural and building services. There is no reason why in the new, more commercial, procurement environment architects should not play an even more important role in the connecting of architectural skills and building resources to different sorts of user.

Source: 'The strategic overview' by Dr Francis Duffy in *Uplifting Architecture*, A Building publication, July 1992

Questions

1 Which other professions involved in the design, construction and maintenance of buildings need economic awareness and why?

2 The extract is part of an introductory set of papers prepared for the **RIBA** which was trying to identify proposals that would enable architects to practise more effectively in a rapidly changing world. Name two equivalent bodies to **RIBA**, ie institutions negotiating on behalf of a specific group of professionals involved in the built environment.

3 To whom have architects delegated the responsibility of building costs?

4 'Fortunately information technology is coming to the rescue'. Explain this statement in the context used in the extract.

5 Why does resource allocation affect the creative design process?

6 Explain in your own words the meaning of the last sentence of the extract.

3

The market mechanism

Chapter Summaries to Review
- *Scarce Resources (1.1)*
- *Free Market (model) Economy (2.1)*
- *Economic Systems (2.1)*

In chapter 2 we began to recognise that the forces of supply and demand underlie the price mechanism. This was highlighted in figure 2.2. To be perceptive in interpreting signals in the property market, building materials sector, or whatever, we need to consider the price or market mechanism in more detail. We can begin to elaborate our understanding of the **price mechanism** by defining it more fully as: an economic system in which relative prices are constantly changing to reflect changes in supply and demand for different goods and services. The price mechanism is synonymous with the term **market mechanism**.

Before any good or service can be produced, the various factors of production need to be employed and again their prices are affected by supply and demand. The forces of supply and demand are, therefore, all – encompassing within the market mechanism. They bring together producers and consumers in such a way that appropriate goods and services are produced, and appropriate incomes are rewarded. To highlight this inter-relationship between supply and demand in literally millions of different markets, we shall first consider an overview of a market-based economy.

Product and Factor Allocation in a Market Economy

In figure 3.1 we display how the wishes of producers and consumers are 'signalled' by the price mechanism. To begin (with the top half of figure 3.1): the consumers (households) supply their economic resources (factors of production) to firms who demand them to undertake productive activity. The supply and demand of these various factors (resources) determine the prices paid for them in the sector in which they are economically active. That is, the various householders receive differing levels of wages for their labour input, interest for the capital services they provide, various rents for the land that they own and profits for their entrepreneurial abilities according to the sector supplied. (These factor incomes are examined in more detail in chapter 11.)

In the product market a similar scenario exists: firms supply various goods and services according to consumers' demand. Again, it is the market price that balances the two parties' interests. (This is shown in the bottom half of figure 3.1.)

Figure 3.1   Product and factor allocation via the price mechanism

In this simplified model there are only two sectors to the economy. Households supply their services—the labour, capital, land and entrepreneurship that they own—to firms that demand them for production. The prices paid in the form of wages, interest, rent and profit are the balancing item that determine factor allocation. Firms, in turn, supply goods and services to households which demand them. Again, prices provide the balancing item which determines product allocation

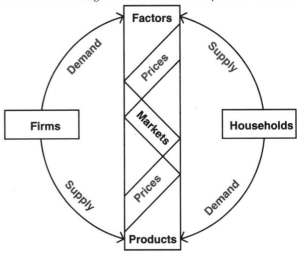

Price Signals and Self-interest

For the market economy to function effectively, it is important that every individual is free to pursue their own self-interest. Consumers express their choice of goods or service through the price they are prepared to pay for them, in their attempts to maximise satisfaction. As the owner of resources used in production (most commonly one's own labour power), the individual seeks to obtain as large a reward as possible, in an attempt to maximise profit.

If consumers want more of a good than is being supplied at the current price, this is indicated by their willingness to pay more, as long as the good is acquired, ie the price is 'bid up'. This in turn increases the profits of those firms involved, ie the incomes paid to the factors producing that good increase. As a result, resources are attracted into the industry and supply expands.

On the other hand, if consumers do not want a particular product, its price will fall, producers will lose money and resources will leave the industry. This is precisely what happened in the 'new build' market during the early 1990s. House prices fell consistently, producers either concentrated on other construction work or went bankrupt. As a result, the completion of new homes fell by over 50 percent.

In simple terms, therefore, the price system indicates the wishes of consumers and allocates the productive resources accordingly. Or, as we suggested in chapter 2, the price mechanism determines what is produced, how it is produced and for whom is it produced.

Chapter Summary 3.1

● The price mechanism is synonymous with the market mechanism.

● The forces of supply and demand in factor and product markets are reconciled by price (see figure 3.1).

● Price movements provide the signals that freely responding individuals interpret, determining what is produced, how it is produced and for whom it is produced.

Graphic Analysis

Analysis of the price (market) mechanism has played a significant role within the history of economics. As far back as 1776, Adam Smith wrote in the *Wealth of Nations* about the 'hidden hands' of supply and demand that determine market prices.

Since then a standard part of any economics course has involved the study of supply and demand graphs. This is probably because it is easier to communicate an idea visually; as the saying goes 'a picture is worth a thousand words'. A supply and demand graph performs much the same function as a picture.

A graph enables the relationship between price and quantity to be explored from the consumers' (demand) perspective and producers' (supply) perspective. The standard layout/notation for each axis is shown in figure 3.2.

Figure 3.2   The axes of a supply and demand graph

On the vertical axis it is customary to plot the price per unit, and on the horizontal axis we plot the quantity demanded and/or supplied per period of time.

Quantity (supplied/demanded) per period of time

What would the pattern of demand look like? (ie can you show on the graph what people would want in relation to the price?) To put the question in more formal terms, can you plot the **demand schedule**? Clearly, as the price of a commodity rises, the quantity demanded will decrease and, as the price falls, the quantity demanded will increase. That is, from the (consumers') demand side there is an **inverse**

relationship between the price per unit and the quantity purchased: higher prices cause smaller quantities of demand.

What would the pattern of supply look like? (ie can you show on the graph how much profit-seeking producers may be willing to supply in relation to price?). To reiterate the question in more formal terms, can you plot the supply schedule? Clearly, as the price of a commodity rises, the quantity supplied will increase and, as the price falls, the quantity supplied will decrease. That is, from the (producers') supply side there is a **direct relationship** between the price per unit and quantity sold: an increase in price usually leading to an increase in the quantity supplied.

As suggested before, these basic principles seem easier to appreciate when plotted on a graph. See if you agree by considering figure 3.3.

Figure 3.3   A simple supply and demand diagram

The demand curve displays the fact that the quantity demanded will fall as the price rises, whilst the supply curve displays the converse, that is, the quantity supplied rises as the price rises.

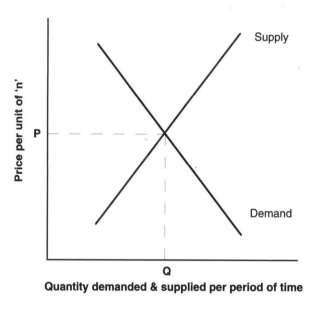

Quantity demanded & supplied per period of time

Three Qualifying Remarks

Economists have devised various methodological procedures to give their statement academic value. Three of these small but important techniques need to be highlighted even though texts fail to enforce them constantly.

Per Period of Time

On the horizontal axis of figures 3.2 and 3.3 we ended the statement with the qualification *per period of time*. This is to highlight that supply or demand is a flow that takes place during a certain time-period. Ideally it should be specified as a month, year, week or whatever. Without a time dimension the statements relating to quantity become meaningless.

Ceteris Paribus

The second qualifying remark relates to the latin phase *ceteris paribus*, which means other things being equal or constant. This is an important assumption to make when dealing with a graph showing two variables. Clearly, price is not the only thing that affects purchases. There are many others which we will cover in chapters 4 and 5. In the above examples, we assumed *ceteris paribus*: for instance, we did not complicate the analysis by allowing consumers' income to change. This is because if, while the price of a good is changing, income is also changing, then we do not know whether the change in the quantity demanded was due to a change in the price or to a change in income. Therefore, we held income constant, along with all the other factors that might affect the quantity demanded. The *ceteris paribus* assumption, therefore, enables the economist to undertake something which approximates to a controlled experiment, studying each significant variable in turn.

Supply and Demand Curves

When using supply and demand curves to illustrate our arguments, they will frequently be drawn as straight lines. Although this is irritating from a linguistic point of view, it is easier for the graphic artist constructing the illustrations and acceptable to economists, since the 'curves' very rarely refer to the plotting of empirical/ actual data. It is worth noting, therefore, that so-called supply and demand 'curves' become straight lines that highlight basic principles.

Chapter Summary 3.2

- On a supply and demand graph, the horizontal axis represents quantity and the vertical axis represents the price per unit.

- Supply and demand curves illustrate how the quantity demanded or supplied changes in response to a change in price. If nothing else changes (*ceteris paribus*), demand curves show an inverse relationship (slope downwards) and supply curves show a direct relationship (slope upwards). See figure 3.3.

- To understand the premise upon which supply and demand diagrams are drawn it is important to remember three criteria: (1) the time–period involved; (2) the *ceteris paribus* assumption; and (3) the shape of the 'curves'.

The Price is Right

Look again at figure 3.3: inevitably there is a point at which the two curves must cross. This point represents the market price. The market price in figure 3.3 is *P* and this reflects the point where the amounts supplied and demanded are equal, namely point *Q*.

At price *P* the market clears. There is no excess supply; there is no excess demand. Consumers and producers are both happy. Price *P* is called the **equilibrium price**: the price when the quantity demanded and the quantity supplied are equal.

Most markets come to rest at an equilibrium price. This could be the labour market, housing market, foreign exchange market, drainpipe market or whatever. All markets have an inherent balancing mechanism. When there is excess demand prices rise and when there is excess supply prices fall. Eventually a price is found where there is no tendency for change. Consumers are able to get all they want at that price and suppliers are able to sell the amount that they want at that price. This special market concept is illustrated in figure 3.4.

The Concept of Equilibrium

We have used the term 'equilibrium price'. The concept of an equilibrium is important in economics and we will be referring to it in different markets and in different

Figure 3.4   The determination of equilibrium price

Only at the equilibrium price is the quantity demanded equal to the quantity supplied. In this example, the equilibrium price per newly built flat is £50,000 and the equilibrium quantity is 2,000 units. At higher prices there would be a surplus: flats would be in excess supply and they will remain empty. For example, at £75,000 the market would not clear; there needs to be a movement along the demand curve from H to E and a movement along the supply curve from h to E. These movements necessitate the price to fall. At prices below the equilibrium, there would be a shortage: flats would be in excess demand and there would be a waiting list. For example, at £25,000, the price would rise, reducing the demand from F to E and supply would then be sufficient, having moved from f to E. £50,000 is where this market will settle.

contexts as we study the economy. **Equilibrium** in any market may be defined as a situation in which the plans of buyers and the plans of sellers exactly mesh. Equilibrium prevails when opposing forces are in balance. In any market, the intersection of a given supply curve and a given demand curve indicates the equilibrium (point) price. If the price drifts away from this equilibrium point—for whatever reason—forces would come into play to find a new equilibrium price. Such a situation is one of **stable equilibrium**. An unstable equilibrium is one in which, if there is a movement away from the equilibrium, there are forces that push price and/or quantity even further away from equilibrium (or at least do not push price and quantity back towards the equilibrium level or rate).

The difference between a stable and an unstable equilibrium can be illustrated with two balls: one made of hard rubber, the other made of soft putty. If you were to squeeze the rubber ball out of shape, it would bounce back to its original form. On the other hand, if you were to squeeze the putty, it would remain out of shape. The former illustrates a stable equilibrium (in terms of physical form) and the latter an unstable equilibrium.

Now consider a shock to the system. The shock can be shown either by a shift in the supply curve, or a shift in the demand curve, or a shift in both curves.

Thus, any shock to the system will produce a new set of supply and demand relationships and a new equilibrium; forces will come into play to move the system from the old price–quantity equilibrium (which is now a disequilibrium situation) to the new one. We shall consider one such example in the next section.

A Change in the Conditions of the Market

To illustrate the dynamics of the market let us imagine what might happen if mortgage rates rise. This will, other things remaining constant, reduce the demand for owner-occupied property *at each and every price*. This decrease in demand is shown in figure 3.5, in the traditional economist's way, by shifting the demand curve to the left from D_1 to D_2. If property prices now stay at P, consumers will only demand Q_a, whilst suppliers (sellers) will continue providing Q. Consequently there will be an excess amount of supply in the market place equal to $Q_a - Q$. However, providing the prices are allowed to move to make the amounts supplied and demanded equal again, suppliers will be able to off-load vacant properties by reducing their prices. As the price falls consumers will be interested in demanding more. Consequently a new equilibrium price will be arrived at. This new price will be P_1 in figure 3.5 and the new quantity being demanded and supplied will now be equal again at Q_1.

Figure 3.5 Changing market conditions lead to a new equilibrium price

The leftward shift of the demand curve indicates that consumers are now willing and able to buy fewer properties in every price range, due to the increase of mortgage rates. The excess supply of properties on the market at the old price P causes a new equilibrium to be found at the lower price P_1, where the quantity demanded and quantity supplied are once again found to be equal.

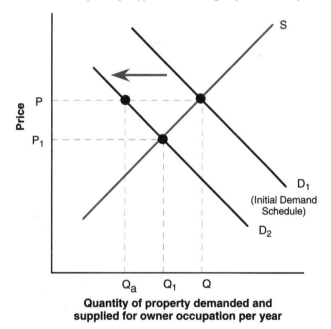

Quantity of property demanded and supplied for owner occupation per year

The shifting of the demand curve (such as occurred in figure 3.5) only occurs when the *ceteris paribus* assumption is violated. In other words, the curves only shift to a new position when the market conditions change. We will explore these 'shifts' in more detail in the next two chapters.

A Closing Note

Finally, to complete our introductory overview of market forces we also need to recognise the existence of **market failure**. So far we have not experienced any market distortions. For example, we have assumed that labour will move freely to wherever work is most profitable and consumers will buy whatever they desire in freely determined markets. Yet in reality, monopolies, oligopolies, subsidies, trade unions and other market rigidities distort the situation. We shall be examining these issues in more detail later, especially in chapter 9.

Chapter Summary 3.3

● When we combine the demand and supply curves we can find the equilibrium price at the intersection of the two curves. The equilibrium price is one from which there is no tendency to change; the market clears. See figure 3.4.

● Equilibrium exists whenever the separate plans of buyers mesh exactly with the separate plans of the sellers. Price points the buyers and sellers in the right direction.

● If conditions in the market change, the relevant curve shifts and a new equilibrium position is established. See figure 3.5.

● In some instances, forms of market failure exist.

Tutorial Preparation

1 Make notes on this chapter using the chapter summaries and another economics textbook. Identify some questions for your tutor.

2 Define in your own words any four of the terms identified in bold. (Pick the ones you think are most important.)

3 Explain why surveyors and related professionals of the built environment need to know the factors that affect the price mechanism.

4 Consider the historical data gathered from a North London estate agent in figure 3.6 and prepare to discuss the following questions.

Figure 3.6   One-bedroom properties for sale in North London

General list of flats and houses for sale   11/05/87   *Page 1*

£39,950   The Terrace Lauradale Road East Finchley N2

Situated in this ever-popular turning just off Fortis Green and close to Cherry Tree Wood is this well-proportioned studio flat. The property itself, although in need of slight redecoration, would represent an ideal first-time purchase. Viewing is strictly by appointment via us, the owner's agents.

1Bds 15×9   Kit 10×7   1Bth
Night Stor

£49,950   Dollis Park Finchley London N3

A convenient located one bedroom flat which is within walking distance of all Finchley Central's local amenities, and northern line underground station. The property has the benefits of fitted carpets and, although it is in need of some decoration, this is amply reflected in the asking price. The property is ideal for the first-time purchaser and should be viewed without delay.

1Bds 9×8   1Rec 14×11   Kit 9×8   1Bth
Lease 90 YRS   Ground Rent 50

£49,950   Manor Cottages Corner of Long Lane East Finchley N2

Earliest viewing is stongly urged of this truly immaculate rather unusual one bedroom ground floor, converted maisonette which is equidistant to both East Finchley and Finchley Central shopping facilities as are various essential amenities.

1Bds 16×11   1Rec 20×12   1Bth
Gas Fired   Lease 97 YRS

£49,950   Nelson Road Crouch End London N8

An ideal first-time purchase is this deceptively spacious, split-level newly converted, luxury, studio flat. The property has been converted to an extremely high standard throughout and affords such benefits as some original features, gas central heating, luxury shower room and possible use of rear garden.

1Bds 16×12   Kit 21×9   1Bth
Gas Fired   Lease 99 YRS

---

a. Why do you think the Lauradale Road property is the cheapest?

b. What is the common factor, if any, between the three properties for sale at £49,950?

c. What explanation can you give for the Dollis Park property not being slightly cheaper than the others?

d. What problems are we going to experience when we discuss property prices?

e. At the top of the data the date is 11/05/87. Try to suggest what will have happened to the prices of the four properties since then?

f. What factors affect house prices in an established area such as North London?

5 The hypothetical record of demand for one-bedroom properties in North London is shown in figure 3.7.

Figure 3.7   Demand for one-bedroom properties in North London during May 1987

Number of enquiries to estate agent	Price ceiling
1	£50,000
2	£48,000
4	£46,000
6	£44,000
8	£42,000

a. Using the data displayed in figures 3.6 and 3.7, construct demand and supply curves for one–bedroom properties in this part of North London during May 1987.

b. What is the probable equilibrium price?

c. What is the equilibrium quantity at that price?

d. What do you understand to have happened to the four properties shown during May 1987?

e. What type of market change may cause the equilibrium to alter?

6 Describe in your own words what you understand by the phrase 'a single market in Europe' and identify what advantages such a market may present for the property developer.

7 a. Describe one price that exists in the UK economy that may not be freely determined by the forces of supply and demand.

b. Explain how the price you have selected is determined.

Tutorial Reading

The International Property Market and Exchange Rate Mechanism

Across the world people speak different languages, wear different types of clothes, share different cultural experiences, live in differently formed structures and use different currencies. The result is an intriguing web of many complex systems. We shall study just one strand of this web and consider its relevance to property.

Before Britain, or any nation, can trade effectively with any other nation, there needs to be a system for exchanging currencies. For example, when you decide to buy a foreign product, such as French wine, you use pounds which ultimately contribute to paying the French wine-maker. French wine-makers, however, would be hard pressed to pay their workers in pounds. The workers are French, they live in France and they need francs. There must therefore be some way to exchange pounds for francs. The necessary exchange occurs in the **foreign exchange market**. The existing exchange rate between France and Britain depends on the interaction of the demand for and the supply of francs and pounds.

Currencies move across the foreign exchange tills for more reasons than just trade and tourism. Indeed the majority of exchanges occur for reasons other than trade/tourism. The central banks of governments around the world sell and buy currencies to stabilise exchange rates; these manoeuvres may be referred to as **official intervention**. Speculators may use short-term deposits of one currency to make a capital gain in another currency. These manoeuvres may be referred to as **hot money**, so called since the deposits involved may switch currency many times as speculators pursue the highest interest rate and/or the best prospect for the **appreciation** of a currency.

These various flows are summarised in figure 3.8. It should be recognised that the foreign exchange market is *not* one big building in a specific country, but a network of bank telephones, telexes and VDUs. Traders communicate via this equipment from one county to another, buying and selling their clients' currencies.

As figure 3.8 suggests, the network of exchanges seems reasonably complex when you consider just two nations. Imagine therefore, the level of boisterous activity in a trading room dealing with all the currencies of the world at once.

To simplify the level of complexity in the real world, let us just consider the trading nations of the European Community. The statistical law of combinations suggests that, without intervention, this community of 12 nations would share 132 exchange rates. In an effort to achieve greater harmony, therefore, a common trading unit (the ECU) and a co-ordinated exchange system (the ERM) have both been developed within the last decade.

These financial developments have encouraged the growth of commercial activity across Europe. In the property sector, Swedish developers have built in Portugal, UK chartered surveyors have begun to link up with their continental counterparts, and French, German and Dutch institutions have bought office buildings in Central London.

Figure 3.8   A simple representation of the Foreign Exchange Market

From the left-hand side sterling is shown to flow for three basic reasons in and out of the UK financial sector; on the right-hand side the same set of flows is represented for France. All of these exchanges occur via the foreign exchange market which is also experiencing changes in the supply and demand of francs and sterling owing to similar activities with all the other nations of the world. Ultimately these movements affect the daily exchange rate.

Key to Flows: ——— Trade and Tourism
– – – Official Intervention (Government)
——— Hot Money (Speculators)

The Exchange Rate Mechanism (ERM)

The UK was a member of the **Exchange Rate Mechanism (ERM)** from October 1990 to September 1992. This mechanism represents an agreement to keep European exchange rates fixed in terms of each other, allowing fluctuations within a narrow band. If the forces of supply and demand operating within one member nation start to push a currency outside of the band, the government concerned would initially adjust its domestic policy. If this proves inadequate central banks and the **European Monetary Fund (EMF)** ensure that funds are available for intervention in the foreign exchange market. If all else fails, a re-alignment of currency values takes place (as has happened with the Italian lira and Irish punt), or ultimately a nation may choose to suspend its membership (as happened in the case of the UK during September 1992).

To illustrate the basic principles, consider figure 3.9. The supply and demand for sterling are shown in relation to the German mark (the Deutschmark, commonly abbreviated as DM). The UK government joined the ERM at a central rate of £1 = DM2.95, agreeing to keep within a 6 percent band. This commitment obliged the Bank of England (the British central bank) to make sure that sterling appreciated to no more than £1 = DM3.13 (ie DM2.95 × 106 percent) and depreciated to no less than £1 = DM2.77 (ie DM2.95 × 94 percent). Maintaining the pound within this band required **official intervention** into the foreign exchange market, and

adjustments of interest rates as and when necessary.

For the purposes of illustration let us follow the scenario that occurred during September 1992. The German economy was experiencing inflationary pressure and therefore the Bundesbank (the German central bank) would not lower its interest rates. As a result, sterling-denominated assets became relatively less attractive. The UK also had a particularly large balance of payments deficit.

Consequently the demand for sterling on the foreign exchange market reduced whilst the supply of sterling increased, as currency traders switched out of sterling into Deutschmarks. This is shown in figure 3.9: the reduced demand for sterling (at each and every price) caused the curve (D) to shift leftwards to D_1, the increased supply (at each and every price) caused the curve (S) to shift rightwards to S_1. The new equilibrium was now below the permitted band. In consequence, the Bank of England had to do something—to intervene officially—to boost the demand for sterling. In this instance it used nearly half of its foreign currency reserves (in excess of £10 billion) to purchase sterling on the foreign exchange market, and raised interest rates by 5 percent. However, the pound could not be lifted from its ERM floor and the decision to suspend Britain's membership was taken on 16 September 1992; this important day was tagged by the press as **'Black Wednesday'**.

Figure 3.9   Management of the Exchange Rate Mechanism

The agreed central (equilibrium) value of the pound against the Deutschmark was £1 = DM2.95. The rate was permitted to fluctuate within a band from DM3.13 and DM2.77. When the demand and supply curves were (D) and (S), no action was needed. However, when the market conditions change and the supply and demand curves shift to D_1 and S_1, intervention becomes necessary, especially when the new equilibrium position falls above or below the permitted band.

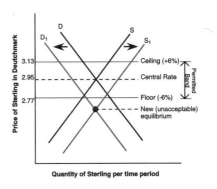

Questions

1 According to a Council of Mortgage Lenders' report in November 1990, foreign currency mortgages would not appeal to residents of the UK.

   a) Why had this become an issue?

   b) Why would foreign currency mortgages not occur?

2 Use the terms ERM, ECU and EMF to write a short account of what is happening in the European foreign exchange market today. (NB Looking at recent press articles may help.)

3 a) Britain withdrew temporarily from the ERM because of 'fault lines'. What do you think the British prime minister was referring to when he coined this phrase in September 1992?

   b) Make an argument either for or against the UK rejoining the exchange rate mechanism.

   c) Identify the member states that are party to the exchange rate mechanism today.

4 Give an account of how the UK exchange rate scene could be affected by some kind of property-related project.

5 a) Apart from exchange rates, professionals working with property will be subject to various other rates which are explicable using supply and demand analysis. State three examples.

   b) Using a supply and demand type diagram (similar to that of figure 3.9), explain how one of these rates may rise or fall due to changes in the market conditions.

6 The general specification of a nation's building stock will be different from nation to nation. Using examples, explain why.

7 Name three non-European trading partners of the UK with whom we have some property-related activities (ideally state the nation and the activity).

8 What relevance does this reading have for the potential fund manager?

9 What aspect of your future career may cause you to refer back to this reading?

10 If a person went round the 12 EC member countries with a £10 note and did nothing except exchange it from one currency to another currency, he would come back with £4.35. Why?

Tutorial Reading

Transactions in the Property Market

The reason individuals turn to markets to conduct economic activities or exchanges is that markets reduce the costs of trading. These costs are generally called **transaction costs** because they are associated with transacting economic exchange. We can define transaction costs as all of the costs enabling exchanges to take place. Thus, they include the cost of being informed about the qualities of a particular product: its price, its availability, its durability record, its servicing facilities, its degree of safety and so on. Consider, for example, the transaction costs in shopping for a lap-top microcomputer. Such costs would include phone calls or trips to sellers in order to learn about product features and prices. In addition to these costs, we must include the cost of negotiating the sale. The specification and execution of any sales contract is thus included, and ultimately transactions costs must take account of the cost of enforcing the contracts.

The transaction costs in the property markets are relatively high. Take, for example, moving home. The cost of selling a £100,000 property in England or Wales during 1991/2 was approximately £3,200. Of this amount, the estate agent's selling fees (**multi-agency**) were around £2,761. The costs of buying the same property were in excess of £1,000; even though the stamp duty of 1 percent on house purchases up to £250,000 had been suspended during the relevant period (December 1991–August 1992).

Figures from: Woolwich Building Society, Annual Survey (1991/92) *'Fall and rise of moving costs'*.

Questions

1 a) Identify the component amounts that make up the £3,200 selling costs.

   b) How could these costs be reduced?

   c) What transaction costs would the buyer experience?

   d) By approximately how much would the transaction cost to the purchaser of the same property have increased by 1993?

2 Identify the extra transaction costs that may be experienced by a seller of commercial property. (Looking back at figure 1.1 may help.)

3 Traditionally, as it becomes less costly to disseminate information, transaction costs in most markets fall. Why is this not the case with property markets?

4 The reason individuals turn to markets to conduct economic activities or exchanges is that markets reduce the costs of trading. Discuss this statement with specific reference to the property market.

4

The theory of demand

Chapter Summaries to Review
● Scarcity (1.1)
● Ceteris Paribus (3.2)
● Supply and Demand Graph (3.2)
● Supply and Demand Curves (3.2)
● Changing Market Condition (3.3)

The concepts of supply and demand are basic building blocks of economics so it is very important that you understand them. In this chapter we will focus on demand and in the next chapter we deal with supply.

The Basic Law of Demand

We have already established in the last chapter that a demand curve has a negative slope, that is, it moves downwards from left to right. This is highlighted in figure 4.1.

Figure 4.1   A standard market demand curve

The normal demand curve for most goods and services slopes downwards from left to right, reflecting that, the higher the price, the lower the level of demand (other things being equal).

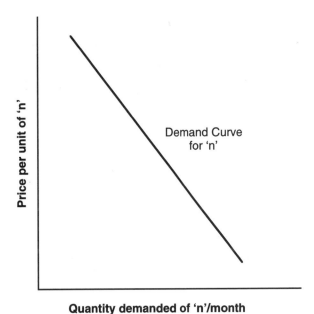

The shape of the demand curve for most goods or service is not surprising when one considers the basic **law of demand.** This may be stated formally as: at a high price, lower quantities will be demanded than at a low price (and vice versa), other things being equal. The law of demand, therefore, tells us that the quantity demanded

of a product is inversely related to that product's price, other things being equal.

To continue with this analysis, we must consider the 'other things being equal' phrase more carefully. Clearly demand is not only affected by price. As already implied in chapter 3, it is easy to see that other factors may also affect demand. The demand curve shown in figure 4.1 may shift to a whole new horizon. Conditions in the relevant market (for product 'n') may change significantly enough to cause consumers to change the quantity demanded *at each and every price*.

Imagine that figure 4.1 represents a product that you are interested in. What event may cause more or less interest in your demand for that product?

We are now beginning to talk formally about market conditions. They may include factors (determinants) such as: changes in income, changes of expectation, the price of other goods (especially substitute and complementary goods), changes in taxation and so on. Each one of these conditions (also referred to as determinants or factors of demand) may be considered one by one, assuming *ceteris paribus*, as we do in the next section.

Changing Market Conditions

There are many, many non-price determinants of demand, for example, the cost of financing (interest rates), technological developments, demographic make-up, the season of the year, fashion and so on. For illustrative purposes we will consider just four generalized categories. Taking each in turn and assuming *ceteris paribus* in each case.

Income

For most goods, an increased income will lead to an increase in demand. The phrase *increase in demand* correctly implies that more is being demanded at each and every price. Thus for most goods an increase in income will lead to a rightward shift in the position of the demand curve.

Goods for which the demand increases when income increases are called **normal goods**. Most goods are 'normal' in this sense. There are a small number of goods for which demand decreases as incomes increase. These are called **inferior goods**. For example, the demand for private rented accommodation falls as more people become able to buy their own accommodation. (It is important to recognise that the terms *normal* and *inferior* in this context are part of the economist's formal language, and no value judgements should be inferred when the terms are used.)

Price of Other Goods

Demand curves are always plotted on the assumption that the prices of all other commodities are held constant.

For example, when we draw the demand curve for lead guttering, we assume the price of plastic guttering is held constant. When we draw the demand curve for carpets, we assume the price of housing is held constant. The price of the goods that are assumed constant may affect the pattern of demand under analysis. This is especially the case if the other good is a **substitute good** (as in the guttering example) or a **complementary good** (as in the carpet and housing example). Economists distinguish between interdependent goods, such as these, in terms of how the change in price of one commodity affects the demand for the related commodity.

Let us consider the guttering example a little more fully. Assume that both types originally cost £10 per metre. If the price of lead guttering remains the same and the prices of plastic guttering falls by 50 percent to £5 per metre, builders will use more plastic and less lead. The demand curve for lead guttering, at each and every price, will shift leftwards. If, on the other hand the price of plastic guttering rises, the demand curve for lead guttering will shift to the right, reflecting that builders are willing to buy more of this product at its present price. Therefore, a price change in the substitute good, will cause a change in the pattern of demand for the good under study. The same type of analysis also applies for complementary goods. But here the situation is reversed: a fall in the price of one product may cause an increase in the demand for both products and a rise in the price of one product may cause a fall in the demand for both.

Expectations

How consumers view future trends of incomes, interest rates and availability may prompt them to buy more or less of a particular good, even if its current price does not change. For example, house purchasers who believe that an increase in mortgage rates is scheduled may buy less property at today's prices. Today's demand curve for houses will shift to the left reflecting that the quantity of properties desired for purchase at each and every price has reduced owing to expectations regarding future mortgage rates.

Government

Legislation can affect the demand for a commodity in a variety of ways. For example, changes in building regulations may increase the demand for double- glazed window units, regardless of their present price. The demand curve for these window units will shift to the right, reflecting the fact that larger quantities of these units are being demanded at each and every price. The government can also influence the level of demand by changing taxes or creating a subsidy. These issues will be considered more fully in chapters 10 and 11, where we shall be reviewing government policy relating to the manipulation of demand.

Chapter Summary 4.1

- The basic law of demand is that as price rises, lower quantities are demanded and vice versa. That is, there is an inverse relationship between the price and quantity demanded, other things being equal. See figure 4.1.

- The other things being equal, in this instance, refers to all of the non-price determinants that affect demand, such as interest rates, technology, demography, fashion and so on.

- Four major non-price determinants are: (1) income; (2) price of other goods; (3) expectations; and (4) government.

Revisiting Ceteris Paribus

When we first introduced the idea of holding other things constant, it may have appeared that these other things were unimportant. The previous two sections should have highlighted how wrong this interpretation would be. Indeed the *ceteris paribus* assumption enables economists to highlight that demand is determined by price and a host of other factors. Thus when you are interested in the level of demand for any good or service you will always need to consider the price and many other related factors (the other related factors will change according to the good or service under analysis), as illustrated by the tutorial preparation exercise number 3 at the end of this chapter).

To highlight this important distinction between the price determinant and the non-price determinants, economists distinguish their terms carefully when they discuss changes in demand.

Terms to Understand Changes in Demand

We have already seen from the preceeding discussion of market conditions that changes of non-price determinants cause the demand schedule to shift to the right or to the left. The opening paragraph to the section on income makes this particularly clear. Changes in demand by any non-price determinant will always cause the entire demand curve to shift to the right or to the left, demonstrating the fact that more or less is being demanded at each and every price. These changes are often referred to as *increases* or *decreases* of demand.

Let us consider one example in detail. How would we represent an increase in the quantity demanded of naturally ventilated commercial buildings (at all prices) due to a respected piece of research concluding that air-conditioned buildings caused **sick building syndrome?** The demand curve for naturally ventilated buildings would shift to the right, to represent an increase in the demand at each and every price. This is shown in figure 4.2.

We could use a similar graphic analysis when discussing decreases in demand owing to a change in non-price determinants. The only difference would be that the demand curve would shift to the left, demonstrating that the quantity demanded is less at each and every price.

By contrast, the price determinant causes a movement along the demand curve. This is obvious when one remembers that the demand curve represents price and quantity relationships on the proviso that all the other determinants remain constant. Changes to the quantity of demand due to price alone are often referred to as an *extension* or *contraction* of demand. This involves a move along the demand curve. When more is demanded at a lower price this may be regarded as an extension from one co-ordinate on the demand curve to another. When less is demanded due to a rise in price, demand contracts. Such movements along the demand curve are described further in figure 4.3.

Figure 4.2   Change in a non-price determinant, causing a shift in demand

If any non-price determinant of demand changes, we can only show its effect by moving the entire curve from D to D₁. We assumed in our example that the move was prompted by some research that proved naturally ventilated buildings would overcome sick building syndrome and the related absenteeism. Therefore, at each and every price a larger quantity would be demanded than before. For example, at price 0P the quantity of naturally ventilated buildings increases from 0Q to 0Q₁.

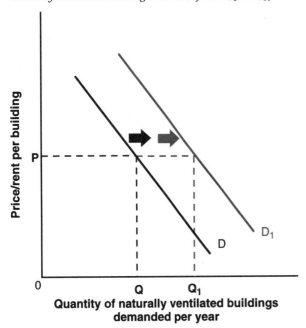

Quantity of naturally ventilated buildings demanded per year

Figure 4.3   Change in price causing a movement along a given demand curve

We show the demand curve for a hypothetical good (x). If the price is P_1, then the quantity demanded will be Q_1; we will be at co-ordinate A. If the price falls to P_2, and all other factors in this market remain constant, then there will be an extension of demand to Q_2. In other words, there has been a downward movement from co-ordinate A to co-ordinate B; this represents an extension of the quantity demanded.

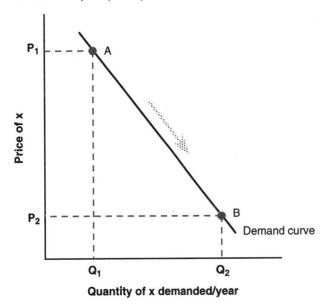

Quantity of x demanded/year

Before we can begin to apply our theoretical knowledge of demand, it is particularly important to remember the distinction between a movement along, and a shift in, a demand curve. These rules will not only help us to understand graphic analysis, but they will also enable us to acknowledge the numerous factors that come into play when considering demand aspects.

Indeed, reliable demand analysis of different markets is the ultimate goal of this chapter. We still need to introduce, therefore, one final technique that summarises the ideas dealt with so far. But first a chapter summary.

Chapter Summary 4.2

● **If any one of the non-price determinants change, the demand schedule shifts to the right or left and we refer to an increase or decrease of demand. See figure 4.2.**

● **Movements along a given demand curve are caused by price changes only and are described as contractions or extensions of demand.**

Demand Equations

Economists sometimes present the relationship between the demand for a good and the various determinants discussed above in the form of an equation. A simple version could be expressed as follows:

$$Q_n^d = f\ (P_n,\ P_n\text{-}1,\ Y,\ G,\ ....)$$

This is formally referred to as a **demand function**. It may look complicated but it is only a form of shorthand notation. The demand function represents, in symbols, everything we have discussed above. It states that (Q_n^d) the quantity demanded of good 'n' is (f) a function of all the things listed inside the bracket: (P_n) the price of the good itself, $(P_n\text{-}1)$ the price of other goods, (Y) income, (G) government policy, (...) a host of other things. We may actually specify some of the other things (...) if we identify what 'n' specifically represents. That is, these equations may be adapted and extended as necessary to aid your analysis accordingly. (See tutorial preparation number 3).

Chapter Summary 4.3

● **The relationship between the quantity demanded and the various determinants of demand can be expressed as an equation.**

● **The shorthand symbols would be amended according to the specific demand analysis being undertaken.**

Tutorial Preparation

1 Economists classify goods into different categories. In this chapter we have introduced four such classifications. In your own words define each of the four types of good and give your own examples. (NB technical terms are highlighted in bold type.)

2 In this chapter, we suggested that price and four non-price determinants affected demand. Write a paragraph on one other determinant that you think would be important to any future demand analysis that you may undertake.

3 Consider the factors of demand that would determine the demand for :

    a. Owner-occupied housing

    b. Privately rented housing

    c. Building surveyors

    d. Architects

    You may find it quicker to complete these exercises in the form of a demand equation.

4 Using a graph, represent the changes in demand experienced over a 10-year period for any two of the sectors listed in question 3. You may complete this exercise in general terms or be accurate by using actual data from official or government statistics.

Tutorial Reading

Some Determinants of Effective Demand for Property

When economists speak of demand, as we have in this chapter, they mean **effective demand**. Effective demand is money-backed desire. It is *not* the demands of a crying baby or spoilt child wanting and grabbing at everything it sees. Demand from an economist's point of view is real, 'genuine' demand backed by the ability to make a purchase.

Many things will therefore influence the effective demand for property. The following edited extract from a newspaper article written during a recession highlights some of the conditions that influence the housing market. Given the questions at the close of the extract and a little thought you should be able generally to appreciate the conditions of demand for property.

This year's mortgage arrears figures make particularly gloomy reading. They are compounded further by the problem of Britain's shrinking wage packet.

The figures themselves are frightening. In 1987 overtime averaged 12.63 hours a week. In 1988, it ballooned to 13.42 hours and in 1989—the last year of the boom—it stood at 13.39 hours. In 1990 it was down to 12.3 hours and in 1991 collapsed to 9.86 hours.

But this is only half the story. The other, even gloomier, side relates to that 1980s wheeze known as 'discounting future earnings' whereby people bumped up their incomes by counting in one-off bonuses and the like. In other words, they fibbed a little.

Average earnings increased in 1987 by 7.81 percent and in 1988 by 8.77 percent. Then in 1989 they hit an annual increase of 9.08 percent, peaking at 9.79 percent in 1990. With those sorts of rises coming year in and year out, it is hardly surprising that a lot of people gambled on the good times continuing indefinitely.

Take the two together—the collapse of earnings that existed during the good times and the non-appearance of earnings that had already been banked on—and it is clear how the talk about 'dry rot' at the heart of the housing market emerged.

The dwindling-income effect is a major problem, according to the Council of Mortgage Lenders. And the stable doors are slamming shut. Expect a chilly smile from your building society manager if you enthuse about the size of your bonus or part-time earnings. Advances based on transient earnings have certainly become less available.

The squeeze on new lending comes not only on the income side, but from the insurance companies, who have seen the easy-money days of mortgage **indemnity insurance** turn into losses of over £1 billion during 1991.

The cost has risen and the conditions have tightened, with Legal & General, Sun Alliance, Eagle Star, Royal Insurance, Commercial Union and General Accident bringing in highly restrictive new policies with mortgage lenders, requiring the latter to shoulder around a fifth of losses and effectively ending mortgage advances in the majority of cases of more than three-quarters of a property's value.

This tighter indemnity cover is expected to be in place by autumn 1992. Taken with much stricter income requirements, the combined effect will be to exclude large numbers of first-time buyers from home ownership.

Source: Adapted from: 'Borrowers who have lost a packet' *The Guardian* 1 August 1992

Questions

1 Define effective demand and discuss the relevance of such a concept to the property market.

2 a) List, in order of importance, the determinants of demand for housing.

    b) How would the determinants alter if we considered the demand for office space?

3 State two factors, other than income, that led to a decrease in the demand for housing during the early 1990's.

4 a) State three financial-type services that most people demand when they buy a house.

    b) Define each of the three services listed for part a.

5 Using a demand graph, illustrate one of the changes between 1987 and 1992 discussed in the extract.

Tutorial Reading

Business Parks: What You Get Is What You Want?

There have been countless studies into the sort of space that business park developers should build and where they should build it. But what of occupiers' requirements?

To get a clearer picture of what tenants actually think, Jones Lang Wootton asked a cross-section of companies occupying space on parks around the country.

One company, located at Stockley Park for six months, has a 20,000 sq ft regional head office with 55 employees. Most of the staff travel to work by car. So far there has been sufficient parking but, bearing in mind the amount of space which the company has taken, possibly not enough for visitors. Amenity facilities for staff were judged adequate, but a bank instead of just a cash point would have been preferred.

The Arena Complex was popular with all staff. All in all, the staff seemed pleased with the working environment.

Building design—an important issue for developers—was not rated so highly by occupiers. Neither were they concerned with the overall image of the park or appearance of the building. Parking provision, property specification, tenure and rent per sq ft were tenants' chief concerns.

An engineering company employing 140 people moved to a 40,000 sq ft office at Aztec West, near Bristol in 1991. The company wanted an out-of-town location near a motorway with a high standard of amenities and sufficient local housing. Availability of staff was also important and this proved to be a deciding factor. In fact, the staff travel from within a 50 mile to 60 mile radius.

As the majority were expected to travel to work by car, the design allowed for sufficient parking to accommodate this. The company continued to find staff access to the park extremely good.

Aztec West also has the great benefit of convenient shops, pubs, wine bars, cafes and leisure facilities.

The only criticism which staff have —and this could be applied to all business parks—is that they would like to see a supermarket on site for domestic and household shopping. The absence of this facility means driving off site during the day for any shopping.

Architect Ian King believes these observations confirm important trends in speculative development.

Source: Adapted from 'Home is where the park is' *Estates Gazette* 20 June 1992

Questions

1   Do you think that house builders face similar problems to those who develop business parks? (Explain your answer fully.)

2   What qualities do you think the tenants of a shopping mall may demand?

3   Construct a small survey for use by a business park developer to research what occupiers may really demand from their location.

4   Does an out-of-town, energy-efficient business park make good use of national resources?

5   What six main factors determine the occupiers' demand for business park space?

6   Name two factors that would cause a marked decrease in demand for business park provision. Use a demand graph to explain fully these factors.

5

The theory of supply

Chapter Summaries to Review
- Law of Increasing Opportunity Costs (1.2)
- Ceteris Paribus (3.2)
- Supply and Demand Graph (3.2)
- Supply and Demand Curve (3.2)
- Equilibrium Price (3.3)
- Changing Market Conditions (3.3)

As the chapter summaries to review may suggest, the theory of supply involves a similar approach to that of the previous chapter on demand. To some extent this gives us an intellectual start. We will not, however, fully appreciate the suppliers' side of the market until we reach chapter 9. Chapters 7 and 8 are particularly significant, since they explore the theory of the firm, which suggests that the number of suppliers within each market affects the price and quantity relationships that exist.

The Basic Law of Supply

Just as there is a relationship between price and quantity demanded, so too is there a relationship between price and quantity supplied. Indeed, we have already encountered the basic idea of supply in chapter 3. We explained that the **supply curve** slopes upwards from left to right demonstrating that, as price rises, the quantity supplied rises and conversely as price falls, the quantity supplied falls. This is the opposite of the relationship that we saw for demand. The basic **law of supply** can be stated formally as: the higher the price the greater the quantity offered for sale, the lower the price, the smaller the quantity offered for sale, all other things being held constant. The law of supply, therefore, tells us that the quantity supplied of a product is positively (directly) related to that product's price, other things being equal. This is displayed in figure 5.1.

Figure 5.1 The supply curve for an individual firm

The standard supply curve for most goods and services slopes upwards from left to right, reflecting that, the higher the price, the higher the quantity supplied (other things being equal).

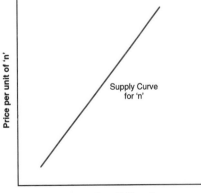

The Market Supply Schedule

The incentives and constraints facing all suppliers within a specific market are roughly the same. Each individual firm seeks to maximise its profits, and each firm is subject to the law of increasing opportunity costs. As we explained in figure 1.4, as a firm (society) uses more and more of its resources to produce a specific item, the cost for each additional unit produced increases more than proportionately. That is, the law of increasing opportunity costs highlights that because resources are generally suited to some activities better than others, it is not possible to increase the quantity supplied of a specific item continually without cost increasing at a disproportionately high rate. In other words, when we utilise less well suited resources to a particular production activity, more and more units of it have to be used to achieve an increase in output.

Similarly, a firm's costs will be affected by its fixed overheads. These vary according to the size of the firm (see chapter 7 for details).

We are now in a position where we can begin to appreciate notionally the concept of a **market supply schedule**. The market supply of a product is given by the sum of the amounts that individual firms will supply at various prices. For example, at a price of £6 per unit, we might find that three firms are willing to supply 400, 300 and 200 units per day, respectively. If these three firms made up the whole industry we could conclude that at a price of £6 the market supply in this industry would be 900 units per day.

Let us consider this example in more detail. The relevant data is presented in figure 5.2.

Figure 5.2 The individual and market supply schedules for a hypothetical three-firm industry

We see from the data that as price increases suppliers are willing to produce greater quantities. At the other extreme, low prices may actually preclude some firms from operating in the market. By combining the supply from each firm within the industry, we can identify the total market supply at each price; we do this in the final column. We have highlighted the combination of supply that would occur at £6, since this price line was discussed in our example above.

Price	Quantities Supplied			
£/Unit	Firm A Units/day	Firm B Units/day	Firm C Units/day	Total Market Supply
4	0	0	0	0
5	300	0	0	300
6	400	300	200	900
7	500	380	250	1130
8	580	460	280	1320
9	620	500	290	1410
10	650	520	295	1465

Here we see how the three firms comprising the industry perform individually at various prices. At low prices, producers B and C offer nothing at all for sale; most probably because their high production costs constrain them. At higher prices the law of increasing opportunity costs begins to take its toll. By adding up each individual firm's output, at each specific price, we can discover the total supply that firms would be willing and able to bring to the market. We have highlighted the combinations at £6 per unit. As a brief educational exercise you may like to plot the market supply schedule on a graph. If you do it correctly, the shape of the supply curve for the market should be similar to that for an individual firm as presented in figure 5.1.

Chapter Summary 5.1

- **The basic law of supply is that, as price rises, larger quantities are supplied and as price falls, smaller quantities are supplied. That is, there is a direct, or positive, relationship between price and the quantity supplied. (Other things being constant.) See figure 5.1.**

- **The size of each individual firm will determine how much it can produce at various prices. Fixed overheads and the law of increasing opportunity costs affect each firm differently.**

- **The market supply of a product is discovered by the horizontal summation of the amounts that individual firms will supply at various prices. Plotting these total amounts against their related prices enables one to construct a market supply curve.**

Supply and the Price Determinant

As the law of supply states, more is supplied at higher prices, other things being held constant. This is because at higher prices there is greater scope for firms to earn a profit. Firms already in the market have an incentive to expand output, while higher prices may also enable those firms on the fringes of the market, with higher production costs, to enter the industry. At higher prices, therefore, the increased quantity supplied is made up by existing firms expanding output and the number of new firms involved increasing. For example, in figure 5.2 we showed that at a price of £5 market supply was 300 units per day, but at higher prices we saw other firms being enticed into the market and total supply increasing.

Supply and Non-price Determinants

Up until now we have discussed supply and its related curve on the assumption that only price changes. We have not considered any other determinants that influence producers' behaviour. We have constantly repeated the qualification that *other things are held constant*. Some of the other things assumed constant are: the costs of production, technology, government policy, weather, the price of related goods, expectations, the goals of producers in so far as they wish to maximise profits or sales, and so on. In the following sections, we shall broadly consider just three of these factors (non-price determinants) in order to reiterate the principles already established about changing market conditions (see chapter 4, on demand).

Cost of Production

We have implied that producers are seeking to maximise their profits. Thus, any change in production costs will, *ceteris paribus*, affect the quantity supplied. To illustrate this principle you may return to figure 5.2. If an input price becomes £1 dearer, the increased cost will be passed on and less will be supplied at each price. Therefore £6 would now secure a market supply of 300 units.

In technical terms, what is happening is that the supply curve has shifted to the left to demonstrate that less is now supplied at each and every price. The opposite would occur if one or more of the inputs became cheaper. This might be the case if, say, technology improved.

Government

In a similar way taxes and subsidies also affect costs and thus supply. For example, a sales tax (such as stamp duty or VAT) will increase costs and therefore reduce supply. A subsidy would do the opposite, since every producer would be paid a proportion by the government for each unit produced.

Expectations

A change in the expectations about future prices can affect a producer's current willingness to supply. (Similarly, as we have already described, price expectations affect a consumer's current willingness to demand.) Builders may withhold from the market part of their newly built or refurbished stock if they anticipate a higher price in the future. In this instance, the current quantity supplied at each and every price would decrease, the related supply curve would shift to the left.

Terms to Understand Changes in Supply

Just as we were able to distinguish between shifts of, and movements along, the demand curve, so we can have the same discussion for the supply curve.

A change in the price of a good itself will cause a movement along the supply curve, and be referred to as an *extension* or *contraction* of supply. A change in any non-price determinant, however, will shift the curve itself and be referred to as an *increase* or *decrease* of supply.

Let us consider one example in detail. If a new computer-assisted design (CAD) package, which incorporates cost estimating, reduces fees relating to new builds, design-and-build contractors will be able to supply more new buildings at all prices because their costs have fallen. Competition between contractors to design-and-build will ultimately shift the supply curve to the right, as shown in figure 5.3, p 35. By following along the horizontal axis, we can see that this rightward movement represents an increase in the quantity supplied at each and every price. For illustrative purposes, only, we follow the increase in the quantity supplied at price $0P$: quantity supplied increases from $0Q$ to $0Q_1$.

If, on the other hand, the costs of production rose, the quantity supplied would decrease at each and every price, and the related supply curve would shift to left.

For analytical purposes, it is helpful distinguish the cause of changes in supply. In the above example about CAD it would have been wrong to conclude that price has simply fallen and quantity supplied expanded accordingly. The reason for the larger supply to the market, at all prices, was due to a change in technology.

Figure 5.3   A shift of the supply curve

If price only changes we move along a given curve. However, if the costs of production were to fall, the supply curve would shift to the right from S to S₁ representing an increase in the quantity supplied at each and every price.

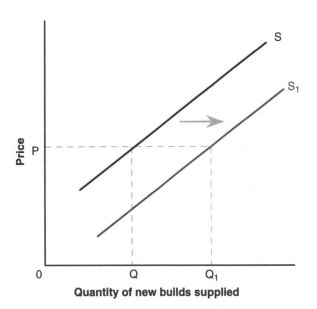

Combining Supply and Demand

In the preceding chapters on demand and supply, we tried to confine our discussion to isolated parts of the market relating to the consumer or producer. Obviously this separation is made for teaching purposes only; in reality there is a very close relationship between the forces of demand and supply. Indeed, we have already discussed in chapter 3 how the interaction of supply and demand determines prices. We introduced the concept of an equilibrium (or market) price where both consumers' and producers' wishes were met. We even extended our discussion to consider the effects of changes to market conditions. Knowing and understanding how supply and demand interact is an essential prerequisite for interpreting many markets, including those of the built environment. It would be worth your while, therefore, to read again the overview of the market mechanism, especially the sections relating to price, equilibrium and changing conditions of the market on pp 19–20.

Meanwhile we will assume that you have grasped the basics, and are ready to consider aspects of supply in a pure or interactive context as assessed by the tutorial activities.

Chapter Summary 5.2

- The supply curve is plotted on the assumption that other things are held constant. Three major non-price determinants are: (1) costs of production (including technological changes); (2) government; and (3) expectations.

- If price only changes, we move along a curve and there is an extension or contraction of supply.

- If any one of the non-price determinants changes, the entire supply curve shifts to the left or right, and we refer to a decrease or increase in supply. See figure 5.3.

Chapter Summary 5.3

- By combining the forces of supply and demand we can begin to understand many markets.

- The concept of equilibrium demonstrates how the wishes of suppliers and demanders are brought together via price.

- In reality the determinants of supply and demand need to be considered simultaneously.

Tutorial Preparation

1   In this chapter we suggested that there were many non-price determinants of supply. We covered three comprehensively. Write a paragraph on one other determinant that you think would affect the supply of property.

2   In chapter 4 on p 29 we discussed demand equations. Complete the following to create an equivalent equation for supply.

$$Q_n^s = f (.....)$$

3   Explain and draw a supply and demand diagram to illustrate why increases in interest rates are likely to depress house prices.

4   Consider the data presented in figure 5.4 (p 36) and answer the following questions.

   a.   Name two firms that have taken up space in this market.

   b.   Name one firm that has been responsible for the supply.

   c.   Which year experienced the most excess supply and what happened to prices/rents in this market during that year?

   d.   Draw a supply and demand diagram to explain what you think has probably happened since 1992 within the Docklands office market.

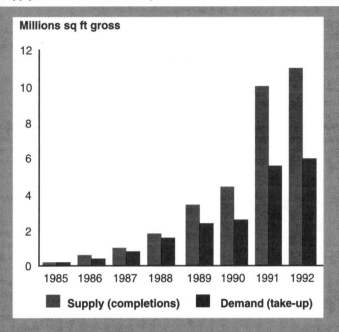

Figure 5.4   The cumulative supply and demand of office space in London Docklands from 1985 to 1992

Millions sq ft gross

■ Supply (completions)   ■ Demand (take-up)

5 Draw on a piece of rough paper a basic supply and demand diagram and consider the changing conditions in the four markets (A to D) described in figure 5.5. Complete the end column each time with details relating to the new price and quantity. (In order to interpret the answers at the back of the book, we suggest you mark each market change on your diagram with the appropriate letter A to D.)

Figure 5.5   Changing market conditions

Market	Product	Changes in Conditions	New Equilibrium Point
A	Energy-efficient buildings	A successful advertising campaign by the energy efficiency office	
B	Computer-assisted design system	Improved microchip reduces cost	
C	Newly built houses	A fall in the cost of a mortgage and an increase in the price of land.	
D	Speculative commercial development	Stock market investments become more stable and consistently increase in value	

Tutorial Reading

Finding a Definition of Market Value for Property

At the beginning of 1992, the **RICS (Royal Institution of Chartered Surveyors)** began to revise its guidelines on valuation in order to cope with the difficulties of valuing property in a falling market. As a consequence, a stream of letters appeared on the correspondence page of *Estates Gazette* between March and September of 1992. The following four extracts represent a brief sample of some of these.

Letter from J Barnett FRICS (21 March 1992)
You have no doubt read that the RICS Assets Valuation Standards Committee are considering updating the definition of 'open market value'.

It is proposed that 'best' be replaced by 'highest'. I believe that this new adjective tends to describe a price level that, by its own definition, is unlikely to be achieved. It is like valuing the tip of

the iceberg and does not, in my opinion, convey to the non-professional a figure that he or she is likely to obtain.

In many years of experience in selling property, I have found that clients prefer to know the band of values in which their property lies rather than the highest 'sunny-day' figure.

Surely the highest price is that which only one purchaser will pay, rather than a figure that can be regularly repeated.

To illustrate this, if six identical properties were sold to different purchasers at prices of £55,000, £56,000, £57,000, £58,000, £59,000 and £60,000, the present, and even proposed, definition of open market value would be £60,000, whereas my band of value advice to a client would be between £55,000 and £60,000.

Letter from B Bridgewood (4 April 1992)

Surely John Barnett (March 21) is right in suggesting that the RICS Assets and Valuation Standards Committee's idea of replacing 'best' by 'highest' is misleading....

In my view there should be three bands:

Band 1: The forced sale valuation – what in the valuer's professional opinion a property can be 'knocked out' for tomorrow.

Band 2: The average plus/minus sort of price that could be obtained in the present market (Barnett's band, in effect).

Band 3: The highest price that is likely to be achieved (according to the old formula) on a good day. Perhaps the RICS would consider sanctifying the bands instead of going for a revised doctrine of total worth?

Letter from S Farnsworth ARICS (4 April 1992)

.... In my view... few clients require a valuation that is representative only of a property at a certain date, except for purposes of capital gains tax. Clients usually require a valuation at today's date that will be valid for perhaps three months so that they can manage their property assets effectively.

I am writing to you in exasperation as I am concerned that the valuation profession does not seem to be getting to grips with the concept of open market value and, until an OMV model is applied to describe what happens in the property market, then valuers will not be giving clients what they are asking for.

Letter from A Cherry (Chairman, Assets Valuation Standards Committee) (18 April 1992)

May I reply to the letters from John Barnett (21 March), Bruce Bridgewood and Stephen Farnsworth (4 April).

Neither John Barnett nor Bruce Bridgewood appear to have noticed that you reported on 22 February that, as a result of the consultation process, the Assets Valuation Standards Committee has decided to retain the expression 'best price' in the definition rather than 'highest price'. Both Mr Barnett and Mr Bridgewood prefer to avoid giving their clients a specific value and suggest a range of values or perhaps an 'average price'. This may be appropriate when advising a client on a potential sale, but valuations to which the Red Book applies require precise figures and it would not be right to report a range of values. 'Best price' is qualified by the words 'reasonably be expected' and in making a valuation the valuer should have a reasonable degree of confidence that the reported figure could have been obtained in the market-place.

Stephen Farnsworth has probably not yet seen the new definition of open market value nor the revised Guidance Notes which have now been approved and are shortly to be published. He correctly suggests that the valuation should take account of market evidence prior to the date of valuation, but I do not share his views that the marketing period should fall either side of the valuation date, and plainly that view is wholly at variance with the circumstances of the notional sale hypothesised by the definition. Most clients have a specific valuation date and the vagueness about the date of valuation for which he argues is precisely the opposite of what the Red Book stands for.

Questions

1 a) What does RICS stand for?

   b) Name the seven divisions into which membership falls.

   c) Which of these divisions would make most use of the definition of open market value?

2 State three different purposes that require a surveyor's valuation on property.

3 Why are valuations in a falling market problematic?

4 Try to explain using economic terms, why values may be difficult to identify in many sectors of the property market.

5 In your opinion should the open market value of property reflect:

   A The value on the date of the survey?
   B The value at some future date after the survey?
   C The value on some date prior to the survey?
   D Some combination of the above?

   Explain the reason for your chosen option.

6 State two problems that may occur if property values are assessed wrongly by a surveyor.

7 Do some library research to discover the existing rules on market valuation as laid down by the RICS.

8 What potential problems can you sense may still exist in relation to the question of property valuation?

Tutorial reading

The Construction Industry and its New Contracts

Construction is a major sector of the UK economy. It creates approximately £50 billion worth of activity each year and accounts for the employment of approximately 1.5 million. Statistics such as these are always approximate because the construction industry is defined and classified in so many ways. For example, the government's Standard Industrial Classification suggests that construction covers the erection, repair and demolition of all types of buildings or civil engineering structures. Other commentators use the categories: **public (non-housing), private commercial, private industrial and housing.**

These approaches beg the question of how related activities are recorded. Traditionally speaking, architects and surveyors working from their own offices are professionals and may be regarded as part of the service industry. Similarly, firms making components for the construction industry may be regarded as manufacturers and so on.

In spite of the problems of definition, construction will always be a significant industry; it encompasses not only new developments, but also redevelopment and refurbishment. To take some examples, you may consider the pages and pages of data on contracts, tenders and planning produced by the **Advanced Building Information Service** on a daily basis, and often published in magazines such as *Building*. Or in more general terms you can read about the supply of new work coming into the market by looking at the *Financial Times*.

To avoid the problem of presenting out-of-date material we have left you to find your own data, and then consider its significance by answering the following questions.

Questions

1 a) What is the date of the column you are reading?

   b) Is this a period of recession or boom?

2 What is the total value of the construction contracts reviewed for the week?

3 What percentage of these new contracts involve refurbishment?

4 In terms of value, what percentage of the contracts can be attributed to the public sector?

5 a) What is the average duration of the building projects reviewed?

   b) When considering the duration of a construction project what other aspects need to be included?

6 Identify two factors operating in the construction market that may affect the rate of supply.

6

Elasticity of demand and supply

Chapter Summaries to Review
- *Supply and Demand Graphs (3.2)*
- *Law of Demand (4.1)*
- *Non-price Determinants of Demand (4.1)*
- *Law of Supply (5.1)*

We have already established the basic laws of supply and demand. You should understand, therefore, that there is an inverse relationship between price and quantity demanded, and a positive relationship between price and quantity supplied—assuming in both cases that other things remain constant.

Consequently, it is possible to predict the direction of change if prices are raised or lowered. We cannot, yet, however tell *by how much* the quantity supplied and the quantity demanded will change.

Clearly some measure of the responsiveness of consumers and producers to changes in price would be beneficial. For example, in August 1985 Sinclair Research announced a 50 percent reduction in the price of its Spectrum computer. This reduction potentially could have led to a loss in total revenue from the sale of Spectrum, unless the sales increased by a great amount. Indeed sales had to increase by more than 50 percent to make the price reduction viable.

Decision-makers within governments also need an idea of how responsive people will be to changes in price. For example, increasing the price of cigarettes through taxation could cause demand to reduce by such a large amount that revenues flowing to the exchequer from sales could be greatly diminished. On recent experience, however, a 10 percent increase in tax reduced consumption by less than 5 percent. Cigarettes have few substitutes and therefore the government can gain higher revenue by increasing the taxes on smoking. The consequent higher prices on tobacco have a less than proportionate effect on the quantity demanded.

Economists have given a special name to the measurement of price responsiveness—it is termed **price elasticity**. It may be defined as a measurement of the degree of responsiveness of demand or supply to a change in price.

Measuring the Price Elasticity of Demand

A numerical value for the price elasticity of demand (PED) may be calculated using the following formula.

$$PED = \frac{\text{percentage change in quantity demanded}}{\text{percentage change in price}}$$

This basic formula may be transcribed in many different formats and you are encouraged to look these up in mainstream economic texts when carrying out tutorial preparation number 1.

What the formula tells us is the *relative* amount by which the quantity demanded will change in relation to

price changes. For example, where a 10 percent increase in petrol prices leads to a reduction in the quantity demanded of 1 percent the price elasticity of demand is 0.1.* That is a very small response.

When do we know if we are dealing with a big or small response? There are three types of price elasticity that economists use as a reference point.

1 Price-inelastic Demand

When the numerical coefficient of the price elasticity calculation is less than 1, demand is said to be 'inelastic'. This will always occur when we divide a small percentage figure for the change in demand by a larger percentage figure for the change in price. A coefficient of anything between 0 and 1 represents a situation of inelastic demand. The above example relating to petrol prices suggests a price-inelastic response: the measured coefficient was 0.1.

2 Price-elastic Demand

When the numerical value of the price elasticity calculation is greater than 1, demand is said to be 'elastic'. This will always be the case when we divide a larger percentage change in demand by a smaller percentage change in price. For example, if a 5 percent fall in price leads to a 50 percent increase in quantity demanded, the coefficient will be 10. In other words, a small change in price has induced a large response in demand.

3 Unit-elastic Demand

This is more of a hypothetical extreme, where the percentage change in price leads to an identical change in demand. This will always produce a coefficient value of 1, since we are dividing the same figure on both the top and bottom lines of the price elasticity formula.

Chapter Summary 6.1

- **Price elasticity is a measure of the responsiveness of the quantity demanded and supplied to a change in price.**

- **The price elasticity of demand is equal to the percentage change in quantity demanded divided by the percentage change in price.**

- **When demand is inelastic, a change in price causes a less than proportionate response in the quantity demanded.**

- **When demand is elastic, a change in price causes a more than proportionate change in the quantity demanded.**

- **When demand is unit elastic, a change in price causes an equal change in demand.**

---

*The mathematically minded student will have noticed that since price and quantity demanded are inversely associated, values showing PED should be negative. By convention we ignore the negative sign in our discussion. See p 40 for more information.

Different Elasticity at Different Prices

Notice that in our elasticity formula, we use *percentage* changes in quantity demanded divided by *percentage* changes in price. We are not considering absolute changes, we are only interested in relative amounts. As a result, the price elasticity coefficient will change as we move from one price range to another. We should, therefore, always bear in mind the price range when discussing price elasticity of demand. An example of this change in pattern of response at different prices can be seen in the housing market. Between 1990 and 1992 large percentage falls in house prices led to very small percentage changes in demand; in the preceding boom, 1987–88, large percentage increases in prices had actually led to relatively large increases in demand. This is because, at higher prices, the price elasticity of demand for housing becomes more elastic, as people begin to regard housing as being an investment as well as somewhere to live.

Calculating the Price Elasticity of Demand for Owner-occupied Housing

To gain a clear idea of the percentage change in the level of demand for owner-occupied housing, it is best to look at the number of transactions that have taken place from one time-period to the next. This is relatively easy to do, since all properties that change hands are processed on a standardised form that is administered by the Stamp (duty) Office and Land Registry. The relevant statistics, therefore, represent the number of particulars delivered (**PD forms**). Ninety percent of these PD forms relate to the purchases of residential property.

The forms are processed about one month after the transaction to which they relate. So the statistics give a fairly up-to-date indication of activity in the property market. Figure 6.1 shows how the number of total transactions has varied year by year since the annual series was started in 1978. Since 1991, more detailed analysis of this data has been presented and the following calculations in figure 6.2 relate to residential property transactions only; the relevant data is replicated as part of tutorial preparation number 1. (See figure 6.8, p 45)

Figure 6.1   Total property transactions 1978-92

The numbers relate to all the property transactions undertaken per year; about 90 percent of these are residential.

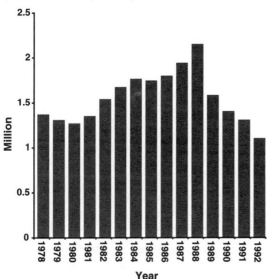

Calculating the percentage change in house prices is also problematic. Many commentators would argue that mortgage interest rates represent the actual money spent on a house. But this is complicated by the cash contributions that owners make to their purchases, and the various maintenance bills and transaction costs. For our purposes, the change in real house prices is the important focus. This is based on an average house price, as calculated by the Halifax and Nationwide building societies, and adjusted to account for changes in the general inflation rate. In other words, we are not considering the changes that are occurring in actual money terms, but in inflation-adjusted 'real' terms. Again the relevant data form part of the data presented for tutorial preparation number 1.

The following equation should now be understood.

PED for owner-occupier housing =

$$\frac{\text{percentage change in transactions}}{\text{percentage change in real house prices}}$$

Some sample figures for the years 1987-91 are demonstrated in figure 6.2.

Figure 6.2   Calculations estimating the price elasticity of demand for owner-occupied housing 1987–91

$$\text{PED} = \frac{\% \, \Delta \text{ in transactions}}{\% \, \Delta \text{ in real house prices}} \quad \frac{9}{11.4} = .78^* \quad \frac{14.1}{17} = .82^* \quad \frac{-4.0}{-7.2} = .55^*$$

* PED coefficient for owner occupied housing

What is it that these figures actually show? The percentage change in demand (the top line) is always smaller than the related percentage change in price, shown on the bottom line. Which suggests that whatever the price change, there is always a less than proportionate change in the number of transactions. In formal terms, therefore, the demand for owner-occupied housing is price-inelastic in the region of 0.82 to 0.55.

The odd feature that these figures highlight is that the quantity demanded is not necessarily inversely related to price. By convention, price elasticity of demand is negative: as price goes up, demand goes down and, as price goes down, demand goes up. Indeed the negative sign is traditionally ignored in the discussion. In our owner-occupied housing example, however, we see prices increasing and demand increasing simultaneously and in 1990/91 both variables decrease at the same time. In all instances, though, the price changes are larger than the changes in demand.

What Influences the Housing Market?

The price elasticity calculations shown in figure 6.2 suggest that price is not a major determinant for housing demand. The PED coefficient is always less than one. This begs the question, what determinant may be important to the housing market? Clearly, expectations relating to future price movements affect the market, and changes in these could help accelerate the market up and down. Interest rates are regarded as important since so many house purchases are based on mortgages. Indeed, figure 6.1 clearly shows the decline in transactions as base mortgage rates rose to around 15 percent, in 1980 and 1990/91. Employment and population trends will also influence the housing market. And finally, time-lags complicate the market since people take time adjusting to changes in income and buildings take time to construct. These latter two aspects, income and construction, will be briefly dealt with in subsequent sections of this chapter. Expectations, interest rates and employment will be covered in later chapters.

Chapter Summary 6.2

- When discussing price elasticity of demand, the price range should always be kept in mind: houses display greater elasticity at higher prices.

- To calculate the price elasticity of demand for owner-occupied housing, we divide the percentage change in the number of transactions by the percentage change in real house prices. The coefficient is always less than one.

Uses of Elasticity

There are two main uses of price elasticity of demand. The one which we shall deal with next relates to maximising revenue; the other relates to gaining insights into market determinants which we already began to develop above. Both have implications for the measuring of elasticity. (eg See tutorial preparation exercise, figure 6.9, p 46)

Elasticity and Revenue

One of the most discussed applications of price elasticity of demand concerns its relationship with a firm's sales revenue. The total revenue (TR) of a firm is calculated by price times quantity. For example, 40 units sold at £1 per unit will create a revenue of £40. If price is cut to 90p and demand increases to 50, total revenue increases to (90p × 50) £45. If, however, demand at 90p only increased to 42, then total revenue would be (90p × 42) £37.80p. In short, what happens to total revenue is determined by the price elasticity of demand. This can be shown graphically. The red coloured rectangle in figure 6.3 represents the total revenue that the firm gets at price £5. It highlights the price multiplied by quantity relationship, since the vertical side of the rectangle equals price and the horizontal side of the rectangle equals quantity. If the price drops to £4, there is a less than proportionate change in demand from 50 to 55. Total revenue clearly falls, which one can gauge by the change in size of the revenue rectangle (eg compare the area marked with the minus and addition signs). Alternatively, calculate 5 × 50 and 4 × 55. Use the way that you understand best. It should, however, be clear that when price changes by a bigger proportion than quantity, price rises will gain the firm revenue, while price falls will lose a firm money. To summarise these price-inelastic demand possibilities:

- Price ↑ Q falls by a smaller proportion; TR ↑
- Price ↓ Q rises by a smaller proportion; TR ↓

In this case of products which have price-inelastic demand, total revenue changes in the same direction as price.

When demand is elastic, the revenue effects are the other way round. If a good or service is price-elastic, the quantity changes more than price. Price falls, causing more than proportionate increases in quantity demanded, will gain the firm revenue. As price rises, decreasing quantity will lose a firm money.

To summarise these price-elastic demand possibilities.

- Price ↑ Q falls by a larger proportion; TR ↓
- Price ↓ Q rises by a larger proportion; TR ↑

In the case of goods or services with demand that is price-elastic, *TR* moves in the opposite direction to price.

Figure 6.3　Revenue rectangles

Price times quantity equals total revenue. The area of the rectangle representing the price and quantity coordinates from a demand curve at different prices can be used to determine if price changes are worthwhile.

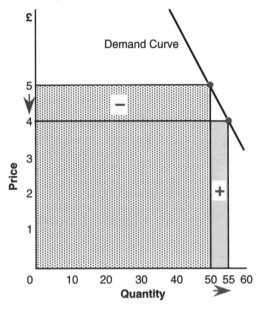

Chapter Summary 6.3

- Price elasticity of demand calculations provide insight into what drives a market.

- Price elasticity of demand is related to total revenues.

- When demand is elastic, a change in price causes a more than proportionate response in the quantity demanded. Consequently total revenues move in the opposite direction to the price.

- When demand is inelastic, a change in price causes a less than proportionate response in the quantity demanded. Consequently, total revenues move in the same direction as the price change.

Non-price Determinant Elasticity of Demand

Changes to the quantity demanded do not only occur due to changes in price. As discussed in chapter 4, there are also many non-price determinants that affect markets. Therefore, just because a market is not particularly responsive to changes in price does not mean that it is not an unchanging market. Indeed, elasticity can be defined more generally as: a percentage change in quantity divided by a percentage change in any related determinant.

An important non-price determinant in the housing market is income. Clearly when house prices increase at a faster rate than income obstacles to purchase increase. The house price-to-earnings ratio is therefore recognised as an important indicator. The ratio's long-term average, since the mid-1950s, has been around 3.5, ie average house prices have been around three and a half times the average annual income. If house prices begin to exceed this value, house price inflation will begin to outstrip wage inflation.

Income Elasticity of Demand

Economists measure the income: house purchase relationship from the perspective of elasticity. It simply involves using the same approach as we did when measuring the sensitivity of demand to changes in price. In this instance, however, we measure the responsiveness of quantity demanded to income changes. The formula for **income elasticity of demand (YED)** is nearly identical to that for price elasticity, only the determinant changes as follows:

$$YED = \frac{\text{percentage change in quantity demanded}}{\text{percentage change in income}}$$

Different Kinds of Income Elasticity and the Housing Market

As before with price elasticity of demand, there are varying ranges of income elasticity depending on whether the percentage change in income results in a larger or smaller percentage change in the quantity demanded.

Positive Income Elasticity

Most goods fall into this category, that is, as income increases so does demand; thus, the income elasticity of demand calculation has a positive value (see figure 6.4). If the income elasticity is less than one but above zero, as with some of the food products shown in figure 6.4, this implies that the good or service is not strongly sensitive to changes in consumer income (but still shows a positive relationship). In most of these cases we are talking about necessity goods and they would be classified as having **income-inelastic demand**. Conversely, if a good or service is said to have an **income-elastic demand**, we are suggesting that a change in income causes a greater change in the quantity demanded. According to the data in figure 6.4 this seems to be the case for items such as wines, spirits and sports equipment.

Negative Income Elasticity

In some exceptional instances a rise in income results in a fall in the quantity demanded. Consumers reduce their spending as they get richer; the coefficient of income elasticity is negative. See some of the examples in figure 6.4. In these situations the relevant goods such as coal, bread and cigarettes are termed **inferior goods**. This is not to convey that there is something wrong with these goods; it is just that people buy less as their increased incomes allow them to switch to higher priced substitutes. Another example of an inferior good would be private rented accommodation.

Income Elasticity and Housing

Housing means different things to different people. The income elasticity of demand for owner-occupied housing would be inelastic for low-income groups and elastic for high-income groups. Data relating to the UK, such as that given in tutorial preparation number 1 (figure 6.8), suggest that home ownership is more sensitively related to income than price, although the erratic nature of the figures imply that other market forces are also at work. In very general terms, for the UK as a whole, income elasticity for owner-occupied housing is thought to lie within the range of 0.75 to 1.25. This implies that, if incomes increase by 10 percent, then house purchases will increase by between 7.5 percent and 12.5 percent—but this increase may take some time to display itself. There is a time-lag involved before people adjust to changes of income.

Figure 6.4 Estimates for income elasticities of demand

The following table has been constructed from two sources. The figures are only estimates but they highlight the YED coefficient value for several goods.

Commodity or service	Elasticity
Cheese	0.29
Cake and biscuits	0.20
Beverages	0.16
Beer	1.22
Catering	1.63
Recreational goods	1.98
Wines and spirits	2.59
Coal	-2.02
Bread	-0.49
Cigarettes and tobacco	-0.03

Source: A. S. Deaton, "The Measurement of Income and Price Elasticities", *European Economic Review*, Vol 6, 1975, p 266 and Ministry of Agriculture, Fisheries and Food 1982.

Chapter Summary 6.4

- **Income elasticity of demand is equal to the percentage change in quantity demanded divided by the percentage change in income.**

- **The value of income elasticity of demand can be either positive or negative. It is more commonly the former.**

- **The degree of income elasticity is complicated by time-lags and consumer wealth generally.**

Measuring the Price Elasticity of Supply

The **price elasticity of supply (PES)** is defined in a similar way as the price elasticity of demand. Supply elasticities are generally positive; this is because, at higher prices, larger quantities will generally be forthcoming from suppliers. The formula used for the calculation is as follows.

$$PES = \frac{\text{percentage change in quantity supplied}}{\text{percentage change in price}}$$

Classifying Supply Elasticities

Just as with price and income elasticity of demand, there are different types of supply elasticities. They are similar in definition. If a 1 percent increase in price elicits a greater than 1 percent increase in the quantity supplied, we say that, at the particular price in question, *supply is elastic*. If, on the other hand, a 1 percent increase in price elicits a less than 1 percent increase in the quantity supplied, we refer to that as *inelastic supply*. If the percentage change in the quantity supplied is just equal to the percentage change in the price, then we talk about *unitary elasticity of supply*.

Price Elasticity of Supply and Time-lags

Time tends to be the main determinant of elasticity of supply. In the immediate time-period supply is fixed, inelastic to the value of zero, while given time for adjustments, supply increases can be organised and responses become elastic. This feature is particularly notable within property markets. Land is characterised by being perfectly inelastic; that is, as price increases the quantity supplied does not alter. Undeveloped areas can be developed, existing areas of land can change use; but both these possibilities take time. (This is discussed further in the tutorial reading, 'What determines land values?')

We therefore talk about short- and long-run price elasticities of supply. The short run is defined as the time-period during which full adjustment *has not* yet taken place. The long run is the time-period during which firms have been able to adjust fully to the change in price. Consequently, in the short run, rental values and house prices are demand-determined because adjustments cannot quickly be made to the supply of property. The property market in the short term is price-inelastic in supply. Indeed, it is the inelastic supply relative to demand that causes property markets to be unstable and characterised by fluctuating prices.

Let us consider just one example in detail: an increase in rent for private accommodation. In the very short run, when there is no time allowed for adjustment, the amount of housing services offered for rent is inelastic. However, as more time is allowed for adjustment, current owners of the housing stock can find ways to increase the amount of housing services they will offer for rent from given buildings. The owner of a large house can decide, for example, to have two children move into one room so that a 'new' extra bedroom can be rented out. In the medium term, some owners of large houses may decide to move into an apartment and rent each floor of their existing house to a family. In the long run, however, greater elasticity of supply will be achieved as the prosperous landlord–tenant market sees more houses being converted into flats, and new developments being purpose-built for the rented sector. Over time, therefore, the quantity of housing services supplied for rent will increase in response to higher rents. This principle is illustrated in figure 6.5.

Chapter Summary 6.5

- **Price elasticity of supply is given by the percentage change in quantity supplied divided by the percentage change in price.**

- **Long-run supply curves are more elastic than short-run supply curves because the longer the time allowed, the more resources can flow into or out of an industry when price changes. This is especially the case in property markets.**

- **It is the inelastic supply of property that causes the related markets to be unstable and characterised by periods of escalating prices.**

Figure 6.5 Short-run and long-run price elasticity of supply.

The longer the time allowed for adjustment, the greater the price elasticity of supply. Consider a given situation in which the price is P_e and the quantity of supplies is Q_e. In the short run, we hypothesize a vertical supply schedule, S_1. In other words, we assume that suppliers are unable to do anything in the very short run, even when there is a price increase. With the given price increase to P_1, therefore, there will be no change in the short run in quantity supplied; it will remain at Q_1. Given some time for adjustment, the supply curve will rotate to S_2. The new quantity supplied will shift out to Q_2. Finally, the long-run supply curve is shown by S_3. The quantity supplied again increases out to Q_3.

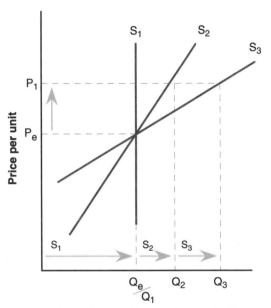

Quantity supplied per time period

Theoretical Extremes

To conclude our discussion of price elasticity of supply and demand it will be useful to consider two theoretical extremes. One is total unresponsiveness, which is called a **perfectly inelastic** situation or zero elasticity, and the other is complete responsiveness, which is called an unlimited, infinite or **perfectly elastic** situation.

Perfect inelasticity is shown for supply in figure 6.6, p 44. It shows that the quantity supplied per year is 100,000 units regardless of price. Hence for any percentage change in price, the quantity supplied remains constant. Look back at our formula for calculating elasticity. If the *change* in the quantity supplied is zero, then the numerator is zero, and anything divided into zero results in an answer of zero. Hence perfect inelasticity. Exactly the same situation can be envisaged for demand: that is, a vertical demand curve represents zero elasticity at every price, too.

At the opposite extreme is the situation depicted in figure 6.7. Here we show that at the price of 30p an unlimited quantity will be demanded. At a price that is only slightly above, or below, 30p, none will be demanded. In other words, there is infinite responsiveness here, and consequently we call the demand schedule in figure 6.7 infinitely elastic. This theoretical extreme does in fact exist in very competitive markets where many small comprising firms have to take their prices from one another. Selling above the market price would result in zero sales, selling below would lead to insufficient profits to stay in business.

Figure 6.6   Perfectly inelastic supply

The supply curve is vertical at the quantity of 100,000 units per year. That means that price elasticity of supply is zero. Producers supply 100,000 units no matter what the price.

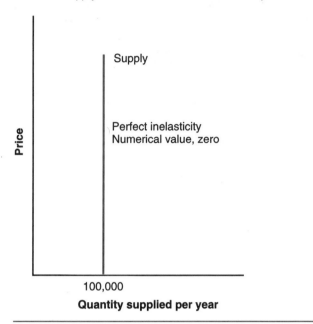

Again we can envisage the same possibility for supply: that is, a horizontal supply curve represents infinite elasticity as there is no limit to the amount supplied at the set market price.

Most of the estimated elasticities relating to markets in the built environment and elsewhere lie between these two extremes.

Figure 6.7   Perfectly elastic demand

The demand curve is horizontal at a price of 30p (in this example); consumers will demand an unlimited quantity. Raising or lowering the price will result in no sales at all. Consumers are completely responsive: there is infinite price elasticity.

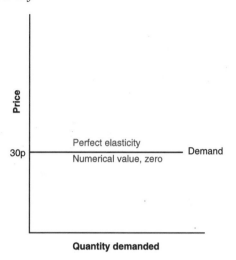

Chapter Summary 6.6

- When a demand or supply curve is vertical, it is completely inelastic; the price elasticity is zero. The same quantity is supplied/demanded at all prices.

- When a demand or supply curve is horizontal, it is completely elastic; the price elasticity is infinite. There is one 'market' price at which unlimited amounts are supplied/demanded.

Tutorial Preparation

Figure 6.8

Panel (a): Statistics relating to the housing market 1984–91

Period	Average price of all houses		Average Earnings		House Price/ Earnings	Change in Real Personal Disposable Income (RPDI)	Increase in Real House Prices
	£	Change %	£	Change %	Ratio	%	
1984	30,812		9,447		3.26	2.3	2.8
1985	33,188	7.7	10,069	6.6	3.30	2.3	1.5
1986	38,121	14.9	10,790	7.2	3.53	3.8	11.1
1987	44,220	16.0	11,648	7.9	3.80	3.2	11.3
1988	54,280	22.7	12,782	9.7	4.25	5.5	17.0
1989	62,135	14.5	14,014	9.6	4.43	5.4	6.2
1990	66,695	7.3	15,371	9.7	4.34	3.2	-2.0
1991	65,593	-1.7	16,817	9.4	3.90	-0.3	-7.2

Panel (b): Number of residential property transactions by type of buyer (000s)

Period	Individuals	Property Companies	Public Sector	Financial Institutions	Other	Total
1986	1,548	26	9	1	15	1,600
1987	1,688	33	10	2	12	1,744
1988	1,927	34	7	3	20	1,990
1989	1,404	29	9	2	23	1,467
1990	1,238	16	7	3	18	1,283
1991	1,188	13	6	3	14	1,225

Notes

1 Increases are over previous year.

2 The source for the number of residential property transactions and real personal disposal income figures is *Economic Trends.*

Source: Various abstracts from *Housing Finance,* Council of Mortgage Lenders August 1992

1 Using the relevant data from the various columns of information presented in figure 6.8, answer the following:
   a. Calculate the price elasticity of demand for owner-occupied housing for 1987/88.
   b. Calculate the income elasticity of demand for owner-occupied housing for any two years.
   c. What do the answers to (a) and (b) suggest about the housing market?
   d. Name three other determinants that you would regard as important influences on the owner-occupied housing market.
   e. Why do you think that figures for property transactions are now used in preference to figures relating to mortgage loans?

2 Again using figure 6.8 as your reference point, select any four of the columns displayed in either panel a or b and:
   a. Define what they show.
   b. Try to extend the data for two of your chosen series to be as up to date as possible.

3 a. Make an argument in favour of adding one more column of data to figure 6.8 to help understand the housing market.
   b. Find this extra data and record it for the years 1984–91.

4 Try to define the following:
   a. Unit-elastic supply.
   b. Interest rate elasticity of demand.

5 Complete the table shown in figure 6.9.

Price	Quantity Demanded	Total Sales Revenue	Elasticity Greater or Less Than One	Elastic Inelastic or Unitary?
13	7	91		
11	9			
9	11			
7	13			

6 'One of the key sources of recession is said to be the housing market'. Using the concept of income elasticity of demand and the related categories of luxury and necessity, begin to explain this increasingly quoted statement (proceed through several phases of a downswing into recession).

Tutorial Reading

What determines land values

The simplest models of land-price determination have always emphasised the importance of supply inelasticity. At the limit, we can argue that the total quantity of land available is fixed. If this is the case, land prices will be entirely demand-determined.

Thus, in figure 6.10, if demand is D_1, the market clearing price will be P_1. If demand increases to D_2, then price increases to P_2, but quantity remains unchanged. Similarly, if demand reduces to D_3, price falls to P_3 but there is no effect on quantity.

Figure 6.10   The demand for land

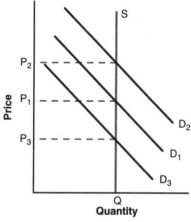

This raises two questions: what determines demand and can land really be regarded as being fixed in supply? With respect to demand, most land is not wanted for its own sake but rather is a derived demand based on the value of the output arising from that land. So in the case of agriculture, the maximum that people will be prepared to pay for a given piece of land will be the value of the most suitable crop less the costs of production, including some profit. Similarly, for housing the developer estimates the expected price that can be

obtained for the dwellings to be built less the costs of building and allowing for some profit. The residual determines the maximum that the developer will be prepared to pay for the land. Different users will bid different prices on the basis of relative profitability—and the most profitable use will win.

It is clear, therefore, that while the total land available may be fixed, the amount supplied to any particular use is not. In particular, different parcels of land have different attributes so their productivity varies between uses. The most important attributes which determine this productivity are:

● the type and quality of soil;
● other physical attributes such as height, gradient, drainage etc;
● environmental aspects which affect the desirability of the land in different uses; and
● accessibility, because all uses involve transport costs which will vary with location. Where the land is used for production, the costs of bringing together factors and sending out final products must be taken into account; where the land is used for housing, the financial, time and other costs of getting to work and other non-residential activities are relevant.

How much different groups — house purchasers, commerce, manufacturing, agricultural, etc — will be prepared to pay for particular parcels of land will vary depending upon the extent of demand and these attributes. In a free market, landowners will offer their land to the highest bidder and uses will therefore be allocated to different parcels of land on the basis of their productivity. The supply curve in each sector will be upward sloping, both because of the different attributes and because there are costs involved in transferring land from one use to another—but it will not be infinitely inelastic.

For example, if the demand for housing land increases, some land will be transferred from other less profitable uses, thus expanding the supply of housing land. In figure 6.11 (p 47) we assume that the only alternative use is agriculture. As demand for housing land goes up from D_H to D_{H1}—eg because incomes are increasing and with them the quantity of housing demanded— land is attracted away from the agricultural sector until the price per unit P_1 is the same in both markets. The price of housing land increases, but so does the supply of that land. In the agricultural sector, on the other hand, prices also go up but the quantity of land available declines from Q to Q_1. Thus, under free-market conditions increased demand for land in one sector affects all other sectors as land is transferred to more productive uses.

Further, although the total supply of land can be regarded as fixed, the quantity actually in use is likely to be very much less than this total because of these varying attributes and the differential costs of bringing land into production (eg drainage, provision of infrastructure, etc). For some types and location of land there may be no profitable use at all. As demand for land increases, it will become worthwhile to bring more land into use, so the elasticity of supply of land, even in total, is not zero.

Source: C. Whitehead in *Economic Review* May 1988

continued on p.47

Figure 6.11   Land in different markets

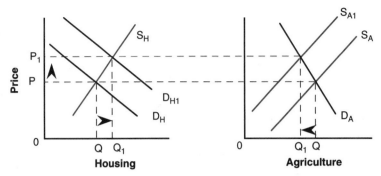

Housing

Agriculture

Questions

1. Land prices in England more than tripled in the 1980s. The price per hectare of housing land rose from an average £111,800 in 1981 to £354,900 in 1990. In Greater London, land cost £2.2 million per hectare in 1990, nearly six times its 1980 cost. In the South East as a whole prices rose from £203,600 to £636,500 per hectare (see *Regional Trends 27* HMSO July 1992).

   a) What determines these values?

   b) What will have happened to prices for agricultural land from 1980 to 1990?

2. As land becomes more expensive, land users will seek to substitute other factors of production.

   a) How will this affect commercial developers?

   b) How will this affect farmers?

3. What other factors apart from price will determine the elasticity of supply for land?

4. How will increasing numbers of house repossessions affect land uses?

5. How would the construction of a Contaminated Land Register affect values for agricultural and commercial uses?

6. Using supply and demand diagrams, explain how the residential and office property markets interrelate within a locality that you know.

7. Using economic terms, describe the income elasticity of demand for land.

Tutorial Reading

Introducing the Property Cycle by Bringing Together Elasticities

Perhaps the essential reason for the post-war success of property as an investment can be summed up by the statement that the occupation demand for property has a strongly positive income elasticity whereas the stock of property is relatively inelastic—in other words, occupation demand varies closely with changes in real incomes, but the stock of property is slow to change. It has been the rise in tenant demand to occupy property in response to the rise in real incomes and prosperity in the post-war period which has caused rental values to rise at a rate in excess of inflation. In the context of a sustained rise in real incomes, office and industrial property values must tend to keep pace with inflation, because the rise in real incomes creates a rise in space needs, and for profitable redevelopment to take place (and therefore new space to be provided), property values must exceed development costs.

Source: 'Retail growth & occupation demand' (p 406) in *Principles of Property Investment and Pricing* by W D Fraser, Macmillan 1984

Questions

1. Explain the statement: 'Occupation demand for property has a strongly positive income elasticity'.

2. Property markets are cyclical; offices, shops and industrial spaces tend to increase reasonably quickly in value and then rapidly decrease. Is this due to income elasticity of demand, price inelasticity of supply, both, or neither? Explain your answer fully.

3. a) The extract was written in the early 1980s; what property market changes have occurred since then?

   b) How do these changes affect the arguments being made?

4. Why must property values exceed development costs?

5. What factor(s) may cause development costs to exceed property value?

6. Explain a possible scenario for property market activity if incomes fell due to increasing unemployment.

Costs of the firm: property construction, development and consultancy

Chapter Summaries to Review
- *Opportunity Cost (1.2)*
- *Productive and Allocative Efficiency (2.4)*
- *Supply (5.1)*
- *Price Elasticity of Demand (6.1)*
- *Perfectly Elastic Demand (6.6)*

We now begin to examine more closely the supply side of an economy. That is, we develop a theory of how suppliers behave. This is known in economics as the **theory of the firm**. How do owners of businesses react to changing taxes, changing input prices and changing government regulations? In order to answer these questions, we have to understand the nature of production costs and revenues for each firm. In this chapter, we examine closely the nature of productivity and costs. These costs may relate to design, construction, maintenance, management, conservation, refurbishment or whatever. In chapter 8 we bring in the revenue side of the picture and conclude by considering the economist's rule for profit maximisation.

The Firm

In general terms we can define a business, or firm, as follows: a firm is an organisation that brings together different factors of production, such as labour, land and capital, to produce a product or service which it is hoped can be sold for a profit.

The actual size of a firm will affect its precise structure but a common set-up involves: entrepreneur, managers and workers. The entrepreneur is the person who takes the chances. Because of this, the entrepreneur is the one who will get any profits that are made. The entrepreneur also decides who runs the firm. Some economists maintain that the true quality of an entrepreneur becomes evident when he or she can pick good managers. Managers, in turn, are the ones who decide who should be hired and fired, and how the business should be generally organised. The workers are the people who ultimately use the machines to produce the products or services that are being sold by the firm. Workers and managers are paid contractual wages. They receive a specified amount for a specified time-period. Entrepreneurs are not paid contractual wages. They receive no specified 'reward'. Rather, they receive what is left over, if anything, after all expenses are paid. Profits are, therefore, the reward paid to the entrepreneur for taking risks.

Profit

The costs of production must include an element of profit to pay for the entrepreneur's services. If the level of profits falls in one area of activity, entrepreneurs may move their resources to an industry where the returns are higher. To illustrate this behaviour economists employ a concept of **normal profit**. Normal profit may be defined as the minimum level of reward required to ensure that existing entrepreneurs are prepared to remain in their present area of production.

Normal profit is included in the cost of production, as it is an essential minimum reward necessary to attract the entrepreneur into economic activity. Normal profit also highlights that all resources can be employed in several ways (ie all resources have alternative uses). Consequently, what is meant by 'profit' in economics differs from its general meaning.

To portray the general meaning of profit the following formula could be used:

Profits = total revenues – total costs

For economists an alternative formula is required:

Economic profits = total revenues – total opportunity cost of all inputs used

What the economic profits formula actually involves will become clearer by looking at two areas of resource allocation and the related cost accounting calculations. The first resource is capital and the second, labour.

Opportunity Cost of Capital

Firms enter or remain in an industry if they earn, at a minimum, a *normal rate of return (NROR)*, ie normal profit. By this term, we mean that people will not invest their wealth in a business unless they obtain a positive competitive rate of return, that is, unless their invested wealth pays off. Any business wishing to attract capital must expect to pay at least the same rate of return on the capital as all other businesses of *similar risk* are willing to pay. For example, if individuals can invest their wealth in almost any publishing firm and get a rate of 10 percent per year, then each firm in the publishing industry must *expect* to pay 10 percent as the normal rate of return to present and future investors. This 10 percent is a *cost to the firm*. The opportunity cost of capital is the amount of income, or yield, foregone by giving up an investment in another firm. Capital will therefore not stay in firms or industries where the rate of return falls below its opportunity cost. Clearly the expected rate of return will differ from industry to industry according to the degree of risk and difficulty involved.

Opportunity Cost of Labour

The self-employed contractor or one-man business often grossly exaggerates the profit because the opportunity cost of the time that they personally spend in the business is forgotten about. A good example is the people you know who run small surveying offices. These surveyors, at the end of the year, will sit down and figure out what their 'profits' are. They will add up all their fees and subtract what they had to pay to staff, what they had to pay to their suppliers, what they had to pay in taxes and so on. The end-result they will call 'profit'. However, they will not have figured into their costs the salary that they could have earned if they had worked for somebody else in a similar type of job. For a surveyor, that salary might be equal to £10 per hour. If so, then £10 per hour is the opportunity cost of the surveyor's time. In many cases, people who run their own businesses lose money in an economic sense. That is, their profits, as they calculate them, may be less than the amount they *could* have earned had they spent the same time working for someone else. Take a numerical example. If an entrepreneur can earn £10 per hour, it follows that the opportunity cost of his or her time is £10 × 40 hours × 52 weeks, or £20,800 per year. If this entrepreneur is making less than £20,800 per year in accounting profits, he or she is actually losing money. (This does not mean that such entrepreneurs are 'stupid'. They may be willing to pay for the non-pecuniary benefits of 'being the boss'.)

We have spoken only of the opportunity cost of capital and the opportunity cost of labour, but the concept applies to all inputs. Whatever the input, its opportunity cost must be taken into account when figuring out true economic profits. Another way of looking at the opportunity cost of running a business is that opportunity cost consists of all explicit (direct) and implicit (indirect) costs. Accountants only take account of explicit costs. Therefore, accounting profit ends up being the residual after only explicit costs are subtracted from total revenues.

Accounting Profits are not Equal to Economic Profits

The term *profits* in economics means the income that entrepreneurs earn, over and above their own opportunity cost of time, plus the opportunity cost of the capital they have invested in their business. Profits can be regarded as total revenues minus total costs—which is how the accountants think of them—but we must now include *all* costs.

We indicate this relationship in figure 7.1. We shall elaborate it further by considering some property developers' ideas on profit in a tutorial reading at the end of chapter 8.

Figure 7.1 Simplified view of economic and accounting profit
Here we see that, on the right-hand side, total revenues are equal to accounting cost plus accounting profit. That is, accounting profit is the difference between total revenue and total accounting cost. On the other hand, we see in the left-hand column that economic profit is equal to total revenue minus economic cost. Economic costs equal explicit accounting costs plus a normal rate of return on invested capital (plus any other implicit costs).

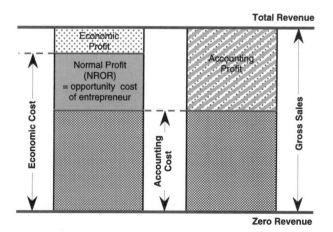

The Goal of the Firm

In most instances, we will use a model that is based on maximisation of profits. In other words, the firm's goal is to maximise profit; it is expected to attempt to make the positive difference between total revenues and total cost as large as it can. We use a profit-maximising model because it allows us to analyse a firm's behaviour with respect to quantity supplied and the relationship between cost and output. Whenever this profit-maximising model produces poor predictions, we will examine our initial assumption about profit maximisation. We might have to conclude that the primary goal of *some* firms is not to maximise profits but rather to maximise sales, or the number of workers, or the prestige of the owners and so on. However, we are primarily concerned with generalisations. Therefore, provided the assumption of profit maximisation is correct for *most* firms, then the model serves as a good starting point.

Chapter Summary 7.1

- A firm is any organisation that brings together production inputs in order to produce a good or service that can be sold for a profit.

- Accounting profits differ from economic profits.

- Economic profits are defined as total revenues minus total costs, including the full opportunity cost of all the factors of production.

- Sole owners often fail to consider the opportunity cost of the labour services provided by the owner.

- The full opportunity cost of capital invested in a business is generally not included as a cost when accounting profits are calculated. Thus, accounting profits overstate economic profits.

- Profit maximisation is regarded as the main objective when considering a firm's behaviour.

The Relationship Between Output and Inputs

A firm takes numerous inputs, combines them using a technological production process and ends up with an output. There are, of course, many factors of production or inputs. We can classify production inputs into two broad categories—labour and capital. The relationship between output and these two inputs is as follows:

Output per unit of time = some function of capital and labour inputs

Short Run versus Long Run

The time-period here is important. Throughout the rest of this chapter we will consider a 'short' time-period as opposed to a 'long' time-period. In other words, we are looking at *short-run* production relationships and *short-run* costs associated with production.

Any definition of the short run will, necessarily, be arbitrary. We cannot talk in terms of the short run being a specific period such as a month, or even a year. Rather, we must deal in terms of the short run having to do with the ability of the firm to alter the quantity of its inputs.

For ease of understanding, we will simply define the **short run** as any time-period when there is at least one factor of production that has a fixed cost. In the **long run**, therefore, all costs are variable. That is, all factors are variable.

How long is the long run? That depends on the individual industry. For McDonald's (hamburgers), the long run may be four or five months—because that is the time during which they can add new franchises. For British Steel the long run may be several years—because that is how long it takes to plan and build a new plant.

In most short-run analyses, the factor that has a fixed cost, or is fixed in quantity, is capital. We therefore state that in our short-run model, capital (as well as land) is fixed and invariable. That is not unreasonable: in a typical firm, the number of machines *in place* will not change over several months or even over a year. After all, the input that changes the most is labour. The production relationship that we use, therefore, holds capital and land constant or given, and labour is variable.

The Production Function—A Numerical Example

The relationship between physical output and the quantity of capital and labour used in the production process is sometimes called a **production function**. The term 'production function' in economics owes its origin to production engineers, for it is used to describe the technological relationship between inputs and outputs. It depends therefore on the available technology.

Look at figure 7.2 panel (a). Here we show a production function that relates total output in column 2 to the quantity of labour input in column 1. When there are no workers, there is no output. When there is the input of five workers (given the capital stock), there is a total output of 50 bushels per week. (Ignore for the moment the rest of that figure.) In figure 7.2 panel (b) we show this hypothetical production function graphically. Note, again, that it relates to the short run and that it is for an individual firm.

Figure 7.2 panel (b) shows a total physical product curve, or the amount of physical output that is possible when we add successive units of labour while holding all other inputs constant. The graph of the production function in figure 7.2 panel (b) is not a straight line. In fact, it peaks at seven workers and starts to go down. To understand why such a phenomenon occurs with an individual firm in the short run, we have to analyse in detail the **law of diminishing (marginal) returns**.

Diminishing Returns

The concept of diminishing marginal returns applies to many different situations. If you buckle one seat-belt over your body, a certain amount of additional safety is obtained. If you add another seat-belt, some more safety is obtained but less than when the first belt was secured. When you add a third seat-belt, again the amount of *additional* safety obtained must be even smaller. In a similar way, the **'U'-values** related to glazing do not decline steadily as glazing units increase. For instance the 'U'-values typically associated with single, double and treble glazing are 5.7, 2.8 and 2.0, respectively. Therefore, assuming the wall construction and other factors remain constant, adding one more unit of glazing from single to double improves the 'U'-value by 2.9, while a third pane of glass only improves the 'U'-value by 0.8.

The same analysis holds for firms in their use of productive inputs. When the returns from hiring more workers are diminishing, it does not necessarily mean that more workers will not be hired. In fact, workers will

be hired until the returns, in terms of the *value* of the extra output produced, are equal to the additional wages that have to be paid for those workers to produce the extra output. Before we get into the decision-making process, let us demonstrate that diminishing returns can be represented graphically and can be used in our analysis of the firm.

Measuring Diminishing Returns

How do we measure diminishing returns? First, we will limit the analysis to only one variable factor of production (or input). Let us say that factor is labour.

Figure 7.2 panel (a)   Diminishing returns: a hypothetical case in agriculture

In the first column, we measure the number of workers used per week on a given amount of land with a given amount of machinery, fertilizer and seed. In the second column, we give their total product; that is, the output that each specified number of workers can produce in terms of bushels of wheat. The third column gives the marginal product. The marginal product is the difference between the output possible with a given number of workers minus the output made possible with one less worker. For example, the marginal product of a fourth worker is eight bushels of wheat, because with four workers, 44 bushels are produced, but with three workers only 36 are produced; the difference is eight.

Input of labour	Total product (output in bushels of wheat per week)	Marginal physical product (in bushels of wheat per week)
0	0	
1	10	10
2	26	16
3	36	10
4	44	8
5	50	6
6	54	4
7	56	2
8	55	-1

Figure 7.2 panel (b)   A production function

A production function relates outputs to inputs. We have merely taken the numbers from columns 1 and 2 of figure 7.2 panel (a) and presented them as a graph.

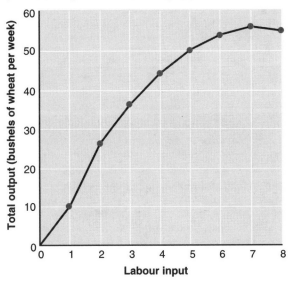

51

Every other factor of production, such as machinery, *must* be held constant. Only in this way can we calculate the marginal returns from using more workers and know when we reach the point of diminishing marginal returns.

Marginal returns for productive inputs are sometimes referred to as the **marginal physical product.** The marginal physical product of a worker, for example, is the *change* in total product that occurs when that worker joins an already existing production process. It is also the *change* in total product that occurs when that worker resigns or is laid off an already existing production process. The marginal productivity of labour therefore refers to the change in output caused by a one-unit change in the labour input.

At the very beginning, the marginal productivity of labour may increase. Take a firm starting without any workers, only machines. The firm then hires one worker, who finds it difficult to do the work alone. When the firm hires more workers, however, each is able to *specialise*, and the marginal productivity of these additional workers may actually be greater than it was with the previous few workers. Therefore, at the outset, increasing marginal returns are likely to be experienced. Beyond a certain point, however, diminishing returns must set in; each worker has (on average) fewer machines with which to work (remember, all other inputs are fixed). Eventually, the firm will become so crowded that workers will start running into one another and will become less productive.

Using these ideas, we can define the law of diminishing returns. For example consider the two following possible definitions:

As successive equal increases in a variable factor of production, such as labour, are added to other fixed factors of production, such as capital, there will be a point beyond which the extra or marginal product that can be attributed to each additional unit of the variable factor of production will decline;

or, more formally,

As the proportion of *one* factor in a combination of factors is increased, after a point, the marginal product of that factor will diminish.

Put simply, diminishing returns means that output does not rise in exact proportions to increases in, say, the number of workers employed.

An Example

An example of the law of diminishing returns is found in agriculture. With a fixed amount of land, fertilizer and tractors, the addition of more labourers eventually yields decreasing increases in output. A hypothetical set of numbers illustrating the law of diminishing marginal returns is presented in figure 7.2 panel (a) and shown graphically in figure 7.2 panel (c). Marginal productivity (returns from adding more workers) first increases, then decreases, and finally becomes negative. When one worker is hired, total output goes from zero to 10. Thus, the marginal physical product is equal to 10. When another worker is added, the marginal physical product increases to 16. Then it begins to decrease. The point of diminishing marginal returns occurs after two workers are hired.

Figure 7.2 panel (c)   Diminishing marginal returns

On the horizontal axis, we plot the numbers of workers as shown in figure 7.2 panel (a). On the vertical axis, we plot the marginal physical product in bushels of wheat (again taking the data from figure 7.2 panel (a)). When we go from no workers to one worker, marginal product is 10. We show this at a point between 0 and one worker, to indicate that marginal product relates to the change in the total product as we add additional workers. When we go from one to two workers, the marginal product increases to 16. After two workers, marginal product declines. Therefore, after two workers, we are in the area of

diminishing marginal physical returns. Total product, or output, reaches its peak at seven workers. In fact when we move from seven to eight workers, marginal product becomes negative.

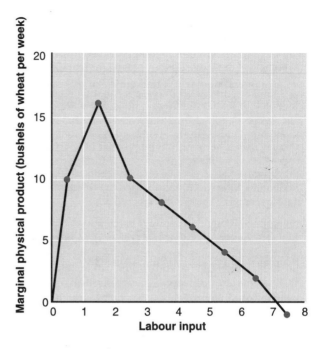

The Relationship Between Diminishing Marginal Returns and the Theory of the Firm

If we now introduce business costs, we can begin to understand the central importance of the law of diminishing returns. For example, consider the relationship between marginal cost, ie the cost of an extra unit of output, and the incidence of diminishing marginal physical returns as illustrated in figure 7.2 panel (a). Let us assume that each unit of labour can be purchased at a constant price. Further assume that labour is the only variable input. We see that, as more workers are hired, the marginal physical product first rises and then falls after the point where diminishing returns are encountered. Thus, the marginal cost of *each extra unit* of output will first fall as long as the marginal physical product is rising, and then it will rise as long as the marginal physical product is falling. Consider figure 7.2 panel (a). Assume that a worker is paid £100 per week. When we go from zero labour input to one unit, output increases by 10 bushels of wheat. Thus, each of those 10 bushels of wheat has a marginal cost of £10. Now the second unit of labour is hired and it, too, costs £100. Output increases by 16. Thus, the marginal cost is £100 ÷ 16 = £6.25. We continue the experiment. The next unit of labour yields only 10 additional bushels of wheat, so that marginal cost starts to rise again back to £10. The following unit of labour increases marginal physical product by only eight, so that marginal cost becomes £100 ÷ 8 = £12.50.

Marginal costs in turn affect the pattern of other costs, eg average variable costs and average total costs. Once these other costs have been discussed the importance of marginal cost analysis (and the above section) will become clearer. In the tutorial preparation section we will consider similar principles by analysing some building costs in relation to rents.

Chapter Summary 7.2

- **The technological relationship between output and input is called the production function. It relates output per unit of time to the several inputs, such as capital and labour.**

- **After some rate of output, the firm generally experiences diminishing marginal returns.**

- **The law of diminishing returns states that, if all factors of production are held constant except one, equal increments in that one variable factor will eventually yield decreasing increments in output.**

- **A firm's short-run costs are a reflection of the law of diminishing marginal returns. Given any constant price of the variable input, marginal costs decline as long as the marginal product of the variable resource goes up. At the point of diminishing marginal returns, the reverse occurs. Marginal costs will rise as the marginal product of the variable input declines.**

Short-run Costs to the Firm

In the short run, a firm incurs certain types of costs. Economists label all costs incurred as **total costs**. These are separated into total **fixed costs** and total **variable costs**, which we explain below. The relationship, or identity, is, therefore:

Total costs = total fixed costs + total variable costs

After we have looked at the elements of total costs, we will find out how to compute average and marginal costs.

Total Fixed Costs

Let us look at a building firm such as Wimpey. The bosses of that business can look around and see the plant and machinery that they own, the office buildings they occupy, and the staff that they are responsible for. Wimpey has to take account of the wear and tear of this equipment, and pay the administrative staff no matter how many houses it builds. In other words, all these costs are unaffected by variations in the amount of output. This

leads us to a very straightforward definition of fixed costs: all costs that do not vary, that is, costs that do not depend on the rate of production, are called fixed costs, or *sunk* costs.

Let us take as an example the fixed costs incurred by a manufacturer of brass door knobs. This firm's total fixed costs will equal the cost of the rent on its equipment and the insurance it has to pay. We see in panel (a) of figure 7.3 that total fixed costs per day are £10. In panel (b) p 54 these total fixed costs are represented by the horizontal line at £10 per day. They are invariant to changes in the output of door knobs per day: no matter how many are produced, fixed costs will remain at £10 per day.

The difference between total costs and total fixed costs is total variable costs (total costs ~ total fixed costs = total variable costs).

Total Variable Costs

Total **variable costs** are those costs whose magnitude varies with the rate of production. One obvious variable cost is wages. The more the firm produces, the more labour it has to hire and the more wages it has to pay. There are other variable costs, though. One is materials. In the production of brass door knobs, for example, brass must be purchased. The more door knobs that are made, the more brass must be bought. Part of the rate of **depreciation** (the rate of wear and tear) on the machines that are used in producing door knobs can also be considered a variable cost. Total variable costs are given in column 3 of panel (a) of figure 7.3. These are translated into the total variable cost curve in panel (b). Notice that the variable cost curve lies below the total cost curve by the vertical distance of £10. This vertical distance represents, of course, total fixed costs.

Short-run Average Cost Curves

In panel (b) of figure 7.3 we see total costs, total variable costs, and total fixed costs. Now we want to look at average cost. The average cost is simply cost per unit of output. It is a matter of simple arithmetic to figure the averages of these three cost concepts. We can define them simply as follows:

$$\text{Average total costs} = \frac{\text{total costs}}{\text{output}}$$

$$\text{Average variable costs} = \frac{\text{total variable costs}}{\text{output}}$$

$$\text{Average fixed costs} = \frac{\text{total fixed costs}}{\text{output}}$$

Figure 7.3 panel (a)   An example of the costs of production

The figures in columns 1, 2 and 3 are given, the others are then calculated according to the formulae shown at the head of each column. The numerical results are translated into graphical formats in panels b and c.

Total output (Q/day) (1)	Total fixed costs (TFC) (2)	Total variable costs (TVC) (3)	Total costs (TC) (4) = (2) + (3)	Average fixed costs (AFC) (5) = (2) ÷ (1)	Average variable costs (AVC) (6) = (3) ÷ (1)	Average total costs (ATC) (7) = (4) ÷ (1)	Marginal cost (MC) (8) = Change in (4) / Change in (1)
0	£10.00	0	£10.00	-	-	-	
							£5.00
1	10.00	£5.00	15.00	£10.00	£5.00	£15.00	
							3.00
2	10.00	8.00	18.00	5.00	4.00	9.00	
							2.00
3	10.00	10.00	20.00	3.33	3.33	6.67	
							1.00
4	10.00	11.00	21.00	2.50	2.75	5.25	
							2.00
5	10.00	13.00	23.00	2.00	2.60	4.60	
							3.00
6	10.00	16.00	26.00	1.67	2.67	4.33	
							4.00
7	10.00	20.00	30.00	1.43	2.86	4.28	
							5.00
8	10.00	25.00	35.00	1.25	3.13	4.38	
							6.00
9	10.00	31.00	41.00	1.11	3.44	4.56	
							7.00
10	10.00	38.00	48.00	1.00	3.80	4.80	
							8.00
11	10.00	46.00	56.00	0.91	4.18	5.09	

Figure 7.3 panel (b)

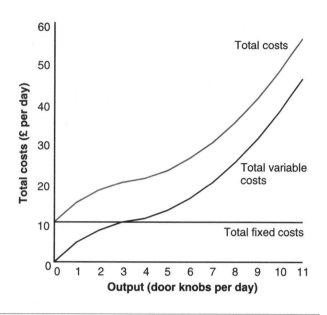

Figure 7.3 panel (c)

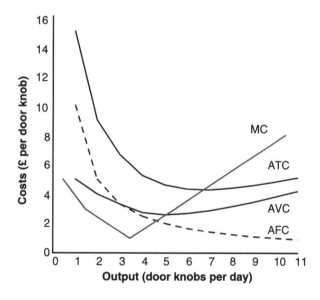

The arithmetic is done in columns 5, 6, and 7 in panel (a) of figure 7.3, while the numerical results are translated into a graph in panel (c). Let us see what we can observe about the three average cost curves in that graph.

Average Fixed Costs (AFC)

Average fixed costs continue to fall throughout the output range. In fact, if we were to continue the diagram further to the right, we would find that average fixed costs would get closer and closer to the horizontal axis. That is because total fixed costs remain constant. As we divide this fixed amount by a larger and larger number of units of output, the result, AFC, must become smaller and smaller.

Average Variable Costs (AVC)

We assume a particular form of the **average variable cost** curve. The form that it takes is U-shaped: first it falls; then it starts to rise.

Average Total Costs (ATC)

This curve has a shape similar to the average variable cost curve. However, it falls even more dramatically in the beginning and rises more slowly after it has reached a minimum point. It falls and then rises because **average total costs** is the summation of the average fixed cost curve and the average variable cost curve. Thus, when AFC plus AVC are both falling, it is only logical that ATC would fall, too. At some point, however, AVC starts to increase while AFC continues to fall. Once the increase in the AVC curve outweighs the decrease in the AFC curve, the ATC curve will start to increase and will develop its familiar U-shape.

Marginal Cost

We have stated repeatedly in this text that the action is always on the margin—movement in economics is always determined at the margin. This dictum holds true within the firm also. Firms, according to economic analysis are very interested in their **marginal cost**. Since the term *marginal* means additional or incremental, marginal costs refer to those costs that result from a one-unit change in the production rate. For example, if the production of 10 brass door knobs per day costs a firm £48, and the production of 11 brass door knobs costs it £56 per day, then the marginal cost of producing that eleventh brass door knob per day is £8.

We find marginal cost by subtracting the total cost of producing all but the last unit from the total cost of producing all units, including the last one. Marginal cost can be measured, therefore, by using the formula:

$$\text{marginal cost} = \frac{\text{change in total cost}}{\text{change in output}}$$

We show the marginal costs of door knob production per day in column 8 of Figure 7.3 panel (a), where marginal cost is defined as the change in total cost divided by the change in output. In our example, we have changed output by one unit each time, so we can ignore the denominator in that particular formula.

This marginal cost schedule is shown graphically in panel (c) of figure 7.3. Like average variable costs and average total costs, marginal costs first fall and then rise.

Finding Minimum Costs

At what rate of output of brass door knobs per day does our representative firm achieve the minimum average total cost? Column 7 in panel (a) of figure 7.3 shows that the minimum average total cost is £4.28, which occurs at an output rate of seven brass door knobs per day. We can find this minimum cost also by finding the point in panel (c) of figure 7.3 at which the marginal cost curve intersects the average total cost curve. This should not be surprising. When marginal cost is below average total cost, average total cost falls. When marginal cost is above average total cost, average total cost rises. At the point where average total costs are neither falling nor rising, marginal cost must then be equal to average total cost. When we represent this graphically, the marginal cost curve will intersect the average total cost curve at its minimum.

The same analysis applies to the intersection of the marginal cost curve and the average variable cost curve. When are average variable costs at a minimum? According to figure 7.3 panel (a), average variable costs are at a minimum of £2.60 at an output rate of five door knobs per day. This is exactly where the marginal cost curve intersects the average variable cost curve in figure 7.3 panel (c).

Chapter Summary 7.3

- Remember the short run is that period of time during which the firm cannot alter its existing plant size.

- Total costs equal total fixed costs plus total variable costs.

- Fixed costs are those that do not vary with the rate of production; variable costs are those that do vary with the rate of production.

- Average total costs equal total costs divided by output, or $ATC = TC \div Q$.

- Average variable costs equal total variable costs divided by output, or $AVC = TVC \div Q$.

- Average fixed costs equal total fixed costs divided by output, or $AFC = TFC \div Q$.

- Average cost equals the change in total cost divided by the change in output.

- The marginal cost curve intersects the minimum point of the average total cost curve and the minimum point of the average variable cost curve.

Long-run Cost Curves

The long run, as you will remember, is defined as the time during which *full* adjustment can be made to any change in the economic environment. That is, *in the long run, all factors of production are variable*. For example, in the long run the firm can alter its plant size. Consequently, there may be many short-run curves as a firm develops over the years, but only one long run. Long-run curves are sometimes called **planning curves**, and the long run may be regarded as the **planning horizon**.

We start our analysis of long-run cost curves by considering a single firm contemplating the construction of a single plant. The firm has, let us say, three alternative plant sizes from which to choose on the planning horizon. Each particular plant size generates its own short-run average total cost curve. Now that we are talking about the difference between long- and short-run cost curves, we will label all short-run curves with an *S*; short-run average (total) costs will be labelled SAC, and all long-run average cost curves will be labelled LAC.

Look at figure 7.4 panel (a). Here we show three short-run average cost curves for three plant sizes that are successively larger. Which is the optimal plant size to build? That depends on the anticipated rate of output per unit of time. Assume for a moment that the anticipated rate is Q_1. If plant size 1 is built, the average costs will be C_1. If plant size 2 is built, we see on SAC$_2$ that the average costs will be C_2, which is greater than C_1. Thus, if the anticipated rate of output is Q_1, the appropriate plant size is the one from which SAC$_1$ was derived.

Note, however, that, if the anticipated permanent rate of output per unit of time goes from Q_1 to Q_2, and plant size 1 has been decided upon, average costs would be C_4. However, if plant size 2 had been decided upon, average costs would be C_3 which are clearly less than C_4.

Long-run Average Cost Curve

If we make the further assumption that during the development of a firm the entrepreneur is faced with an infinite number of choices regarding plant size, then we can envisage an infinite number of SAC curves similar to the three in figure 7.4 panel (a). We are not able, of course, to draw an infinite number; we have drawn quite a few, however, in figure 7.4 panel (b).

By drawing the envelope of these various SAC curves, we find the **long-run average cost curve (LAC)**. The long-run average cost curve, by result, represents the cheapest way to produce various levels of output, ie provided the entrepreneur is prepared to change the size and design of his plant. Consequently long-run average cost curves are sometimes referred to as planning curves.

Figure 7.4 panel (a)   Preferable plant size

If the anticipated permanent rate of output per unit time-period is Q_1, the optimal plant to build would be the one corresponding to SAC$_1$ because average costs are lower. However, if the rate of output increases to Q_2, it will be more profitable to have a plant size corresponding to SAC$_2$, as unit costs can fall to C_3.

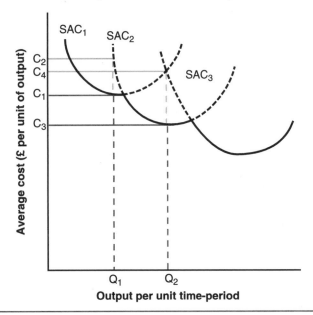

Figure 7.4 panel (b)   Deriving the long-run average cost curve

If we draw all the possible short-run average curves that correspond to different plant sizes and then draw the envelope to these various curves, SAC1 ... SAC8, we obtain the long-run average cost curve, or the planning curve.

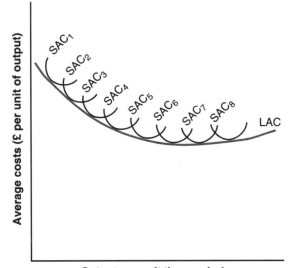

Why the Long-run Average Cost Curve is U-Shaped

Notice that the long-run average cost curve, LAC in figure 7.4 panel (b) is U-shaped, similar to the U-shape of the short-run average cost curve developed previously in this chapter. The reason for the U-shape of the long-run average cost curve is not the same as that for the short-run U-shaped average cost curve. The short-run average cost curve is U-shaped because of the law of diminishing marginal returns. However, that law cannot apply to the long run, because in the long run all factors of production are variable, so there is no point of diminishing marginal returns since there is no fixed factor of production. Why, then, do we see the U-shape in the long-run average cost curve? The reasoning has to do with changes in the scale of operations. When the long-run average cost curve slopes downwards it means that average cost decreases as output increases. Whenever this happens the firm is experiencing **economies of scale**. If, on the other hand, the long-run average cost curve is sloping upwards, the firm is incurring increases in average costs as output increases. That firm is said to be experiencing **diseconomies of scale**. Finally, if long-run average costs are invariant to changes in output, the firm is experiencing **constant returns to scale**. In figure 7.5 we show these three stages. The first stage is for a firm experiencing economies of scale; the second stage constant returns to scale; and the third stage diseconomies of scale.

Figure 7.5   Economies of scale, constant returns to scale and diseconomies of scale

Long-run average cost curves will fall when there are economies of scale, as shown in stage 1 up until $0Q_1$. There will be constant returns to scale when the firm is experiencing output $0Q_1$ to $0Q_2$, as shown in stage 2. And, finally, long-run average costs will rise when the firm is experiencing diseconomies of scale, beyond $0Q_2$ in stage 3.

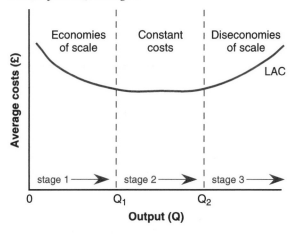

Returns to Scale: in Three Stages

Savings (economies of scale) are possible as firms progress to larger and larger production. Following Professor EAG Robinson's approach there are five basic reasons for the economies of scale. He termed these:
1   Technical economies: these relate to taking full advantage of the capacity of machinery.
2   Managerial economies: relating to specialised management and its benefit over larger and larger numbers.
3   Commercial economies: such as buying in bulk and advertising.
4   Financial economies: larger firms have a greater variety of sources for funds and often at favourable rates.
5   Risk-bearing economies: larger firms may achieve distinct advantages by diversifying into several markets and researching new ones.

When economies of scale are exhausted constant returns to scale begin. Some economists regard the commencement of this stage as the **minimum efficient scale**, since it represents the lowest rate of output at

which long-run average costs are minimised. It would be represented by point $0Q_1$ in figure 7.5.

After a point, however, average unit costs may start to rise, ie a firm can expect to run into diseconomies of scale. For example, it might be possible to hire from one to 10 workers and give them each a shovel to dig ditches, however, as soon as 10 workers are hired, it may also be necessary to hire an overseer to co-ordinate the ditch-digging efforts. Thus, perhaps, constant returns to scale will remain until 10 workers and 10 shovels are employed; then decreasing returns to scale set in. As the layers of supervision grow, the costs of communication grow more than proportionately, hence, the average cost per unit will start to increase.

A Final Note on Technical Terms

The economies (listed above) are all *internal* to the firm. That is to say, they do not depend on what other firms are doing or what is happening in the economy. They are formally referred to as **internal economies (or diseconomies) of scale** This phrase is necessary to distinguish them from **external economies** which arise through the growth of the whole *industry*.

External Economies of Scale

When expansion of a *whole industry* occurs *all* the comprising firms benefit. Firms can buy in services more easily; firms can combine to fund research and/or training; firms often become more specialised; a trade association and/or journal may be started. These developments normally lead to savings for *all* the firms involved.

Therefore it is possible to envisage a firm benefiting from internal and external economies of scale. The former are the direct result of internal company policy, and the latter the by-product of being a firm involved in an expanding industrial sector.

These terms are particularly important to remember if you intend to use other texts for the tutorial preparation at the close of this chapter.

Chapter Summary 7.4

- The long run is often called the planning horizon.

- The long-run average cost curve is derived by drawing a line tangent to a series of short-run average cost curves, each corresponding to a different plant size.

- The firm can experience economies of scale, diseconomies of scale and constant returns to scale, all according to whether the long-run average cost curve slopes downwards, upwards or is horizontal (flat).

- Economies of scale refer to what happens when all factors of production are increased and average costs fall. This may occur for any one of five reasons: (i) managerial, (ii) commercial, (iii) financial, (iv) technical and (v) risk–bearing.

- The minimum efficient scale occurs at the lowest rate of output at which long–run average costs are minimised.

- The firm may experience diseconomies of scale because of limits to the efficient functioning of management.

- Internal economies of scale arise from the growth of one firm, regardless of what is happening to other firms.

- External economies of scale relate to the whole industry.

Tutorial Preparation

1 The following exercise is designed to help students consolidate their understanding of the various business costs identified in this chapter.

    a. Give a brief definition and an example for each of the eight column headings shown in figure 7.6.

    b. Copy figure 7.6 and complete the missing information from the costs given.

    c. Once you have completed the cost information, can you identify the profit maximising position? (Explain your answer as fully as possible.)

Figure 7.6   Short-run cost behaviour

Q Output (Col 1)	FC Fixed Costs (Col 2)	VC Variable Costs (Col 3)	TC Total Costs (Col 4)	ATC Average Total Costs (Col 5)	MC Marginal Costs (Col 6)	AFC Average Fixed Costs (Col 7)	AVC Average Variable Costs (Col 8)
0	100	0					
10	100	100		20			
20		180					
30		230					
40		260					
50		350					
60		500					
70		670					
80		860					
90		1160					

2 Internal and external economies of scale.

    a. Make comprehensive notes on internal economies of scale and give examples that relate to professions within the built environment.

    b. Give an example of an external economy of scale experienced by any surveying practice.

3 Using the most up to date *Housing and Construction Statistics* (HMSO, Department of Environment), find the number and size of private contractors, and the value of work done by these contractors. Tables 3.1, 3.3, 3.4 and 3.8 in the annual publication are the most relevant. Having found this data, answer the following questions.

    a. Of the total number of private contractors in the construction industry, what percentage of firms employs less than 25 people?

    b. What percentage of output in value terms are firms with less than 25 employees responsible for within the private construction industry?

    c. Are big firms or small firms more efficient in the construction industry? (NB In economics, firms with less than 25 employees are often regarded as small firms.)

    d. Why do you think the construction industry has so many small firms?

Tutorial Reading

Graveyard Management

Avoiding too many puns about being a deadly topic and confirming the idea of economics as a dismal science, a study of graveyard management and the costs of funerals clearly illustrates many basic economic concepts. To state just one example, funerals illustrate the theoretical extreme of perfectly inelastic demand more effectively than most other goods.

Indeed, it was partly due to their odd market characteristics that the **Office of Fair Trading (OFT)** investigated funeral businesses and issued a report in

January 1989. This report was reviewed by the media and some edited highlights from one such article follow:

About 12,500 people were buried in Britain last week. The services, ceremonies and assorted arrangements cost their nearest and dearest some £7.3 million. They also paid out a further £1.9 million for flowers, urns, plots of land, entries in books of remembrance and rose bushes with bronze plaques. Did the grieving relatives get value for money, or were they taken for a funeral ride?...

Overall, the OFT found that less than 25 percent of the people surveyed had seen or been given a price-list to help them choose a funeral to suit their pockets and circumstances, and 40 percent had been given no price information *at all*. A third were never given an estimate of the total cost, and realised the true figure only when they saw the final bill.

The OFT says: 'For many this will be their first experience of death and its aftermath. Some may be too embarrassed to tell a funeral director that what he is offering seems expensive. Others may simply not take in what is said or realise what they have agreed to...'

'We accept the situation is not perfect', says Graham Barber, vice president of the Funeral Directors' Association, who runs his own firm in Norwich, 'but it's not as black as it sounds. In my experience, the public's expectation of the cost is far greater. They are pleasantly surprised when it doesn't cost £1,000.'

When customers walk into a funeral parlour, they are shown a brochure. The range from which they are invited to choose usually starts with the cheapest (the veneered chipboard job) at around £525, to a silk-lined oak casket that could set them back £1,250 or more. Included

in this, however, just to make the comparison more difficult, is the provision of a hearse and one mourners' car. Hidden in this package is the funeral director's fee for the use of his premises and services as liaison man between the family and officialdom.

Anything else is extra and goes under the heading of disbursements, which can include: the cost of removing the body from the hospital or home, £60; the minister's fees, £25; grave diggers' fees, £45–£110; crematorium, £60–£90; extra cars, £60; medical certificate fees in the case of cremations, £42.40–£104.

The price of a burial plot varies greatly in different parts of the country. Some church land is free but in east London a private grave for two people will cost £500; a grave in a Jewish

cemetery in Willesden runs as high as £7,000.

The average cost of a burial is currently £630 and a cremation £567, according to the OFT survey. Costs vary, however, throughout the country. Another study carried out for the Independent Order of Oddfellows, the Manchester-based friendly society, shows that the south-east is the most expensive place to die. The average interment there involves £665. A typical basic funeral, according to the Oddfellows, is now running at £736, up by a solid-looking £200 since 1986—well above even present rates of general inflation.

Source: Adapted from A Wilson 'Cost of dying: are we being conned into the grave?' *Sunday Times* 28 February 1989

Questions

1   For those who own and manage graveyards the law of diminishing returns sets in quickly. Fully explain this statement using any diagram and/or examples that seem appropriate.

2   a) Explain, using a diagram, why the concept of perfectly inelastic demand is relevant in the case of funeral services.

   b) Can you think of any other good or service that illustrates the theoretical concept of perfectly inelastic demand?

   c) How does a firm faced with a nearly perfect inelastic demand schedule benefit when it comes to covering costs?

   d) What does (c) imply for firms faced with a perfectly elastic demand schedule?

3   When it comes to funerals, it seems that market forces may not operate as effectively as they do in other sectors. A possible way of correcting the type of market failure that benefits funeral directors would be to introduce a tax. The tax could be of two types: a unit tax per burial or a lump-sum tax per year for being licensed to bury people.

   a) Explain and illustrate, using diagrams, the effect on some of the different costs displayed in figure 7.3 (panel c) of (i) a unit tax and (ii) a lump-sum tax.

   b) Which of these two taxes, if any, would you advise a government to adopt? (How else may funeral directors be made more accountable to market forces?)

   c) Give examples from the article that suggest funeral directors benefit from a type of market failure.

   d) How could those involved in the funeral industry be accused of wasting resources?

4   a) What does the Office of Fair Trading do?

   b) Which other industries might the OFT be interested in researching?

   c) Why do you think the supply of mortgage valuations has been an issue raised by the OFT, and subsequently investigated by the Monopolies and Mergers Commission?

5   Explain the economic reasons why a plot in a Jewish cemetery in Willesden would be so expensive.

6   During 1987 Westminster City Council, under the leadership of Dame Shirley Porter, sold three of their cemeteries for £1. Within the next 12 months the sale of these cemeteries caused much controversy in the press, especially as the assets exchanged hands for significant profits, before being returned to council ownership. Research the reasons behind these dealings, or discuss the possibilities that may have led to such an odd sequence of events. (Fraud was not involved.)

Tutorial Reading

The Costs of Sick Building Syndrome

Sick building syndrome is not, as the term may suggest, a problem explicitly describing a structural fault. Rather the term seeks to describe a group of specific symptoms that employees may experience owing to the nature of the building they work in. In one way or another they are sickened by the

building. (See the dictionary for symptoms.) Interest in sick building syndrome has become prominent since the mid-1980s. Research has taken on many guises in many nations—but as yet no definite cures have been identified.

There are now many possible causes

of sick building syndrome, but it seems probable that it is in some way associated with air-conditioned buildings; in fact in the States it is frequently referred to as 'tight building syndrome'.

Next we shall consider the costs of this syndrome and its possible cure.

There may be some short-term value in increasing the level of natural ventilation, but this would increase the energy costs. The positive trade-off would be improved productivity and the related decrease in staff costs. Putting the costs in a broader context, the higher energy use would have an impact on the supply of non-renewable resources and increase pollution at the power generating stations. The broader positive aspect would include a reduction in absences due to sickness, time spent complaining and the time needed for extended breaks.

Questions

1   Using a diagram similar to figure 7.4 panel (a) explain the context and meaning of the phrase 'The positive trade-off would be improved productivity and the related decrease in staff costs'.

2   Why do the costs related to sick building syndrome often get overlooked in the management accounts?

3   What other 'hidden costs' may you need to quantify when considering a building project.

4   Use the costs of sick building syndrome to compare the concept of 'profit' as employed by an economist and an accountant.

5   Using the concept of opportunity cost, try to explain how you might put a monetary value on the benefits of curing sick building syndrome.

Tutorial Reading

Design and Build

The one-stop approach to construction is catching on in many sectors and in many guises across the UK... The overriding appeal of **design and build** is its perceived package holiday-like qualities —one ear to bend, one cheque to sign, no unexpected surcharges.

Like it or lump it—and architects mostly lump it—about a fifth of all projects are now procured along this route.

Growth is mainly in the public sector. Housing associations are almost entirely design and build. Health, food manufacture and leisure are also target areas.

The private sector has been slower on the uptake but some pundits are predicting that the use of design and build for commercial projects will surge in the second half of this decade.

Contractors of course are pleased this method of procurement is gaining prominence. Even in these rough times, it is still possible to make more from a design and build contract than from any other form, though this route is no less competitive.

But many contractors are less gleeful about the benefits than might be expected. In theory, design and build puts the contractor in charge of the whole project. But in practice clients are demanding more and more say in the design.

Instead of giving a contractor a brief on an A4 slip of paper, as they might have done in the past, clients are employing their own consultants to come up with a concept design. They see this as a necessary precaution to ensure they get the building they want.

Clients' consultants are now designing buildings up to stage D on the RIBA architect's appointment scale— that is roughly the layout and look of the building. When the contract is let the contractor then has the responsibility of thrashing out the details. To some critics, this so-called develop and construct hybrid is like letting architects in through the back door. Contractors call it 'cynical design and build...'.

'The up side of taking detailed design,' says Tom Barton, a Mowlem South East director with responsibility for design and build, 'is that it doesn't cost so much to put together the bid.' Mowlem, however, has no in-house design staff, arguing that it is best to use different designers to suit the project.

A current fashion is for the client to pass the architect on to the contractor — so called 'novation'. But novation can also have its problems, causing near schizophrenia in the architect. Ray Moxley, senior partner with Moxley Jenner and Partners says: 'The problem with novation is that the client still thinks the architect is working in his interest. Of course he's not, and when the contractor comes under financial pressure then the quality is still going to be trimmed.'

One architect currently being novated has mixed feelings about it: 'As architects we want to be able to see the design through, but it can become contractually difficult.' He says novation also has a down side for the client because the contractor may claim against the client if the architect defaults.

Novation can work well, but the whole point about design and build is that the client should be offered a cohesive team.

Source: Adapted from special feature 'Design and build' *Building* 14 August 1992 pp 24-36.

Questions

1   In your own words describe what is meant by a design and build contract.

2   Which economic concept could be used to explain the development of design and build?

3   a) Name three firms involved in design and build.
    b) State two of the sectors that they have specifically specialised within.

4   What arguments could a traditional practice-based architect make against the design and build contractors?

5   'Most practitioners of design and build agree that the success of a project depends on the client's initial brief.' What economic implications does this statement carry for future design and build contracts?

6   'It is possible to make more from a design and build contract than from another form.' Explain why this is the case in 1992?

7   As more firms gear themselves up for design and build, will profits rise or fall? Explain your answer as fully as possible.

8   a) Find an example of a completed project that was constructed on a design and build basis.
    b) Critically assess the performance of this building
    c) What recommendations would you make if this project were to be repeated?

8

Theory of the firm (Part 2): property construction, development and consultancy

Chapter Summaries to Review
- Demand (4.1)
- Supply (5.1)
- Horizontal Demand Curve (6.6)
- Accounting and Economic Profits (7.1)
- Economies and Diseconomies of Scale (7.4)

Firms have to know not only about costs, discussed in the last chapter, but also about revenues when they make pricing and output decisions. Indeed, it is impossible to identify a profit-maximising position until firms know of revenue, especially as the cost curves include an element of normal profit. In order to understand the precise relationship between output, revenues, and price, a firm has to know the structure of the market, or industry in which it is selling its product. There are various **market structures**, all dependent upon the extent to which buyers and sellers can assume that their own buying and selling decisions do not affect market price. At one extreme there is a **monopoly** where one producer dominates the market, and controls the price and output decisions alone. To the other extreme both buyers and sellers correctly assume that they cannot affect market price—this market structure is known as **perfect competition**. Whenever buyers and sellers must take into account how their individual actions affect market price, we are not in a market structure of perfect competition, but have entered an *imperfectly competitive market*. We examine such markets towards the close of this chapter.

The Purpose of Perfect Competition

To begin, we will consider in some detail the hypothetical extreme of a perfectly competitive market. Although no real-life industry meets all the requirements of such a market, it provides an important reference point for economists. The perfectly competitive market acts as a benchmark from which other market situations can be judged. As will be seen, an optimum allocation of resources arises from perfect competition, because every firm is producing at minimum unit cost. Consequently, we will be able to proceed with common notions of what is meant by a 'fair' price, a 'normal profit' and an 'efficient' industry.

The term perfect competition relates to a specific (model) market structure, the characteristics of which are set out below.

The Characteristics of Perfect Competition

1   The product that is sold by the firms in the industry is *homogeneous*. This means that the product sold by each firm in the industry is a perfect substitute for the product sold by every other firm. In other words, buyers are able to choose from a large number of sellers a product that the buyers believe to be the same. The product is thus not in any sense differentiated regardless of the source of supply.

2   Any firm can enter or exit the industry without serious impediments. Resources must be able to move in and out of the industry without, for example, government legislation preventing such resource mobility.

3   There must be a large number of buyers and sellers. When this is the case, no one buyer or one seller has any influence on price. Also, when there are large numbers of buyers and sellers, they will be acting independently.

4   There must be the fullest information available to both buyers and sellers about market prices, product quality and cost conditions.

Now that we have defined the characteristics of a perfectly competitive *market* structure we shall consider the position of an individual firm. We define a **perfectly competitive firm** as one that is such a small part of the total industry in which it operates that it cannot significantly affect the price of the product in question. This means that each firm in the industry is a **price-taker**—the firm takes price as given: as something that is determined *outside* of its individual control.

This definition of a competitive firm is obviously idealised, for in one sense the individual firm has to set prices. How can we ever have a situation where firms regard prices as set by forces outside their control? The answer is that even though every firm, by definition, sets its own prices, a firm in a perfectly competitive situation will find that it will eventually have no customers at all if it sets its price above the competitive price. Let us now see what the demand curve of an individual firm in a competitive industry looks like.

Single-firm Demand Curve

We have already discussed the characteristics of demand schedules. We pointed out that for completely elastic demand curves, if the individual firm raises the price by one penny, it will lose all its business. Well, this is how we characterise the demand schedule for a purely competitive firm—it is a horizontal line at the going market price. That is, it is completely elastic (see chapter 6). And that going market price is determined by the market forces of supply and demand. Figure 8.1 is the *hypothetical* market demand schedule faced by an individual brass door knob producer who, we assume, controls only a very, very small part of the total market for brass door knobs.

Figure 8.1   The demand curve for an individual brass door-knob manufacturer

We assume that the individual door–knob producer represents such a small part of the total market that he cannot influence the price. The firm accepts the price as given. At the going market price it faces a horizontal demand curve, dd. If it raises its price even one penny, it will sell nothing. Conversely the firm would be foolish to lower its price below £5, because it can sell all that it can produce at a price of £5. The firm is a price-taker and its demand curve is completely, or perfectly, elastic.

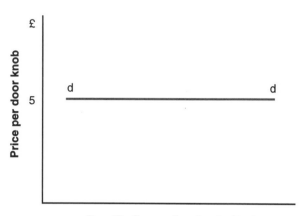

Quantity (brass door knobs/day)

At the market price of £5 per unit, which is where the horizontal demand curve for the individual producer lies, people's demand for brass door knobs from that manufacturer is perfectly elastic; the firm can sell as much output as it wants, providing it does not alter the price. If the firm were to raise its price, consumers will buy the same door knobs from another producer.

How Much Does the Perfect Competitor Produce?

As we have shown, a perfect competitor has to accept the given price of the product. If the firm raises its price, it sells nothing. If it lowers its price, it makes less money per unit sold than it otherwise could. The firm has only one decision variable left: how much should it produce? We will apply our model of the firm to this question to come up with an answer. We shall use the *profit-maximisation* model and assume that firms, whether competitive or monopolistic, will attempt to maximise their total profits, that is, the positive difference between total revenues and total costs.

Total Revenues

Every firm has to consider its **total revenues**. Total revenues are defined as the quantity sold multiplied by the price. (They are also the same as total receipts from the sale of output.) The perfect competitor must take the price given.

Look at panel (a) of figure 8.2. Much of the information comes from panel (a) of figure 7.3 but we have added some essential columns for our analysis. Column 3 is the market price of £5 per door knob, which is also equal to average revenue (AR), since each door knob is sold for the same price.

Column 4 shows the total revenues, or TR, as equal to the market price, P, times the total output in sales per day, or Q. Thus, $TR = P \times Q$. We are assuming that the market supply and demand schedules intersect at a price of £5,

and that this price holds for all the firm's production. We are also assuming that since our door-knob maker is a small part of the market, he can sell all he produces at that price. Thus, panel (b) of figure 8.2 shows the total revenue curve as a straight line. For every unit of sales, total revenue is increased by £5.

Total Costs

Revenues are only one side of the picture. Costs must also be considered. **Total costs** are given in column 2, panel (a) of figure 8.2. Notice that when we plot total costs in panel (b), the curve is not a straight line but, rather, a wavy line that is first above the total revenue curve, then below it, and then above it again. When the total cost curve is above the total revenue curve, the firm is experiencing losses. When it is below the total revenue curve, the firm is making profits. Where the two curves intersect represents break-even points.

Comparing Total Costs with Total Revenues

By comparing total costs with total revenues, we can figure out the number of brass door knobs that the individual competitive firm should produce per day. Our analysis rests on the assumption that the firm will attempt to maximise total profits. In figure 8.2 panel (a) we see that total profits reach a maximum at a production rate of between seven and eight brass door knobs per day. We can see this graphically in figure 8.2 panel (b). The firm will maximise profits at that place on the graph where the total revenue curve exceeds the total cost curve by the greatest amount. In our example, that occurs at a rate of output and sales of either seven or eight door knobs per day; this rate may be called the profit-maximising rate of production.

Another way to find the profit-maximising rate of production for a firm is by looking at marginal revenues and marginal costs. This method is formally termed marginal analysis, and we consider this method after we have clarified the meanings of marginal revenue and marginal cost.

Marginal cost has already been introduced in chapter 7. It was defined as the change in total cost due to a one-unit change in production. As you will remember, the resulting schedule of costs was based on the law of diminishing returns: at first costs fall and then they begin to rise (column 9 of figure 8.2 (panel a) is taken from figure 7.3). This leaves only **marginal revenue** to be clarified.

Marginal Revenue

What amount can our individual door-knob making firm hope to receive each time it sells an additional (marginal) brass door knob? Since the firm is such a small part of the market and cannot influence the price, it must accept the price determined by the market forces of supply and demand. Therefore, the firm knows it will receive £5 for every door knob it sells in the market. So the additional revenue the firm will receive from selling one more door knob is equal to the market price of £5; marginal revenue, in this case, equals price.

Marginal revenue represents the increment in total revenues attributable to selling one additional unit of the product in question. Hence, marginal revenue may be calculated using the following formula:

$$\text{marginal revenue} = \frac{\text{change in total revenue}}{\text{change in output}}$$

In any market structure, therefore, marginal revenue will be closely related to price. In a perfectly competitive market, the marginal revenue curve is exactly equivalent to the price line or, in other words, to the individual firm's demand curve, since the firm can sell all of its output (including the last unit of output) at the market price.

Marginal Analysis: Comparing Marginal Cost with Marginal Revenue

Notice that the numbers for both the marginal cost schedule and the marginal revenue schedule in figure 8.2 (panel a) are printed *between* the figures that determine them. This indicates that we are looking at a change between one rate of output and the next.

In figure 8.2 (panel c), the marginal cost curve intersects the marginal revenue (or *dd*) curve somewhere between seven and eight door knobs per day. Consider a rate of production that is less than that. At a production rate of, say, six door knobs per day, marginal cost is clearly below marginal revenue. That is, at an output of six, the marginal cost curve is below the marginal revenue curve. Since it can receive £5 per door knob, and since marginal cost is less than this marginal revenue, the firm has an incentive to increase production. In fact, the firm has an incentive to produce and sell right up to the point where the revenue received from selling one more door knob equals the additional cost incurred in producing that same door knob. Profit maximisation, therefore, is always at the rate of output at which marginal revenue equals marginal cost. (To be strictly correct, we should add: 'and the MC curve cuts the MR curve from below'.) For a perfectly competitive firm, this is at the intersection of the demand schedule, *dd*, and the marginal cost curve, MC. In our particular example, the profit-maximising, perfectly competitive brass door-knob manufacturer should produce at a rate of between seven and eight brass door knobs a day. If he chooses to stop output at three or four units per day, he will not have maximised profits: he will not have squeezed the pips until they squeak. The profit maximiser should not be satisfied until the last penny has been earned. This will only be achieved at the point where marginal costs equal marginal revenue (point E in figure 8.2 panel (c).

Figure 8.2 (panel b)   Finding a profit-maximising position

Total revenues are represented by a straight black line, as each door knob is sold for £5. Total costs represented by the red wavy line, first exceed total revenues, and a loss is made, then they become less than total revenues, and a profit is made. We find maximum profits where total revenues exceed total costs by the largest amount.

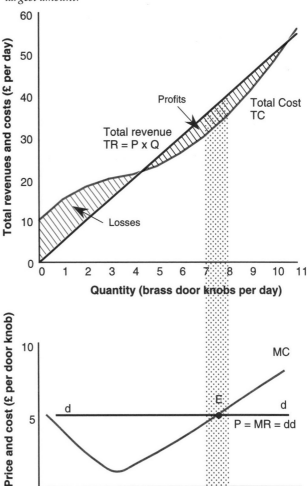

Figure 8.2 (panel c)   Finding a profit-maximising position, using marginal analysis

Marginal revenue is represented by the individual demand curve, dd. The marginal costs curve is represented by MC. Both have been plotted from the data in panel (a). Profit maximisation occurs where marginal revenue equals marginal cost, ie somewhere between seven and eight door knobs per day.

Figure 8.2 (panel a):   A table showing the costs of production and the revenues from the sale of output

As the asterisks highlight, many of the columns on costs are taken from panel (a) of figure 7.3. Alongside these, we need to consider the revenue data, in order to establish a profit-maximising position. The short formulas used to calculate the various items are shown at the head of the relevant columns, either on this table or its counterpart in figure 7.3.

Total output and sales per day (1)	Total costs (TC) (2)*	Market price (P) (3)	Total revenue (TR) (4) = (3) x (1)	Total profit (TP) (5) = (4) – (2)	Average total cost (ATC) (6)*= (2) ÷ (1)	Average variable cost (AVC) (7)*	Marginal revenue (MR) (8) = Change in (4) / Change in (1)	Marginal cost (MC) (9)*= Change in (2) / Change in (1)
0	£10.00	£5.00	0	-£10.00	-	-		
							£5.00	£5.00
1	15.00	5.00	£5.00	-10.00	£15.00	£15.00		
							5.00	3.00
2	18.00	5.00	10.00	-8.00	9.00	4.00		
							5.00	2.00
3	20.00	5.00	15.00	-5.00	6.67	3.33		
							5.00	1.00
4	21.00	5.00	20.00	-1.00	5.25	2.75		
							5.00	2.00
5	23.00	5.00	25.00	2.00	4.60	2.60		
							5.00	3.00
6	26.00	5.00	30.00	4.00	4.33	2.67		
							5.00	4.00
7	30.00	5.00	35.00	5.00	4.28	2.86		
							5.00	5.00
8	35.00	5.00	40.00	5.00	4.38	3.12		
							5.00	6.00
9	41.00	5.00	45.00	4.00	4.56	3.44		
							5.00	6.00
10	48.00	5.00	50.00	2.00	4.80	3.80		
							5.00	8.00
11	56.00	5.00	55.00	-1.00	5.09	4.18		

*Taken from Figure 7.3 (Panel A)

Two Profit-maximising Rules

You will notice that the same profit-maximising rate of output is shown in panel (b) of figure 8.2, where the total revenue and total cost curves are the point of reference, and in panel (c) of figure 8.2 where the marginal revenue and marginal cost curves are drawn. We can, therefore, find the profit-maximising output solution in two ways:

1   By finding the output where TR exceeds TC by the greatest amount.

2   By finding the output where MC = MR.
    These profit-maximising rules apply to all forms of market structures.

Chapter Summary 8.1

- There are various market structures, for example, a monopoly where one producer alone controls price and output decisions alone, and perfect competition where no single producer can control the market.

- The perfectly competitive market is a hypothetical extreme which acts as a benchmark by which the imperfect markets of reality can be judged.

- The hypothetical model of perfect competition has four main characteristics: (1) homogeneous product; (2) freedom of entry and exit; (3) large number of buyers and sellers and; (4) adequate information.

- A perfectly competitive firm is a price-taker. It takes price as given. It can sell all that it wants at the going market price. The demand curve facing a perfect competitor is a horizontal line at the market price.

- Profit is maximised at the rate of output where the positive difference between total revenues and total cost is greatest.

- Using marginal analysis, the profit–maximising firm will produce at a rate of output where marginal revenue equals marginal cost.

- Profit-maximising rules apply to all types of market structure.

Towards the Notion of an Efficient Industry

To consider an entire industry, the cost and revenue schedules of all its constituent firms would need to be aggregated. For an industry with a perfectly competitive market structure, this is not a problem since the costs and revenues for each firm will be identical. This theoretical extreme will prove relevant when we consider the notions of efficiency that exist in reality. Indeed, it should be particularly useful to those concerned with the performance of firms in the industrial sectors that make up the built environment. Most of the firms in this sector do seek to maximise their profits, they often have a large degree of freedom to enter and exit the various activities, and they rarely set their prices without regard to the terms expressed by their competitors.

Short-run: Super-normal Profits for a Firm and its Industry

Before taking an industry-wide perspective we need to understand what our individual, competitive manufacturer of brass door-knobs is actually making in terms of profit. To do this, we have to add the average total cost curve (ATC) to figure 8.2 panel (c). We take the necessary information from column 6 in figure 8.2 panel (a) and add it to figure 8.2 panel (c) to get figure 8.3. Again, the profit-maximising rate of output is where marginal revenue and marginal cost are equal—ie, between seven and eight door knobs per day. If we have production and sales of seven door knobs per day, total revenue will be £35 per day. Total costs will be £30 per day, leaving a profit of £5 per day. If the rate of sales is eight door knobs per day, total revenue will be £40 and total costs will be approximately £35, again leaving a profit. This can be seen graphically in figure 8.3. The total revenue (price × quantity) is shown as a coloured rectangle. Superimposed over this is a grey striped rectangle, showing total cost, which is designated by quantity times the ATC. The remaining slice where total revenue exceeds total cost (TC) is the profit at that output level.

Figure 8.3   Measuring supernormal profits
The profit-maximising position is where marginal revenue equals marginal cost. Profits are the difference between total revenues and total cost. Total revenues equal price times quantity sold. Total costs equal quantity produced times the average total cost (costs/unit). Profits are represented by the difference between the total cost and total revenue.

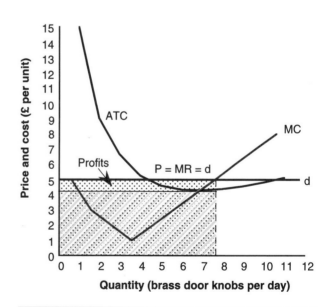

In a perfectly competitive market, it is easy to move from this single-firm presentation to an industry-wide perspective. The price on the vertical axis remains the same because all firms comprising the industry take their price from the market. The quantity on the horizontal axis simply changes by a multiple of output of the number of firms involved. The interesting factor, however, is that it now appears that firms in this industry are making more than 'normal profit'. The area where total revenue exceeds total cost is known as **supernormal profits**.

Long-run: 'Normal Profits' for a Firm and its Industry

In a perfectly competitive market, supernormal profits will not continue indefinitely. In the long run, new firms will be attracted into the industry to share 'the supernormal profits'. The consequential increase in market supply will, in time, force the equilibrium price of the product down, until each firm is making only normal profit. This situation is shown in figure 8.4.

In the long run, the perfectly competitive firm/industry finds itself producing at a rate Q. At that rate of output, the price is just equal to the minimum average total cost. Obviously, it is possible for supernormal profits to cause too many firms to enter the market, in which case the market price would fall below P and firms would make a loss—**subnormal profits**. Firms would then leave the industry and the decrease in supply would cause market prices to rise again to P. In this sense, perfect competition results in no 'waste' in the production system. Goods and services are produced using the least costly combination of resources. This is an important attribute of a perfectly competitive long-run equilibrium, particularly when we wish to compare the market structures that are less than perfectly competitive.

Figure 8.4 Long-run perfectly competitive equilibrium

In the long run, perfectly competitive firms move towards a position where marginal revenue equals marginal cost and average total costs. In short, 'where everything is equal' as shown by point E.

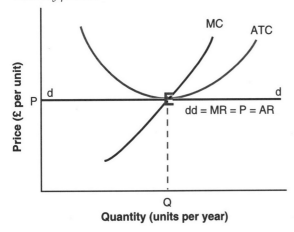

Quantity (units per year)

The Behaviour of Firms in the Built Environment

This sector contains a wide diversity of firms ranging from the small estate agent to the large developer such as Tarmac. All these businesses share one common objective—the maximisation of profits. Consequently, they seek to differentiate the products and services that they provide by brand-naming, packaging or advertising. Also, firms may collude to prevent competition entering into their market. This may be achieved by price-rigging or other discriminatory behaviour.

Therefore, the theory of the firm may not seem directly applicable to many of the businesses that you study. The principles that it highlights, however, are relevant and this will become apparent in the tutorial sections and your future careers.

Chapter Summary 8.2

- Short-run profits (and losses) are determined by comparing average total cost with price at the profit-maximising rate of output.

- In the short run, the perfectly competitive firm can make supernormal profits.

- In a perfectly competitive market, supernormal profits will be absorbed by new firms entering the industry.

- In the long run, a perfectly competitive firm (industry) produces where P = MR = MC = ATC.

- In reality, firms differentiate their products and collude in order to maximise their profits.

Tutorial Preparation

The following five exercises are designed to help you think more carefully about the types of market structure that exist in reality and the various implications for profits etc.

1
   a. Using a graph show the relevant cost and revenue schedules for a perfectly competitive firm making a subnormal profit (loss).

   b. What features would alter if the graph portrayed a firm involved in imperfect competition?

2
  In 1933, Edward Chamberlin, an American economist, revolutionised the theory of markets through his work on the monopolistic competition model. An extract and some related questions on this work follow:

> Differentiation may be based on certain characteristics of the product itself such as: exclusive patented features; trade marks; trade names; peculiarities of the package or container, if any; or singularity in quality, design, colour or style. It may also exist with respect to the conditions surrounding its sale. In the retail trade, to take only one instance, these conditions include such things as the convenience of the seller's location, the general tone or character of his establishment, his way of doing business, his reputation for fair dealing, courtesy, efficiency and all the personal links which attach his customers either to himself or to those employed by him. In so far as these and other intangible factors vary from seller to seller the 'product' in each case is different, for buyers take them into account more or less and may be regarded as purchasing them along with the commodity itself.

Source: *The Theory of Monopolistic Competition* by E Chamberlin

   a. According to Chamberlin, what is the major difference between his model of monopolistic competition and that of perfect competition?

   b. Give two examples of monopolistic competition within the built environment.

   c. How does monopolistic competition affect an industry's profit?

   d. What is the purpose of any economic model?

3
  In figure 8.5 we present a spectrum showing the different types of competition reviewed in most economic textbooks.

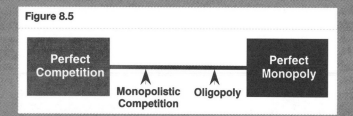

Figure 8.5

   a. Define each of the four market structures displayed.

   b. Give an example of firms functioning within the built environment for each form of competition.

   c. Which type of competition would be most efficient from a resource point of view?

   d. Which type of competition would be most efficient from a profit point of view?

   e. Give a generic term for the types of competition that exist between the two boxed extremes.

   f. Discuss the freedom of firms to enter into each of the four market categories.

   g. Give an example of malpractice (unfair trading) that you know takes place within any of the industries related to the built environment.

   h. What is the purpose of competition policy?

4
  Complete the table shown in figure 8.6.

Figure 8.6

Type of market	Number of firms	Freedom of entry	Nature of product eg homogeneous or differentiated	Examples from the built environment	Implication for competition policy
Perfect competition					
Monopolistic competition					
Oligopoly					
Monopoly					

5 'An increase in standardisation of product and service are common developments within professions of the built environment'.

    a. Give three examples of standardisation within the built environment.

    b. Give some economic reasons to explain this statement.

6 The table shown in figure 8.7 relates to a hypothetical development of a building that, when complete, will be rented. The yields that are to be calculated relate to the expenditure on buildings only and do not (until the penultimate question) relate to any capital outlay on the purchase of the site.

Figure 8.7

Capital Outlay £	Annual Net Income £	Average Net Return %	Marginal Units of Capital Outlay £	Marginal Net Income £	Marginal Net Return %
200,000	40,000				
400,000	76,000		200,000	36,000	18
600,000	108,000				
800,000	136,000				
1,000,000	160,000				
1,200,000	180,000				
1,400,000	196,000	14			

    a. Copy and complete the table from the information given

    b. What kind of development might the figures represent?

    c. What are the obvious pitfalls of hypothetical information such as this?

    d. State two reasons why the marginal net return would have a downward trend in reality.

    e. The cost of borrowing is not included in the figures. If the cost of borrowing was 14 percent, what would be the profit-maximising capital outlay? If the cost of borrowing increased to 16 percent, what would be the profit-maximising outlay?

    f. A basic proposition of economic analysis is that site value is determined by the demand for the buildings which occupy the land. Site value is thus a residual value determined by the development process. Try to calculate the annual site value, given a 14 percent cost of borrowing funds.

    g. Site value has many uses; name two of them.

Tutorial Reading

An Alternative Theory of the Firm

At almost exactly the moment when Britain's 10 biggest housebuilders decided to abandon their attempt to build a patchwork of new towns across the home counties, newly-weds Maria and Lee Davies moved into a £48,000 two-bedroom house in Tircoed, 10 miles north of Swansea.

It is a coincidence that will not be lost on the Pentref Development Company, a non-profit-making group set up in 1981 to build Tircoed Forest Village. Its housebuilder-with-a-heart approach was realised on Valentine's Day when the Davies became the first occupants of what will eventually be a 500-house community of more than 1,000 people.

Tircoed is a blueprint for housing in the 1990s, feels Pentref chairman Bernard Williams, head of his own 35-strong firm of building economists in London. 'Developers are now altering their ideas to produce the sorts of development that match what we are doing at Tircoed'.

But the blueprint had taken over 10 years to turn into working drawings. Inspiration came from a Town and Country Planning Association meeting in 1979 to discuss the setting up of new communities.

At this were Williams, Cardiff architect Jim Grove and Dr Nicholas Falk, a community development expert whose London-based company URBED is marketing the development. The three, together with Sydney Issacs of Cardiff solicitors Merrils Ede, formed Pentref in 1981. They then set out to find the land; that wasn't too difficult. And money; that was much more difficult.

It took eight years for philanthropy to move bricks and mortar—work started in October 1989. Even then the £4 million funding eventually came from a French bank.

'I have to say the British banks and building societies did not understand what we were trying to achieve. What they really could not understand was why we did not want to make a profit,' says Williams. 'They were suspicious of our motives'.

Planned for the 125 hectare site is a series of 40 to 50 unit hamlets, which will be four-fifths private and one indistinguishable fifth rented homes. 'They will be in ones or twos threaded into the private homes. We don't want a single area of rented homes all managed by one housing association—it would create a ghetto'. Williams says that individual units will be offered to housing associations, 'or we might form our own'.

Grove has designed the houses in the Welsh rendering-under-slate vernacular. A row or two of 'workhouses' is planned. Pentref's photographer John

Fry has put down a deposit on one house that has a workspace where the double garage would have been on a more traditional developer's development.

More than £1 million has been spent on the initial roads and sewers contract which went to Wrekin Construction. Builder GEE Walker & Slater is completing the contract to build the first 44 units.

'It's a blueprint that could be used for many other developments,' says Williams. 'Planners can see that we have taken the greed part of the profit away, so they are much more amenable.

We are actively looking for the opportunity to build on our success. We would like to think that now we have a track record that finance would become less of an obstacle—perhaps coming this time from a British source'.

Source: Adapted from 'How not to make money and still influence people' *Building* 1 March 1991

Questions

1   The article suggests that some firms have other goals than profit-maximising. Can you think of at least two other goals that may motivate a firm other than profit?

2   Name some other firms that do not seek to maximise their profits.

3   Name six firms that do seek to maximise their profits.

4   Why is the profit-maximising goal so important to British and European firms?

5   Give some economic reasons to explain why in February 1991 'Britain's ten biggest housebuilders decided to abandon their attempt to build a patchwork of new towns across the home counties'.

6   Does the law of diminishing returns apply to non-profit-making firms?

7   Draw some short-run cost curves that a non-profit-making firm may face.

8   When considering long-run cost curves for a non-profit-making firm, what shape might they exhibit? What can you deduce from this question and questions 6 and 7?

9   'The Pentref Development Company is a non-profit-making group'. How far do you agree with this statement?

10   What findings would the Office of Fair Trading report if it investigated the Pentref Development Company?

Tutorial Reading

Profit-maximising and the Price Developers Pay for Land

What is a piece of land worth? The obvious answer is that it is worth what you can sell it for. But how do you calculate what price a piece of land might be expected to fetch? How, indeed, do you calculate what you can afford to pay for a piece of land if you are the prospective buyer? There is, let us assume, no building on the land at present, nor is it producing any rental income. Since property valuation is usually a matter of putting a capital value on a future flow of rental income, where do you start?

The answer is that the value of a piece of land depends on what can be done with it. It could have one value if its use was restricted to farming, a totally different value if you were allowed to build houses on it and a different value yet again if you had permission to erect an office block on the land. In other words, to see what a piece of land might be worth you have to visualise it in its developed state, then work backwards. This is a 'residual' basis of valuation; formally referred to as the **residual method**.

Take a simple example. On the piece of land in question—assume that it is freehold—you have planning permission to build an office block. So you begin by adding up the costs of erecting your office block. There will be the construction cost itself and the fees to architects and other professional advisers. Then there will be the finance cost: the interest on borrowed money while the block is under construction and before it is producing any revenue. You may also, depending on the climate, want to build in a significant sum for marketing the block once it is completed and a further amount to cover the period for which you expect it to be empty; when the block is empty and producing no revenue it is still clocking up interest charges, which add to the overall financing cost.

Let us suppose that all these costs add up to £10 million. But that is not the end of the story, because you are taking a risk if you decide to develop an office block and there is also no point in doing it unless the developer can make a profit. So you build in an extra 20 percent, say, to cover the **developer's profit**. On top of the £10 million of costs that brings the total to £12 million.

Then you look at the project from the other angle: what will it be worth on completion? What benefits in the form of revenue will roll in? In the prevailing economic climate you may estimate that you should be able to let the offices with a **full repairing and insuring lease** (FRI) at a rent of £1 million a year.

Investors are currently prepared to buy properties of this type to show themselves an **initial yield** of 7 percent. This is the same thing as saying that they will be prepared to buy at about 14.3 **years' purchase** of the rent. So, if somebody is prepared to buy the completed building at 14.3 times the £1 million rent which you expect it to produce, it will be worth £14.3 million once it is completed and let. (Question 1 may help to clarify this concept.)

Therefore, if total costs—plus the profit allowance—are expected to be £12 million, you could afford to pay a maximum of £2.3 million for the land: the £14.3 million end-value, less the costs and profit allowance of £12 million.

Source: Adapted from 'Beginner's guide: the price of land' *Estates Gazette* 21 March 1992

Questions

1   Put simply, years' purchase is a reciprocal of the yield. It is calculated by the formula $\frac{100}{\text{Yield}}$.

Therefore, it shows that if you buy a building at a price showing a 7 percent yield you would be paying 14.3 times the rent it initially produces. If you buy on a 5 percent yield you are buying at a 20 years' purchase and so on. Valuers use this concept to convert rental income into capital value as the following example illustrates:

Net income (rent)	£1 million
Years' purchase at 7 percent	14.3
Capital value	£14.3 million

a) What would happen to the capital value if the rental market improved during the development and the completed building is let for a sum of £1.25 million?
b) What would happen to the land value if the rental value of the completed property decreased?
c) Define the term initial yield.
d) What economic factors would determine the expected yield?
e) Calculate the years' purchase of a 6 percent yield and of a 10 percent yield.

2   What problems would have been overlooked if the developer actually bid up to the ceiling price and paid the full £2.3 million available for the land?

3   Compare and contrast the concepts of 'economic profit' and 'developer's profit'.

4   What does it mean when offices are let on full repairing and insuring terms?

5   According to economic theory, there are two rules that can be applied to a profit-maximising position. To what extent can property developers benefit from these ideas?

6   In a couple of sentences, highlight the main features of the residual method of valuation.

7   a) In what type of market structure would most office blocks be found?

b) What implications would this have when it came to rent reviews?

8   In economic terms, is property development an efficient or inefficient industry?

Tutorial Reading

The Cement Cartel has Cracked Up

According to estimates carried out for *Building* illegal price fixing by Britain's three largest cement suppliers cost the construction industry more than £100 million in rigged prices, during the 7 year period 1981-1987.

Davis Langdon & Everest (DL&E) examined 1987 delivery prices for London and Milton Keynes, where price rings existed, and South Buckinghamshire where they did not.

'In Milton Keynes prices were around £43 per m³ and in Buckinghamshire £37 per m³, said Peter Fordham who carried out the investigation for DL&E.

In London, Peter Fordham compared the prices in mid-1987 when the **cartel** was operating with mid-1988 figures after the cartel's exposure.

It seemed that price-fixing had raised the average price of readymix by around 10 percent, a figure that was backed up by the OFT. This suggests an unjustifiable increase of at least £3 per m³—or more than £100 million at today's prices for the 38.2 million cubic metres sold in price-rigged areas in the 7 year period.

Common price agreements for cement had been in existence since 1934. The cement manufacturers maintained that it was in the public interest for prices to be fixed countrywide. However, faced with a declining market after the construction industry peak in 1973, the major cement manufacturers became vulnerable; especially as the excess capacity that occurred in Britain was accompanied by a surplus in the rest of the world.

Source: Adapted and extended from 'Concrete cartel hits industry for £100m' *Building* 19 March 1991

Questions

1   Name Britain's three largest cement suppliers.

2   Define the term 'cartel'.

3   State some factors that may have caused the cartel to be disbanded.

4   How might the cement manufacturers have argued that the cartel was in the public interest?

5   How may Blue Circle Cement (the market leader) proceed during the 1990s to maintain its dominant market share.

6   Name some other construction firms that have experience of cartel-like behaviour.

Tutorial Reading

34,000 Pubs and What Have You Got?

In March 1989 **The Monopolies and Mergers Commissions (MMC)** reported on the lack of competition in the brewing industry. It highlighted the need to break down the big brewers' **oligopolistic** control of the beer market. The six biggest brewers were in control of 75 percent of the market: producing 75 percent of the beer and owning 75 percent of 'tied' pubs.

The MMC stipulated that by November 1992 brewers owning more than 2,000 pubs must sell or lease free of 'tie' at least 50 percent of the remaining pubs in their estate. The biggest five breweries owned more than 5,000 pubs each.

The subsequent proceedings up until April 1992 were reviewed in *Estates Gazette*, and some edited highlights follow.

Deals between the big brewers have taken huge blocks of pubs off the market. The 'pubs-for-breweries-swap' between Grand Met and Courage led to the formation of the 7,355-pub 'Inntrepreneur' estate and meant that only 1,096 of the two brewers' pubs actually came up for sale.

Bass has sold a large proportion of the 2,740 pubs of which it was obliged to dispose in blocks to various management operations, including 370 to Enterprise Inns, 291 to Century Inns and 150 to the Centric Pub Co.

A new breed of independent specialist pub operators has also emerged, owning and managing anything from five to 500 outlets. Century Inns, purchaser of Bass pubs among others, is one such company, established by the former managing director of Brent Walker's Hartlepool brewery, Alistair Arkley, with initial capital of £60 million. The company intends to build a managed estate of 500 houses throughout the North and East of England and has recently bought 30 pubs from Grand Met—separately negotiating a supply contract with Courage to provide a full range of Courage ales and lagers to its entire estate.

While the big brewers have been negotiating large-scale deals with other multiple operators, the individual and entrepreneurial end of the market has also seen activity, although there have been a few freehold sales of pubs to date...

Whitbread has targeted both experienced licensees and newcomers with its 'One-Stop Pubs Shop' roadshow throughout the country, which offers a preview of the freehold properties on its books. The company had some 2,300 pubs to free from the tie and still has to dispose of another 500 by the November deadline.

David Street, Whitbread Property's sales director, says his firm has sold about 1,000 pubs, but has decided to retain flexibility by leasing a number of properties short-term. 'It is not the best market to sell into at the moment. We have introduced some five-year leases with a view to sell the freeholds of the pubs in five years' time.'

One of the more significant changes to the licensed trade's market profile has been the requirement to adopt traditional institutional leases. Institutions have always been more interested in acquiring properties with vacant possession and, as a result, no proven market of pubs as investments yet exists. However, according to the big operators, institutional leases are simply a response to the MMC's recommendations. Longer leases were already being developed and implemented on a test basis before the recommendations came into effect.

However, the Beer Orders have speeded up the transformation process and focused the brewers' attention more firmly on their estates. No longer can the estates be viewed as simply a retail outlet for the parent company's product. They must now operate in an efficient and profits-orientated manner in their own right.

The new breed of (FRI) full repairing and insuring longer lease gives tenants greater security of tenure via the protection of the Landlord and Tenant Act.

But how far will the new leasing agreements go to making licensed premises viable institutional property investments? The valuation of licensed premises is still, by and large, based on profitability and barrelage methods rather than the 'four-walls-and-a-roof' square footage technique applied to other forms of property.

Source: Adapted from 'Time gentlemen, please!' Karen Lennox *Estates Gazette* 25 April 1992

Questions

1   Name at least four of the six breweries that constituted the oligopoly that made up the beer market during the 1980s.

2   What kind of pricing policy would oligopolistic firms adopt?

3   How would the demand curve of a firm involved in oligopolistic competition differ from those in perfect competition?

4   Why do you think the brewing industry was referred to the Office of Fair Trading?

5   What is meant by the term inntrepreneur?

6   What is meant by the phrase 'traditional institutional leases'?

7   State some reasons that explain why institutional investors have not traditionally bothered with the pub market.

8   The property-related manoeuvres that the breweries have undertaken since 1989 are generally disapproved of by the Office of Fair Trading. Explain why.

9   In which other industries are there tied tenants?

10   Which other property assets are not valued according to their square footage?

11   a) What oligopolies exist in the industries of the built environment?

b) Which of these do you think should be referred to the Office of Fair Trading? (You must explain why.)

12   Explain why the FRI longer lease gives tenants greater security.

Market failures and government remedies

Chapter Summaries to Review
- *What, How, and For Whom (2.1)*
- *Productive and Allocative Efficiency (2.4)*
- *Supply and Demand Equilibrium (3.3)*
- *Shifting Supply Curves (5.3)*
- *Perfect Competition (8.1)*
- *Equilibrium of the Firm in the Long Run (8.2)*

So far in this text we have emphasised that markets allocate resources effectively. Firms have been seen to freely move in and out of markets in their search for profits. Prices have been flexible. All markets have cleared as equilibriums have been arrived at. Indeed the text has implied that all of an economy's problems can be resolved by allowing the free market to work.

The 'market', however, does not always work. That is to say, there are problems in the way some markets operate that prevent the price system from actually attaining productive and allocative efficiency.

In those cases where the market cannot attain efficiency, non-market alternatives need to be considered. One of the most important non-market forces is government. It is the government's role within failing markets that will be reviewed in this chapter. But we shall also recognise, towards the end of the chapter, the possibility that governments fail too. It is not, however, our intention to paint a picture of complete failure; this chapter, therefore, must be kept in perspective.

Market failure may be defined as any situation where the unrestricted price system causes too few or too many resources to be allocated to a specific economic activity.

The world is full of many instances of market failure. Two topical examples can be seen on the banks of the Thames in London. People have to resort to sleeping in cardboard boxes as the free market system allocates too few resources for their needs. Further down the Thames, the empty office blocks of Canary Wharf represent a classic over-allocation of resources.

What Causes Market Failure?

In this chapter we shall deal with five basic causes:

- Time-lag
- Unequal distribution of income
- Producer power
- Externalities
- Free-rider problems

Time-lag

Owing to the inflexible nature of certain markets, the forces of supply and demand are not very sensitive to price changes. These markets are often structured in such a way that aspects such as trade union practices, training requirements, information flows and legislation restrict the dynamics of the market. Economists refer to these problems as **structural rigidities**.

The property markets are a good example, as shown by the cyclical booms and slumps which represent the struggle to arrive at stable market prices. The cobweb theorem can be used to explain the circumstances.

The Cobweb Theorem

Property construction is typified by a lengthy production process. For example, it takes approximately 18 months to two years to complete a house from the initial planning stages and up to five years for a modern office block. Because of this time-lag problem, price instability within property markets is not unusual. Indeed, we can see in figure 9.1 that house price fluctuations have taken the form of *fairly regular* cycles over time.

Figure 9.1   House price booms and slumps 1970-91

The graph shows three cycles between 1970 and 1991. The cobweb theorem, illustrated in figure 9.2, helps to explain these price fluctuations.

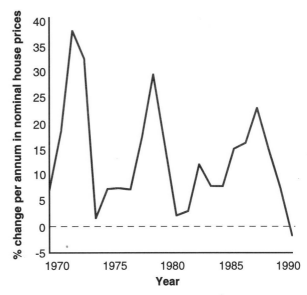

Source: Housing Finance (page 12), Aug 1992.
Published by Council of Mortgage Lenders

To account theoretically for these successive cycles, we need to accept two distinguishing features of the construction industry.

1   The decision of builders to change their output is heavily influenced by the current market price. Thus, house supplies in two years' time are dependent on prices actually received in the past.

2   There are many building firms and they each take decisions to adjust their scale of production in isolation from each other.

The result of these distinguishing features is that, if property supplies happen to be scarce in one time-period, the high level of the market-clearing price will prompt construction firms to begin major building programmes. This rise in production will in due course depress market prices, setting off a major contraction in the scale of production. We show this in figure 9.2. The fixed amount available in the short run means that the market-clearing price may rise to P_1. The supply curve indicates that, at price P_1, construction firms would like to produce Q_2. But they cannot do so immediately. Building contractors begin to make plans to adjust output to the current market price and try to produce Q_2. After a time-lag, a potentially unstable situation is likely. Indeed, if output Q_2 is actually built, the market-clearing price will have to drop to absorb the excess supply. This will ultimately result in a contraction in production and higher prices. Note that in this example market prices move above and below the equilibrium level P and are not stable. Depending on the elasticity of the supply and demand curves, this instability of prices could be greater or less than as shown in figure 9.2.

Figure 9.2   A cobweb diagram showing how property prices can fluctuate

The market equilibrium price is P and quantity Q. If there is a change to the demand or supply, the market will move to a disequilibrium. For example, supply may be restricted owing to weather conditions affecting starts. Consequently, a perfectly inelastic supply curve will exist, as shown by the dashed line (P_{es}). The longer-run supply curve, S, indicates that at price P_1 construction firms would like to build Q_2. These structures will take some time to construct. However, when Q_2 is eventually completed, the price will need to fall to P_2 to absorb the excess supply. This will result in a subsequent contraction of supply as shown by position 3. The shortage of supply will cause prices to be bid up and the process continues.

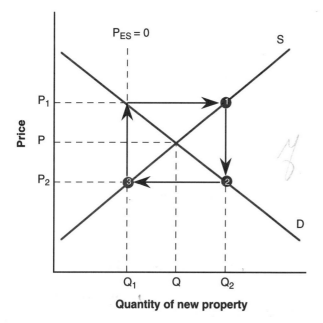

Quantity of new property

The pattern of oscillation around the equilibrium point is accounted for by time-lag, imperfect information and, to a lesser extent, the inflexible nature of the construction industry. The oscillating pattern also provides the explanation for the name of this model—the **cobweb theorem**.

Obviously, there are limitations to this generalised theoretical model. First, builders are aware of the cyclical nature of their industry and attempt to make adjustments to relate starts to expected rather than current prices. Secondly, they can choose to manipulate their stocks by holding property off the market during the low price part of the cycle. Nonetheless, the economic analysis is still useful since it highlights the root of a problem.

Unequal Distribution of Income

According to economists, who gets what, when and how is resolved by the market system. (This approach has already been explained in chapter 2.) Clearly, for the price (or market) mechanism to operate fairly we all need to be able to 'cast our votes' with purchasing power. Left to its own devices the free market will allocate nothing to those who cannot pay. That is, those who can sell their labour, or other factors of production, will have significantly better life chances than their retired, unemployed, disabled or underprivileged counterparts. Consequently, all post-war governments have used policies, with differing levels of commitment, to redistribute income from the rich to the poor. These policies and others, designed to resolve failings of the market, will be reviewed in the middle section of this chapter. For now, it is enough to say that those who have no money are not able to function in the market.

Producer Power monopolies.

It is clear from the last section that, for consumers who have no money, the free market structure is far from perfect. In contrast, for producers who dominate a specific sector or work in close collusion with their competitors, unfettered markets can prove to be very rewarding.

Firms in dominant market positions do not have to 'price-take'. They can 'price-make' or become involved, through **collusion**, in price-fixing. Several of these possibilities were considered in the tutorial sections of chapters 7 and 8.

It has been acknowledged since the beginning of economics, for example, in the writings of Adam Smith in 1776, that 'people of the same trade seldom meet together for fun and merriment, but the conversation ends in a conspiracy against the public, or in some contrivance to raise prices'. Consequently, it is recognised that as competition declines, the price (or market) system often becomes less efficient in allocating resources.

Externalities

These are **third-party** effects that occur as spill-overs from market activity. In the traditional market agreement, there is a deal struck between a buyer and seller: a good or service is exchanged for money. Alongside this two-party activity exist various spill-overs to third parties. That is, people external to the market activity are affected—hence **externalities**. These externalities may be classified as positive or negative: as benefit or cost.

For example, consider a hypothetical world where there are no government planning departments. A property developer moves into a street and converts two large Victorian houses into eight flats. The price (rent) eventually charged will reflect only the costs incurred by the developer during the refurbishment. On completion of the development, however, neighbourhood costs are created. There are now parking constraints, traffic congestion and related road problems as eight couples try to negotiate the two generous spaces initially allocated to the two houses. The indirect costs that the neighbours inevitably experience are referred to as a negative externality or external cost.

Not all externalities are negative. Some property developments may improve the value of nearby residences. That is, some of the benefits associated with the development may spill over to third parties. These positive externalities may be termed external benefits.

One way of taking into account the positive and negative externalities is via **cost-benefit analysis**. This will be dealt with in the next section of this chapter (see p 74) but first of all some related terms need clarifying.

Private Costs and Benefits

Up until now we have been dealing with situations where the costs and benefits of any market activity have been accounted for directly by individuals. The prices paid were assumed to cover all the costs and justify all the benefits that occur.

Social Costs and Benefits

In this chapter, however, we have raised the possibility that, in some instances, third-party costs and benefits are experienced. Hence, not all of the costs and benefits remain private (ie internal to the two parties involved). External costs and benefits also exist. When we add these external costs and benefits to the private (internal) costs and benefits we can identify a total picture: a (net) **social price**. The following definition may help to clarify: a social price involves considering the private costs and benefits alongside the external cost and benefits. This analysis of costs and benefits will be considered further when looking at the cures of market failure.

Free-rider Problems

The last piece of analysis leads us to the *free-rider* problem. Whenever external benefits greatly exceed private benefits, the good or service concerned becomes unprofitable. For example, if you pay for several lampposts to light your pathway and pavement, the private benefit would be too small relative to the cost. Yet the external benefit to your neighbours from the lighting would be significant, especially as they would get a brighter pathway for free. The problem is, therefore, that the market cannot easily supply goods, or services which are jointly consumed. For the market to work efficiently, a two-party agreement is preferable. In those few instances where non-paying parties cannot easily be excluded, we have the problem of the free rider. Markets for sewerage services, paving, street lighting, flood control, drainage and fire-protection services are some examples. A common solution is to have the government finance and organise services for these types of market.

Chapter Summary 9.1

- Market failure occurs whenever the free forces of supply and demand over-allocate or under-allocate resources to a specific economic activity.

- There are five main causes of market failure: (1) time-lag; (2) unequal distribution of income; (3) producer power; (4) externalities and (5) the free-rider problem.

Correcting Market Failure

The government can intervene in various ways to correct these failings. We shall deal with each of these in turn

before considering their effectiveness in the next section. To preview the approach, figure 9.3 (on p 74) provides a general summary.

Supply-side Policy

In order to reduce the problems related to time-lags, markets can be made more dynamic and responsive by removing as many **barriers to entry** as possible. For example, regulations relating to minimum wages and union practices can be abolished. Taxes may be reduced and training possibilities increased. These aspects encourage the labour market to become more flexible. Indeed, they are part of the whole process of **deregulation** that has been occurring in many sectors since 1979. We shall discuss this concept more fully in chapter 14, when we consider in detail the example of financial deregulation.

Four Systems to Redistribute Income

All post-war governments have concerned themselves with the distribution of income. This is understandable, since one requirement for political stability is to avoid glaring inequalities between the rich and poor. In fact, without government intervention, many of the poorer sections of society would be homeless and starving. Ultimately, such situations could lead to a loss of political favour and even possible revolt.

Consequently, governments support systems that redistribute income. The system of taxation, especially **progressive income tax**, which involves taxing high-income earners more than the lower-paid, is one system employed throughout Europe. **Transfer payments**, which represent various forms of state benefit (for which no services are concurrently rendered) are paid out selectively on a means-tested basis to support the poor; housing benefit is an example. **Maximum price legislation**, which fixes the permissible price below the market equilibrium price, has kept rents low in several countries. And finally, **merit goods**, which make essential services such as housing available to all.

For our purposes it will be interesting to take a closer look at the last of these four systems. Merit good provision differs from country to country since it depends upon what the government of the day regards as socially desirable. The decision involves selecting certain goods or services and providing them free, or below cost, to all citizens either through subsidy or government production.

Examples of merit goods in the UK are museums, ballet, health, education and council housing. The important feature is that there is nothing inherent in any of these particular goods that makes them different from **private goods**; they can be supplied through the market (and in some countries they are) but because they are deemed important, due to their related positive externalities, the government becomes involved.

Some aspects of government intervention designed to correct market failure relating to income distribution within the housing market are discussed further in the tutorial reading, entitled 'The failing market for rented housing'.

Competition Policy

Our focus in this section is to recognise that successive UK governments have attempted to promote competition. Various bits of legislation designed to prevent monopolies and unfair practices between firms have been put in place over the last 40 years. The Office of Fair Trading (OFT) and the related Monopolies and

Mergers Commission (MMC) now employ over 100 staff to investigate markets which appear uncompetitive.

Alongside these established government regulatory agencies exist policies to promote small firms and, more recently, the privatisation process has been engineered to break up state monopolies.

Internalising Externalities

We have seen that, when there are external costs, the market will tend to over-allocate resources to the production of the good in question (as these costs are not borne by the producer). Conversely, when there are external benefits, the market forces will under-allocate resources to the production of that good or service. When there is an over- or under-allocation of resources we have cases of market failure. By definition, therefore, externalities creating market failure will only be resolved by non-market forces. Clearly the case of negative externalities can be seen as problematic and is common within property development.

The government can attempt to correct negative spill-overs in a number of ways. Let us consider some examples.

Taxation and Legislation

When drivers get into their cars, they bear only the private costs of driving. That is, they pay for the petrol, maintenance, depreciation and insurance for their cars. They cause, however, an additional cost—that of air pollution. The air pollution created by exhausts is a cost that individual drivers do not bear directly. The social (or total) costs of driving include all the private costs plus the cost of air pollution, which society bears. Decisions made only on the basis of private costs lead to too much driving; global resources are taken for granted. Consequently, governments have intervened and created laws relating to catalytic converters and higher tax on leaded petrol. Similar arguments have been used to justify the revision of building regulations and the imposition of VAT on fuel bills from 1994.

These taxes and legislative changes are designed to reduce the carbon dioxide emissions which cause global warming. The government is, therefore, introducing instruments to benefit the community at the expense of the individual, or to put it in official terms: the principle is that the polluter pays.

Cost-benefit Analysis (CBA)

Another option for the government is to use an investment appraisal technique known as cost–benefit analysis. This method of resource allocation, popular with government economists since the 1960s, involves setting the external costs and benefits alongside the conventionally accounted internal (private) costs and benefits, thus creating a total picture of resource utilisation. To paraphrase the Heineken advertisement: CBA identifies the parts that other methods of resource allocation cannot reach.

Two problems with this technique are acknowledged. First, the externalities that are identified rely upon value judgements and subsequently all the issues need to be expressed in monetary terms for a 'total price' to be arrived at. The second problem is resolved by employing the concept of opportunity cost. For example, when completing the cost–benefit analysis of London's third airport, noise pollution was quantified on the principle of how much it would cost in double- and treble-glazing to restore the houses to their foregone quiet existence.

Regardless of these limitations, cost–benefit analysis studies have been used to assess the building of motorways, the channel tunnel and the Victoria underground line in London. It may be worth your while to look at one of these or a similar example in detail before considering the reading on planning gain at the close of this chapter.

Public Goods

The fifth area which we identified as a cause of market failure related to the free-rider problem. The basic problem here is **excludability**. Owing to the nature of some goods or services, non-payers can not be excluded from the benefits. Consequently throughout history, supporters of the free market, from Adam Smith to Milton Friedman, have recognised that there are a few goods and services that the market mechanism does not effectively supply. These are called **public goods**. In these instances, the principles of exclusion cannot be applied. Another feature of these goods is that they can be utilised several times. In other words, public goods can be jointly consumed by many people simultaneously without any discriminatory price system being applied. National defence, street lighting and overseas representation are the standard examples. **Quasi-public goods** could include parks and the enforcement of law and order.

Chapter Summary 9.2

- Governments can use several devices to correct market failure. For example there are four systems to redistribute income, various policy options to influence competition or supply, and the provision of public goods.

- CBA involves identifying monetary values for *all* the internal and external costs and benefits of a project, thereby enabling a total (social) price to be arrived at. This type of analysis helps to identify externalities.

- Externalities can be internalised by taxation and/or legislation.

Are Government Corrections Effective?

The assumption that the alternative to a failing market is a brilliant government is wrong. Governments can fail, too! As evidence, several of the corrective measures discussed above have related problems. These problems are briefly summarised in figure 9.3 and will be examined further in this section.

Figure 9.3   Market failure and government remedies

Cause	Correction	Effectiveness
Time-lag	Supply-side policy Deregulation	Do incentives work? Imperfect information
Unequal distribution of income	Progressive income tax Transfer payments Maximum price legislation Merit goods	Does the right group benefit?
Producer power	Competition policy Privatisation	Assessment problems Enforcement problems
Externalities	Tax Legislation CBA	Measurement problems Enforcement problems
Free-rider problem	Public goods	Tax burden

Inefficient Policy

Just because a government policy has been debated and successfully passed through Parliament does not automatically mean it will work. A good example is the lowering of income tax to encourage people to look for work. As the UK government believed during the 1980s, 'lower rates of tax sharpen up incentives and stimulate enterprise'. Consequently, basic rate income tax fell from 33 percent to 25 percent between 1979 to 1989 and is destined to become 20 percent by the end of the century.

Whether these manoeuvres actually improve the incentive to work is debatable. Although logic suggests that what is important to those seeking work is the after-tax, or take-home pay, it is easy to recognise that changes in the tax rate will also influence attitudes to leisure. For example, a decrease in income tax would boost disposable income and this could increase the demand for leisure in preference to more work, especially by those already in employment.

This whole debate was expressed rather elegantly by an American economist named Arthur Laffer during a social party for congressmen. His explanation centred round a diagram which he drew on a dinner serviette. His theory now forms part of modern supply-side economics.

The Laffer Curve

Laffer's central theme rests on the premise that zero tax rates would obviously produce zero tax revenues. Similarly tax rates of 100 percent also produce zero revenues, as taxpayers would cease to work (at least for money), since their incomes would be entirely taxed away. Maximum revenue would, therefore, be achieved by some rate in between. This idea was portrayed on the serviette in a similar way to figure 9.4.

Tax rates are shown on the vertical axis and tax revenues on the horizontal axis. Tax rate T_1 identifies the maximum rate that the government can impose before the relationship between tax rates and revenues becomes negative. For example, at a higher tax rate (T_2) revenues drop to $0R_2$.

Figure 9.4 The Laffer curve

The Laffer curve is a representation of the relationship between tax rates and tax revenues. Tax revenues can go on the horizontal axis and tax rates on the vertical axis. The maximum tax revenues collectable, $0R_{max}$ may result when the tax rate T_1, is imposed. If the government insists on having a tax rate of T_2, tax revenues collected fall from $0R_{max}$ to $0R_2$. This suggests that a tax rate reduction can lead to an increase in tax revenues as indicated by the arrows.

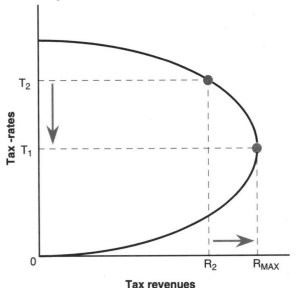

Although it is difficult to argue with the theoretical logic of the Laffer curve, the practicalities of identifying how near an economy is to T_1 is more complex. Consequently, whether reductions in rates of taxation will sufficiently stimulate the economy to increase the total tax revenue is difficult to assess. Indeed, research carried out on behalf of the Treasury in 1987 suggested that cuts in tax would not make people work harder.

Enforcement Problems

Not only does a government face the problem of knowing how effective a policy will be, but there is also the related issue of *enforcement*. For example, how many people working unofficially, 'for cash in hand', will transfer to official working, 'through the books', if income tax rates are reduced?

In a similar way we may consider whether the increase in VAT on domestic energy bills from 1994 will provide the necessary incentive to reduce fuel consumption by encouraging the purchase of energy-efficient appliances, wall insulation and double-glazing. In short, can the related target for carbon dioxide emission be enforced?

Each of the examples presented within this enforcement section highlights the fact that government policy is often a blunt instrument. The tax devices discussed are categorised as **market-based instruments**, since they affect prices and thus decisions taken in the market place. These instruments, although problematic, are regarded as sharper and more efficient than their legislative counterparts, since regulatory bodies and laws can be evaded.

Assessment Problems

When some form of ignorance is the reason for a market failure, the provision of information by government may help. This information, however, will depend upon government judgement. For example, if the government decides to enforce competition via various regulatory bodies, they need to be able to monitor effectively whether firms are behaving in the public's interest. What constitutes 'the public's interest', however, is ambiguous. Consequently, there is a problem of assessing each case consistently.

Measurement Problems

Government attempts to minimise negative externalities require measurement. The **polluter pays principle** is all well and good, providing that the guilty party is easy to identify and that it is possible to determine a fair price for him to pay. Given that many externalities manifest themselves in global or national issues, and involve free goods such as air, measurement (and assessment) causes endless problems.

It may help to consider these problems graphically, as presented in figure 9.5. Here we have the demand curve (D) and the supply curve S for product X. As usual, the supply curve includes only the private costs (internal to the firm). Left to its own devices, the free market will arrive at an equilibrium with price P and quantity Q. We shall assume, however, that the production of good X involves externalities that the private business did not take into account. These externalities could be air pollution, destruction of the green belt, noise pollution or any neighbourhood-type cost.

We know, therefore, that the social costs of producing X exceed the private cost. This can be illustrated by shifting the supply curve to the left, since it indicates that theoretically the costs of producing each unit are higher. (You may remember from chapter 5 that an increase in input prices always shifts the supply curve to the left.)

The diagram highlights the fact that the costs of production are being paid by two groups. At the lower price (P) the firm is paying for its necessary private inputs. The difference between the lower price P and the higher price P_1 is the amount paid by the community, or external costs. For these external costs to be internalised, the government would need to introduce a tax equal to P, P_1. This should result in there being less demanded and supplied (Q_1), owing to the higher price. (The tax income could be used by the government to clean up the environmental damage.)

Figure 9.5   Internalising external costs

We show the demand and supply for good X in the normal way. The supply curve, S, represents the summation of the private costs, internal to the firms producing the good. The curve to the left, S_1 represents the total (social) costs of production. The grey arrows indicate the external costs that have been added. In the uncorrected situation the equilibrium would be P, Q. After imposing a tax equal to P, P_1 the corrected equilibrium would be P_1, Q_1

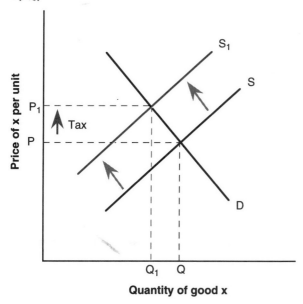

Quantity of good x

Theoretically, therefore, it is easy to see that in an unfettered market, external costs are not paid for, and resources are over-allocated to environmentally damaging production. A tax should help to alleviate the problem. But the practical issues of how much tax and who will be burdened with the expense remain as difficult questions to resolve.

Universal Versus Selective Benefits

If the government intervenes to protect the poorer classes of society, can we be confident that it is the poor who actually benefit?

There are two possible routes to follow. The universal route involves benefits being made available to *everyone* regardless of need. For example, interest payments are reduced by a quarter on the first £30,000 of a mortgage loan. This subsidy is available to everyone—providing they are buying their own house. The other route involves selective payments; these are paid according to need and often involve some form of means test. For example, housing benefit is only available to those who exist on incomes below a certain level.

The irony is that these payments systems, initiated to redistribute income, often do no more than maintain the existing differentials.

Rent Control

A classic example of a system which was set up to promote welfare but which distorted the market even further is **rent control**. Obviously, if a price is fixed below

the equilibrium this will lead to shortages as suppliers (landlords) move into more profit-making areas which are not regulated. The outcome is that the poorer tenant ends up with less choice of accommodation. Again, a supply and demand diagram helps to paint a fuller picture. In figure 9.6 the demand for rented accommodation at the controlled maximum price of P_1 is Q_3. At this controlled price, however, landlords are only willing to supply Q_1. The distance Q_1Q_3 represents the demand that remains unsatisfied owing to the imposition of rent control. The final result is that the rent control only benefits the relative few who are fortunate enough to find and live in rented accommodation. This theme is revisited in the tutorial reading entitled 'The failing market for rented housing'.

Figure 9.6   Rent control: maximum price legislation

The free market equilibrium price is P_2. The government impose a maximum price for rented accommodation of P_1. Consequently demand increases to Q_3 but supply is reduced to Q_1. The final outcome is an excess demand of $Q_1 Q_3$.

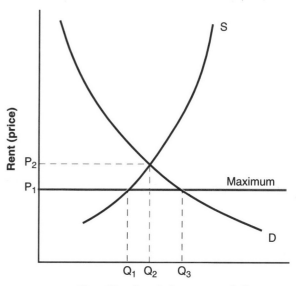

Quantity of rented accommodation

Chapter Summary 9.3

- Just because the government has passed some legislation does not automatically mean it will be efficient.

- The Laffer curve shows the relationship between tax rates and tax revenues, and enables economists to discuss whether lower taxes will increase revenue and/or work incentives.

- Policy enforcement is difficult, regardless of whether the government uses market-based instruments or regulatory procedures.

- One method for internalising external cost is to impose a tax. But whether this effectively means that the polluter pays is difficult to judge.

- Universal and/or selective systems devised to benefit the poor do not necessarily have the desired effect. A classic example of this problem can be seen in rent control.

Government Failure

To conclude the theoretical parts of this chapter, we should recognise that market failure cannot simply be remedied by government action. That is, imperfect markets are not resolved by perfect governments. In fact, modern economic texts also acknowledge the occurrence of **government failure**.

Government failure is understandable, since the political process by its very nature is likely to be inefficient in allocating resources. When individual choices are expressed through the price mechanism, the price forces the individual to absorb most of the costs and benefits. Politicians, however, allocate resources more on the basis of judgement.

Government judgements are skewed by lack of financial incentives, gaps in information and pressures applied by different interest groups which need to be acknowledged for re-election.

Furthermore, the sheer scale of managing a nation from the centre is problematic. As discussed above, there are problems of enforcement, assessment and measurement. These problems of inefficiency lead to a wasteful use of resources. Indeed, the more wide-reaching and detailed the intervention becomes, the greater the costs in terms of resources employed.

In recent years, therefore, the tendency has been to have reduced confidence in government solutions, especially as government systems have become bureaucratic and inflexible, and excessively expensive to run. Furthermore as government intervention increased, individual liberty had been reduced and the profit motive declined. The present trend, therefore, is to give more opportunities to the market. How far the trend should go before we arrive at an 'optimum' level of government intervention is debatable. Indeed, it is not solely a question of economic efficiency—but one of politics too!

Chapter Summary 9.4

- Government failure is a recently acknowledged phenomenon which highlights the fact that constitutional intervention via policy does not necessarily improve economic efficiency.

- Government failure is caused by a number of factors, such as poor judgement, lack of information, inadequate incentives and the scale of the problems to be resolved.

Tutorial Preparation

1   Continue to create a glossary by defining in your own words any five of the terms identified in bold in this chapter. (Pick the ones you think are most important.)

2   Construct and complete a chart showing five causes of market failure and the related attempts at government correction. A suggested outline follows.

Cause of market failure	Government's corrective device
1	1
2	2
3	3
4	4
5	5

3   Consider three press statements made in January 1993 and then answer the following questions relating to the cobweb theory in practice.

Statement one: The total number of houses started during 1992 is projected to be 126,000, the lowest since 1981.

Statement two: House sales grew steadily during the last four months of the year, rising from 490 per day in September to 555 per day in December.

Statement three: The director of the House Builders Federation (HBF) said there were tentative signs of a recovery—but house prices were unlikely to rise during 1993.

a. Explain, using a cobweb diagram, how the data could lead the director of HBF to suggest that: 'there were tentative signs of recovery'.

b. State at least two features of the housing market that may disturb the 'tentative signs of recovery' during the forthcoming years.

4   The government is considering a road building project, incorporating a toll gate. The benefits, costs and externalities arising from four possible routes are outlined in the table below (externalities have been given monetary values).

	Route A £m	Route B £m	Route C £m	Route D £m
Private benefits	125	130	100	140
Private costs	100	110	120	130
Positive externalities	50	55	55	60
Negative externalities	70	50	40	50

a. Give one example for each of the four accounting categories.

b. Which of the routes (A, B, C or D) would maximise profit in conventional accounting terms?

c. Which of the routes (A, B, C or D) would maximise economic welfare generally, and what would be the net social gain in monetary terms?

5   A report by the Standing Advisory Committee on Trunk Road Assessment (SACTRA) published in March 1992 concluded that 'some environmental effects of road schemes cannot sensibly be valued or expressed in economic terms'.

a. Give two examples of environmental effects of road schemes that may not sensibly be expressed in terms of money.

b. Give two examples of externalities relating to road schemes and explain how these may be expressed in money terms.

Tutorial Reading

Professional Deregulation: ARCUK—R.I.P.

The Construction Industry Council (CIC), an organisation representing 24 professional bodies, responded to the government's decision to scrap compulsory registration for architects by saying it will press for a new voluntary register for all building professionals.

Construction minister Sir George Young had told the House of Commons that 'there is no reason why architects uniquely among the construction professions should be regulated by statute'. Therefore, the government has terminated the 62-year-old legal requirement that limits the term architect to the 31,500 members of ARCUK (the Architects Registration Council of the UK).

Most professional bodies welcomed the move, regarding it as the end of an anachronistic division between architects and others. Most professions operate voluntary chartered schemes, to co-ordinate their members' standards and activities.

Source: Various press articles during February 1993 (Especially *Building* 5 and 12 February 1993)

Questions

1   Name at least four of the professional organisations that are probably represented by the CIC.

2   Which professional organisation may you become a member of after graduation and what benefits will this membership give?

3   Distinguish between ARCUK and RIBA.

4   On hearing the government's decision to scrap ARCUK, the Director General of RIBA said: 'The government doesn't see any difference between buses and architects'.

   a) Explain this statement.

   b) Do you think that most members of the RIBA executive would be for or against the move to scrap ARCUK?
      (Explain your answer fully.)
   c) What has happened to the registration of architects since February 1993.

5   What economic arguments support the government's decisions to scrap ARCUK?

6   The government's decision to abolish compulsory registration of architects is against international trends. In Australia a federal law of registration has recently been introduced, and in the USA there is both state registration and a national organisation. Give an example of a professional registration scheme in Europe, describing how the representation works.

Tutorial Reading

Planning Gain

The first, and only, formal definition of **planning gain** appears in a Department of Environment circular (22/83). The official terminology reads as follows: 'a term which has come to be applied when, in connection with a grant of planning permission, local authorities seek to impose on a developer an obligation to carry out works not included in the development for which permission has been sought and make some payment in cash, or confer some benefit in return for letting the development take place'.

This seems unnecessarily long-winded. Using the terminology and ideas of CBA, it is possible to simplify planning gain as a trade-off agreement between a local authority and developer which involves permitting some external costs to occur in return for some community benefits being provided free. For example, in 1985 Merton Borough Council signed an agreement in connection with a superstore of 38,500 sq ft, whereby Tesco would provide a new community hall and also carry out flood prevention works in the vicinity. Similarly, Bromley Borough Council achieved a community gain of a new sports centre in return for development permission for 113 houses on a 5.9 acre site.

In fact, in recent years community gains have become a recognised feature of planning negotiations. Nowadays private development companies often take the initiative and offer community facilities, cash pay-outs, infrastructure developments or social housing almost without being asked. In fact, from a developer's perspective, planning gain is often viewed as some sort of 'blackmail or sweetener'.

From the local authority perspective, planning gain is frequently perceived as a community benefit that involves issues that are broader than the development itself. In consequence, the deal may involve benefiting the community on the other side of town. Examples might include providing new changing rooms for local stadiums and building bandstands in parks. In some instances, developers have even been requested to refurbish historically interesting buildings.

It is because of the wheeling and dealing nature of these negotiations that the 'deals' remain low profile. Both parties endeavour to secure their own broad interests. The 'exchange' or 'bribe' that is agreed as a result may seem underhand. The practice of planning gain, however, is encouraged in some legislation, for example, Section 52 of the Town & Country Planning Act of 1971, but to date there is still relatively little published material.

Questions

1 Define the concept of planning gain in your own words.

2 Give one example of a planning gain agreement that has been negotiated in your home town.

3 Why do you think that some private developers take the initiative and offer incentives to local authorities without being asked?

4 Recently the provision of social housing and/or contributions to infrastructure services have been common aspects of planning gain agreements. Choose one of these types of agreement and explain why they will be acceptable to both the local authority and the developer.

5 How do you think the value of each community benefit may be justified?

6 Explain why so few publications on planning gain exist.

Tutorial Reading

The Failing Market for Rented Housing

The Private Rented Sector

The history of the private rented sector is closely associated with various forms of rent control. These controls were first introduced in 1915, when 90 percent of UK families resided in homes rented from private landlords. By 1992 this figure had fallen to less than 7.5 percent. This rapid decline was largely caused by the constant renewal of legislation relating to rent in various attempts to keep the cost of housing as low as possible.

Rent control, like any maximum price legislation, causes a disincentive to the supplier, becauase the control enforces a 'price ceiling'. Consequently, private landlords respond by reducing the number of dwellings available for rent. They either sell their property on the open market for higher-priced uses, such as owner occupation, or put less funds into maintaining them. The result is that the supply of rented accommodation decreases and deteriorates.

The reality of this unfortunate scenario, initiated to help the poorer tenant, is well illustrated with a supply and demand diagram, such as that portrayed in figure 9.7.

Using a supply and demand diagram makes it easy to recognise that, given a regulated price below the market equilibrium, the quantity demanded exceeds the quantity supplied. It is also evident that the effect of applying such a control distorts the free-market solution.

This is not what the present government supports. Consequently, the private rented sector has been largely deregulated since 1988, and provided with tax incentives to try and revive it.

The Local Authority Sector

As the private rented sector declined, local authority accommodation developed from 1919 onwards. The initial idea was that the government should pay an 'explicit subsidy' towards housing units to make up for the shortage of accommodation available to low-income families. (This contrasts with the 'implicit subsidy' discussed above ie the difference between the regulated rent and market rent.)

Again a diagram makes the distinction clear. In figure 9.8 we assume that volume house builders, such as Tarmac, Wimpey or Barratts, can easily identify their average total costs (ATC). These are represented by the horizontal line ATC, suggesting an optimum long-run position of constant returns. Left to their own devices the house builders proceed from this position by adding a healthy profit margin. This effectively increases the unit cost and reduces the supply that is made available at each and every price. This is shown by a shift of the supply curve to the left, shown by S_1, giving a market price of P_1 and quantity Q_1 when demand is D. If the government pays an 'explicit subsidy' per unit equal to P_1, P_2, the builders' costs are reduced and the supply curve

shifts to the right, S_2, indicating a willingness to supply more at every price. The market price can now be lowered to P_2 and more houses bought (Q_2), given that demand remains constant. In the case of council housing, construction was often undertaken by the local authority and offered for rent below market cost.

Another way of understanding council property is as a merit good. A merit good is one that the government wishes to make available to all, regardless of income. These goods can be supplied via the market, but a freely determined price restricts some people's use. The government intervenes, therefore, and provides the good below the market price or free. Traditional textbook examples of merit goods are health and education, but council housing is also appropriate.

Clearly, the merit good approach does not sit comfortably with free-market ideology, especially as subsidies cause the **tax burden** to increase. Consequently, whenever politically viable, merit goods have been subject to reduced funding. Indeed, since the **Right to Buy Act** of 1980, council tenants have been actively encouraged to purchase their rented property. They have been offered substantial discounts below the market price.

Source: Adapted from 'Housing markets and government policy' *Economic Review* November 1993.

Figure 9.7

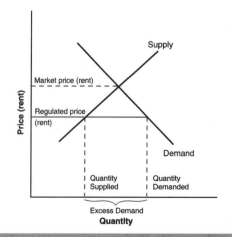

Figure 9.8

Questions

1 Distinguish between the public and private rented sector.

2 a) Figure 9.7 suggests that the imposition of a price ceiling below the market equilibrium will cause excess demand. State how the limited supply may be allocated.
  b) Subsidised council rents have also caused excess demand. State how the limited supply may be allocated.

3 Using up to date data, for example, from *Housing and Construction Statistics* published by HMSO, answer the following three questions.

  a) In 1979 6.5 million dwellings were rented from the local authorities. How many dwellings have been sold since?
  b) What percentage of dwellings are still rented from local authorities?
  c) Has the private rented sector seen any revival since 1988?

4 Employing the concepts of market failure, government failure and deregulation describe briefly the history of rented accommodation during the 20th century.

5 What other government housing policy has affected these two rental sectors since 1979? (For example, legislation relating to housing associations?)

6 Consider carefully the title of this reading and discuss the basic cause.

7 An eminent American economist, Professor Galbraith, once remarked `that Capitalism has nowhere in the world solved the problem of building affordable housing for the poor'. Discuss this statement in relation to the UK's past experience and comment on opportunities for the future.

Tutorial Reading

Commercial Property: Cycles and Leases

The property cycle may be exacerbated by anti-market leases, at least this was the message conveyed by the Governor of the Bank of England when he addressed the annual British Property Federation conference on 20 January 1993. The theme of the conference was 'Property in the 1990s: an approach to recovery'. The Governor's views are highlighted by the following extracts from his speech.

We all recall that, over the last two decades there have been three main booms in the commercial property market: during the early 1970s, at the end of the 1970s and at the end of the 1980s. The first and last of these episodes witnessed the most dramatic rises in property values over this period and in each case boom was followed by a severe slump in values, while the smaller property boom of the late 1970s was followed by a somewhat more muted decline in values in the downswing. This broad picture conceals differences between the various segments of the market...

We all know only too well how the recession has affected property companies and the property assets of other enterprises. Comparisons have been widely drawn between this recession and that of the mid-1970s, but there are two important differences. First, investment and development have been funded in recent years much more by bank finance rather than institutional money. Second, in this recession, property rental values have declined in absolute as well as in **real terms**.

There is no doubt, however, that the existence of **privity of contract**, as it now stands, can have apparently absurd outcomes ...

I also believe that market pressures will bring about adjustments to other terms of long-lease contracts, which will bring a better balance between flexibility for users of property and acceptable risk for those who provide the finance.

Upwards-only rent review clauses seem designed for a world which had the certainty of an upwards-only pattern of property values. This pattern is not in the interest of the economy as a whole and the thrust of our anti-inflationary policy is intended to make it obsolete.

What else might we do to aid the process? One of the classic obstacles to a perfect market is a lack of transparency. I have been surprised at the relative lack of consistent comprehensive data on the property markets and the apparent lack, until quite recently, of research into the functioning of those markets. The availability of data is limited by many factors but one reinforcing factor is the widespread use of confidentiality clauses. A diminished use of such clauses and a greater willingness to make data available would encourage a more efficient market and aid research and perhaps policy-making.

Source: *Bank of England Quarterly Bulletin* February 1993

Questions

1 How do the main booms in the commercial property market since the early 1970s relate to the cyclical pattern of the residential market (as portrayed in figure 9.1 p 71)?

2 How may the cyclical patterns be explained?

3 Give at least two instances that exemplify structural rigidity within commercial property markets.

4 Compare and contrast the present upwards-only rent review of most commercial property leases and the past rent control of residential accommodation.

5 In your own words try to define what you understand by a 'confidentiality clause'.

6 Could market failure relating to the commercial property market be remedied by:

  A the government
  B the Bank of England
  C market forces

  Choose one option (a, b, or c) and explain how a set of remedies may operate.

10

Managing the macroeconomy

Chapter Summaries to Review
- *Macroeconomics (1.3)*
- *The Mixed Economy (2.3)*
- *Government Devices to Correct Market Failure (9.2)*

We have already recognised that cycles occur within property markets (eg see figure 9.1). These cycles are related to activity in the broader economy. At times the overall business climate is buoyant: few workers are unemployed, productivity is increasing and not many firms are going bust. At other times, however, business is not so good: there are many unemployed workers, cut-backs in production are occurring and a significant number of firms is in receivership. These ups and downs in economy-wide activity are termed **business cycles** (or trade cycles). Inevitably, such cycles affect all markets. Therefore, some knowledge of government macroeconomic management geared towards stabilising these business fluctuations will help us to understand the built environment within a broader context.

Trade Cycles: Business and Property

In most years, output, income and employment increase. Consequently, a steady upward trend is experienced in most property markets. In fact, over the last 100 years the economy has averaged approximately a 1.5 percent annual increase in economic activity. There are, however, periodic fluctuations which detract from this steady trend. At times business activity slows right down and even becomes negative. Whilst at other times it accelerates rapidly and may even double in pace. We call the former a **recession** and the latter a **boom**.

Figure 10.1 The trade cycle
The coloured line represents the long-term growth path around which economic activity fluctuates, moving with some regularity from boom to recession and back again.

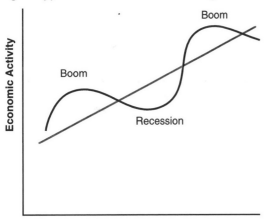

In figure 10.1 we portray a typical trade cycle. When it was first identified in 1860, (by Juglar) it was suggested that it took eight to 11 years to progress through a complete cycle from one boom to another. Since then, however, other economists have challenged this time measurement with various cycles being identified ranging from three to 50 years.

In other words, there are many explanations for the cycle of which the following is only one. A situation leads to 'over-heating'; this is characterised by shortages of labour and stock, and a consequent rising of prices. This leads into a down-turn, characterised by falling output, and rising unemployment and stock levels. Properties become vacant and cheaper to rent or buy. Eventually this generates opportunities for a new upswing which takes advantage of the various cheap unemployed resources.

Five Macroeconomic Objectives

The typical trade cycle is not, however, left to its own devices—governments intervene. It does not matter which political party they belong to or which nation they govern, all governments seek certain broad economic goals. These goals can technically be referred to as **macroeconomic objectives**. It is generally recognised that five main ones dominate.

Stable Prices

Persistently rising prices cause problems within many sectors of an economy. Consequently, since 1947, governments have monitored price increases via the Retail Price Index (RPI). For example, the statistics for the period 1986–91 are presented in figure 10.2. More discussion of this important macroeconomic objective occurs in chapter 13.

Full Employment

To have a large amount of unemployed labour represents wasted resources. Unemployment clearly has many costs in terms of human suffering, loss of dignity and loss of output. Consequently, all governments are concerned with recording the number of workers without a job. The precise way this is executed changes from time to time. At present 'official' unemployment in the UK is calculated according to the number registering for unemployment benefit. These claimants are then expressed as either a percentage of the total workforce of 28 million, or as an absolute number. In figure 10.2 it is easy to see that percentage unemployment was over 10 percent in 1986/7. Recently, it has reached these high proportions again, as the tutorial preparation will highlight.

Sustained Economic Growth

A long-term objective of all governments is to achieve steady increases in productive capacity. Consequently, economic growth is measured by the rate of change of output. In the UK a commonly used measure of economic output is GDP—**gross** (total) **domestic** (home) **product** (output). To portray accurately the rate of change of actual output, we must correct GDP for changes in prices. When this is done, we get what is called real GDP. Hence, a more formal measure of economic growth may be defined as the rate of change in real GDP over time. As the footnotes to figure 10.2 highlight, the growth data has been corrected accordingly. It is, therefore, a clear indicator of boom or recession: the earlier years in the chart showing high rates of activity and 1991 representing a recession with a negative growth rate. A fuller coverage of GDP and how it is calculated will be given in the next chapter.

An Equilibrium on the Balance of Payments

All international transactions are recorded in a country's balance of payments statistics. The ideal situation represents a position where over a number of years one nation spends and invests abroad no more than other nations spend or invest in it.

Obviously, economic transactions with other nations can occur on many levels and for accounting purposes these transactions are often grouped into three categories, namely current account, capital account and official financing. Of these three, the most widely quoted is the current account transactions. This involves all transactions relating to the exchange of visible goods (such as manufactured items), the exchange of invisibles (such as services) and investment earnings (such as profits from abroad). Clearly, therefore, in any one year, one nation's balance of payments deficit is another nation's balance of payments surplus—ultimately, however, in the long run, debts must be paid. The data in figure 10.2 show a worrying trend, but the figures need to be considered in a broader historical context. It also needs to be recognised that these specific figures are notoriously difficult to record accurately. (In fact all the statistics shown in figure 10.2 are subject to subsequent amendments—but the balance of payments amendments are by far the biggest.)

Figure 10.2 Macroeconomic statistics for the UK economy 1986-91

The data displayed is taken from various government sources (which are referred to in the tutorial preparation for this chapter). Two points need to be emphasised: the figures are subject to revision and calculated in different ways in different nations. The footnotes are, therefore, important for proper comprehension.

	1986	1987	1988	1990	1991
Inflation [1]	3.4	4.1	4.9	7.7	6.5
Unemployment [2]	3.29	2.95	2.37	1.66	2.30
Economic Growth [3]	3.1	4.7	4.5	0.7	-2.5
Balance of Payments [4]	-66	-4482	-16179	-17029	-6321

Footnotes: 1. Retail prices (percentage increase on previous year)
2. Total unemployment (annual average, in millions)
3. Annual percentage increase in "Real" G.D.P.
4. Current account (total for whole year, £ millions)

Preventing Environmental Damage

As discussed in chapter 9, free markets do not deal effectively with the spill-over (third-party) effects of many economic activities. Consequently, governments frequently step in to influence resource allocation; in fact, this issue is at the heart of many of the new political parties that are developing throughout Europe. At present, there is no agreed way of measuring the performance of this objective, although one possibility being tested by **OECD** nations is to express various toxic emissions as a ratio of GDP.

Priorities: An Historical Perspective

The order of priority in which these five objectives are attacked depends on the government in office. But all governments, in all nations, ultimately desire these same objectives in their quest for economic stability.

This notion—that the government should undertake actions to stabilise business activity—is, in historical terms, a relatively new idea. In Winston Churchill's budget speech of 1929, he said: 'It is the orthodox Treasury dogma that, whatever the social and political advantages, ... no permanent additional employment can ... be created by state borrowing and public expenditure'. Since then, however, economic advisers have been appointed by the government to measure and analyse economic trends, and suggest policy for their manipulation.

The turning-point for governments being responsible for economic objectives occurred after World War II. For example, the White Paper on Employment published in May 1944 stated that the government accept 'as one of their primary aims and responsibilities the maintenance of a high and stable level of employment after the war'.

Since this statement of intent in 1944, employment policy has been an important criterion for all governments. During the 1980s, it dropped from the number one spot to allow a more concentrated effort on curbing inflation. In the 1990s, we will see environmental protection become an increasingly important economic issue.

Chapter Summary 10.1

- The trade cycle represents fluctuations above and below a steady upward growth path. (See figure 10.1)

- The cyclical behaviour of an economy leads to governments throughout the world attempting various stabilisation policies.

- To achieve economic stability, five macroeconomic objectives are pursued, as follows: (1) full employment; (2) stable prices; (3) equilibrium on the balance of payments; (4) steady growth; and (5) a clean environment.

- The macroeconomic objectives change in their order of priority according to the government in office.

Government Policy Instruments

In their attempts to achieve these objectives, all governments, regardless of political colour, employ the same types of policy. Again, it is only the emphasis that seems to change. For organisational purposes, these policy instruments will be explained in three categories, namely fiscal, monetary and direct.

Fiscal Policy

This emanates, on the government's behalf, from the Treasury and consists largely of taxation (of all forms) and government spending (of all forms).

The word *fiscal* is derived from Latin for 'state purse', and this is most appropriate, as taxation is the main source of income from which governments finance their spending. In short, fiscal policy is concerned with the flow of government money in and out of the Treasury.

Monetary Policy

This emanates, on the government's behalf, from the Bank of England and is largely concerned with influencing, through various channels, the interest rates, exchange rates and the availability of credit. We shall deal with some specific examples in chapter 14.

An important point to note at this juncture is that fiscal and monetary policy are equally important in the government's attempts to manage the macro-scene. Changes to either set of instruments have broad effects on many of the objectives at once. Consequently, governments employ both sets of policy; it is only the emphasis that alters. As Professor Arthur Okun put it: 'The debate over whether the nation should rely only on monetary policy or only on fiscal policy, is a bit like arguing whether a safe car is one with good headlights or one with good brakes. It is not very wise to drive at night unless you have both'.

Direct Policy

This emanates from the government assembly and tends to be more 'objective specific' than either of the broad macro-policy options discussed above. Prices and incomes policies to influence price stability, or research and development policies to influence growth, are two examples of direct policy. The trends of this type of policy will vary according to the government in office.

Some commentators of the macroeconomic scene would refer to this type of policy as *non-market*, since it tends to be legislative and has less specific impact on market prices than either of the other options discussed.

Inter-relationship between Government Objectives and Policy

By now, you should understand that all governments desire a stable economy. This is easier said than done. Some of the means and ends involved are summarised in figure 10.3. The scales imply that there are trade-offs to be made between policy and objectives. Trade-offs, however, also occur between one objective and another, and one policy and another.

Let us just consider one scenario as an example. Interest rates are put up to reduce spending and prevent further pressure on price rises. In turn, such action will affect employment opportunities as consumer spending is cut back. Increasing unemployment will put a strain on fiscal policy as the unemployed will stop paying taxes and begin to receive benefits from the state. Consequently, the **public-sector borrowing requirement (PSBR)**—the government's 'overdraft'—will increase. This may necessitate government spending cuts in other areas, leading to further unemployment. As output falls, then obviously economic growth slows down. As economic growth declines, less environmental degradation should occur.

The scenario has two purposes: to highlight the complex nature of macroeconomic management and to emphasise that some of the objectives are incompatible.

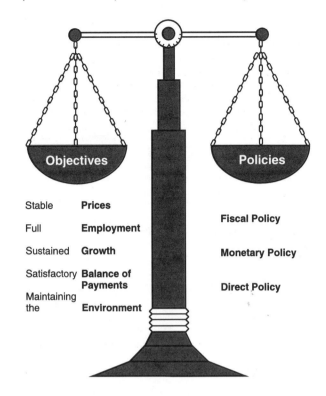

Figure 10.3   Government objectives and government policy
The scales in this figure are meant to suggest that the macroeconomic objectives are balanced by various government policies in an attempt to create a stable economy.

Objectives		Policies
Stable	**Prices**	
Full	**Employment**	**Fiscal Policy**
Sustained	**Growth**	**Monetary Policy**
Satisfactory	**Balance of Payments**	**Direct Policy**
Maintaining the	**Environment**	

Chapter Summary 10.2

- All governments utilise the same range of instruments, namely fiscal policy, monetary policy and direct policy.

- Fiscal policy is concerned with government expenditure and taxation.

- Monetary policy is concerned with the availability of credit.

- Effectively managing the macroeconomy is difficult, especially as some of the objectives are incompatible.

Economic Forecasting

The interpretation of economic events is a complex process. Macroeconomic policy instruments can affect several variables at once. As a consequence, government economists can only hypothesise regarding economy-wide interaction. To make their assumptions seem more scientific, however, they can present their views as sets of mathematical equations that link a number of economic variables.

The 1992 version of the Treasury model contained 386 equations which enabled forecasts based on past relationships to be made. These variables are known as **endogenous**, which means they have *'end-on'* relationships affecting one another. For example, one of the Treasury equations states a relationship between house prices and consumer spending. There are also 127 **exogenous variables** which need to be put into the model since they are *external* to the system, being determined by world events and policy (eg oil prices and interest rates). The overall program, once fed into a computer, enables forecasts to be made about macroeconomic behaviour.

Problems of Forecasting

Understandably, these Treasury forecasts are often wrong, since it is difficult to predict accurately the behaviour of millions of consumers and businesses to the last detail. Furthermore, forecasts are limited, owing to false assumptions about policy which may need to change course owing to sudden changes of events or revised statistics. Finally, there are problems relating to time-lags, since it will often take years for a specific monetary or fiscal instrument to fully work through an economic system.

Consequently, government economic forecasting is subject to much criticism, to the extent that many academic and private agencies compete over the task. Some of these forecasters specialise in property markets, which form a central part of most forecasting models.

It would be wrong to conclude, however, that the whole exercise of economic forecasting is futile, because it is quite inevitable that it will be undertaken so long as policy-makers, property developers and other entrepreneurial types have to make decisions and assess options. Indeed, Alfred Marshall emphasised in 1919 (before forecasting had really been established) that: 'the chief purpose of every study of human action, should be to suggest the probable outcome of present tendencies and thus to indicate, tacitly if not expressly, such modifications of these tendencies as might further the well-being of mankind'. In other words, forecasting is easily recognised as the natural outcome of economic analysis.

Chapter Summary 10.3

- The Treasury model used for forecasting is based on a computer program containing hundreds of equations representing endogenous and exogenous relationships.

- Economic forecasting is an unreliable science owing to unforeseen events, revised statistics and time-lags.

Tutorial Preparation

1 Taxation comes in various forms and often affects property.
   a. Find details relating to the following: capital gains tax, stamp duty, council tax, corporation tax, uniform business rate (UBR).
   b. Explain the impact that each category of taxation described in part (a) may have on property transactions.

2 Find up-to-date statistics for each of the macroeconomic objectives. The following official sources may help. The *Employment Gazette* is published monthly and includes the most recent figures relating to unemployment and the Retail Prices Index. The *Blue Book* and *Pink Book* are published annually and provide official data relating to GDP and balance of payments respectively. (Your library should stock copies of these publications.)

3 Professor F. Paish once likened managing an economy to 'driving a car with the front and side windows blackened and just a rear view mirror to see where the car is going, and with a brake and accelerator pedals that take effect some time after they are applied'.
   a. Explain and discuss this analogy.
   b. Compare the problems of managing an economy to managing a property investment fund.

4 Using any daily newspaper, find an article covering one macroeconomic objective and consider:
   a. How the issues raised will affect the other macroeconomic objectives.
   b. How different sectors of the property market may be affected.

5 A fall in PSBR is likely to occur, other things remaining the same, if
   A. the interest rate on government borrowing rises
   B. the level of unemployment falls
   C. the value added tax on energy remains at zero
   Select one option and explain your choice.

6 a. In your own words, define monetary policy.
   b. Describe how changes in monetary policy may affect property markets.

Tutorial Reading

The 1993 Budget

Among the many tax changes announced by the Chancellor in his budget, the reduction in **MIRAS (mortgage interest relief at source)** is perhaps the one with the greatest long-term significance.

The change in the rate at which MIRAS is calculated (from 25 percent to 20 percent) is not in itself very dramatic, and it won't have an enormous impact on individual household incomes. People will pay a little more on their mortgage, but the impact will be nowhere near as severe as the extension of VAT to domestic fuel supplies.

However, although the immediate short-term impact of the change to MIRAS is not that great, it nevertheless marks a sea change in housing subsidies. For the clear implication of the Chancellor's announcement is that MIRAS is on the way out. Its death may not come that soon, but there can be no doubt that its days are numbered.

What a remarkable reversal of policy this is. Seven years ago, when Michael Meacher suggested something similar, the entire Tory establishment denounced it as a wicked Labour ploy which threatened the very existence of every home owner in Britain.

Indeed, such was the sensitivity of the issue in the run-up to the 1987 General Election that the very word MIRAS became a shibboleth to every Labour politician; not to be mentioned under any circumstances other than when reciting the official reassurance that Labour would, or course, continue to pay MIRAS to every standard rate taxpayer. The only difference between the parties was that the Tories promised to pay it at the higher rate to higher rate taxpayers.

That distinction disappeared two years ago when Norman Lamont removed entitlement at the higher rate. Now, by reducing entitlement to standard rate taxpayers, the Tories are taking the axe to the benefit that they once so proudly defended.

In one respect, I am delighted. MIRAS was always an indefensible subsidy—expensive, untargeted, inequitable, inefficient and in some ways inflationary. So I will rejoice over the Tory sinners who have seen the error of their former ways and repented ...

Source: 'Only a muted cheer to mark the death of MIRAS.' *Building* 30 April 1993

Questions

1 a) Explain what you understand by the MIRAS scheme.
   b) Give a numerical example of how MIRAS would affect payments on a mortgage of £30,000 at 10 percent interest.
   c) Why was it considered to be a regressive instrument up until 1991?
   d) Identify two economic events that would cause the Treasury's MIRAS bill to increase.

2 a) What do the initials VAT stand for?
   b) Explain the statement 'the extension of VAT to domestic fuel supplies'.
   c) Which sector(s) will benefit from this extension of VAT?
   d) Which sector(s) will be disadvantaged by the change?

3 Do the examples from the 1993 budget discussed above constitute fiscal or monetary instruments?

4 Have there been any further amendments to housing subsidies since the April 1993 budget?

5 'MIRAS was always an indefensible subsidy:

   expensive, untargeted, inequitable, inefficient and in some ways *inflationary*'.

   a) Explain any two of the five features written in italics.
   b) Give two positive features that this subsidy could be linked to.

6 Suggest other possible ways that housing subsidies could operate.

7 Make a note of the details relating to the most recent budget and try to account for the changes that occur.

Tutorial Reading

UBR—For Those not in Business?

Property owners and developers are, naturally, not overjoyed by slumps in demand for their product and, equally naturally, continue to try to secure tenants where at all possible. The entrepreneur, meanwhile, revises his profit forecast or makes provision against loss and endeavours to conduct his business as best he can in difficult market conditions. He could, however, be forgiven for thinking that the Government which did so much to foster the spirit of enterprise and fuel his activities has effectively double-crossed him and is helping to hamstring his attempts to ride out the recession. Receiving no income from vacant property is painful enough, but being obliged to pay the 50 percent unoccupied property rate is adding insult to injury. With little prospect of dramatically improved demand in the near future, developers are looking very closely at their rate liabilities and considering how,

if at all, they can reduce the burdensome bills. Not surprisingly some are turning to 'constructive vandalism' to render their buildings incapable of beneficial occupation. This may mean removing ceilings and raised floors or simply taking out the toilet facilities, although safety standards must be maintained ...

Developers are not the only ones affected: all sections of the business community may face the same iniquitous tax. For example, a tenant seeking to assign a lease on unwanted property has to pay the same penalty. Alternatively, he may seek his landlord's permission to take to the sledgehammer and, if he obtains it, contract to make good all damage—which could cost as much as the rates bill he is paying. He must also pay the full rate on his new accommodation: a double whammy for business! Further, the prospect of a country and, in particular, the nation's capital scarred by empty shells would hardly act as a testament to

the ruling party's economic policies. The arguments for action are powerful, but none has been forthcoming. Why? Clearly the Government is reluctant to lose the cash generated by rates levied on vacant buildings. And there is some reluctance to tinker with a system which has been the cause of much political bloodletting.

But the time has come to bite the bullet. Property practitioners should support their professional bodies and lobby their MPs to make sure the voice of the industry is heard and its suggestions acted upon. One possible method of removing the worst aspects of the existing 50 percent rate would be to introduce a sliding scale, say 50 percent on the first six months after the quarter void period, 25 percent for the next three months and no liability after one year.

Source: 'Hammer horror' *Estates Gazette* 27 June 1992

Questions

1 How can tenants be enticed to rent vacant property during the low part of a cycle?

2 How could the government justify the need for landlords of empty buildings to meet a proportion of their rate bills?

3 What problems would there be with a sliding scale for rates on empty premises (as proposed in the final sentence)?

4 Are landlords of all empty commercial buildings still faced with this rates dilemma?

5 Make out a case in favour of either the government or landlord in relation to business rates payment on empty buildings.

Tutorial Reading

The Problems of Policy and Forecasting

A big problem for forecasters, during 1993, is at the long end of the market and this warrants some explanation. The starting point is the savage deterioration in the state of Britain's public finances. From a position in the late 1980s where the public sector borrowing requirement (PSBR) was actually negative, we have switched to red figures so far as the eye can see. Next year the PSBR is expected by many to be £55 billion-plus on present policy, equivalent to around 9 percent of GDP.

That rivals the darkest days of the 1970s. And, since it is largely a reflection of the rise in such expenditure as unemployment benefit that results from recession, a slow recovery, which is the best that we can hope for in an economy overburdened by debt, means that the pressure on Government finances will continue for some time. But the increase in the PSBR is not purely cyclical. Public spending has been racing away since John Major became leader of the Tory party. Though the Treasury disagrees, the Organisation for Economic Co-operation and Development argues, in its latest report on the British economy, that around 30 percent of the budget deficit is structural. That is to say, 30 percent of it will not disappear when the economy returns to a normal growth path.

This will put huge pressure on the capital markets and the backwash will inevitably be felt in property. With institutional cash flow running at between £45 billion and £50 billion, a PSBR of £55 billion threatens to absorb much of the money, at a potentially high cost to property values. The question is, how will the Government pull off the funding trick?

Source: Adapted from 'Plender's Perspective' *Estates Gazette* 13 February 1993

Questions

1 Define PSBR.

2 During the late 1980s there was reference to the PSDR. What do these initials stand for?

3 Apart from the effects of recession, such as unemployment, what will cause the PSBR to increase?

4 What does the phrase, 'institutional cash flow running at between £45 billion and £50 billion' mean?

5 Why will government action to fund the PSBR impose high costs on property?

6 What relationships exist between fiscal and monetary policy?

7 Do you think that the total of public and private sector debt would exceed 20 percent of GDP during any year of the 1990s? Explain your answer fully.

8 Why is long-term forecasting so difficult for economists?

11

The circular flow of income: its measurement and manipulation

Chapter Summaries to Review
- *Scarce Resources (Factors of Production) (1.1)*
- *Equilibrium (3.3)*
- *Trade Cycles and Economic Objectives (10.1)*
- *Macroeconomic Policy Instruments (10.2)*

In the last chapter we introduced the idea of government objectives and government policy. To use the terms of a medical analogy, we know that in managing an economy there is medicine to be dispensed, so that instabilities that may occur owing to the cycle of an economy can be remedied. To develop this further we need to improve our understanding of the flow of funds between various organs (sectors) of the economy, and to recognise how they may be measured and manipulated.

Circular Flow Model

To begin our analysis we ignore the government sector, the financial sector and the overseas sector. That is, our starting point is a simple two-sector economy and we analyse only the relationship between households and businesses. The complications of the real world will be considered later.

To make our starting model effective the following assumptions are made:

1. That households receive their income by selling whatever factors of production they own.

2. That businesses sell their entire output immediately to households, without building up any stocks.

3. That households spend their entire income on the output of the businesses.

These three assumptions seem realistic. Businesses will only make what they can sell. Production will involve buying in land, labour, capital and enterprise, and these services will generate income payments—rent, wages, interest and profit—which in turn will be spent.

The concept of the circular flow outlined in this way suggests that there is a close relationship between income, output and expenditure. These relationships are highlighted in a traditional format in figure 11.1.

From figure 11.1 it is apparent that businesses generate income to the factors of production (land, labour, capital and enterprise) by paying those that own them rent, wages, interest or profit. In turn, these incomes form the basis of consumer expenditure which the businesses receive to recycle to the households in the form of more income.

This suggests that it is possible to measure the amount of economic activity in an economy by adding up the value of total output, or total income, or total expenditure

Figure 11.1   The circular flow of income, output and expenditure
The diagram highlights two flows: the flow of money in pink and the flow of goods and services, and factors of production in grey. The two lower flows indicate the factor market, wherein households exchange their factors of production with businesses in return for payment. The two upper flows show another exchange. Businesses provide a flow of goods and services in return for monetary expenditure.

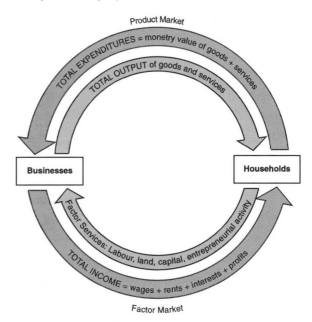

during a specified time period. It should only be necessary to calculate one of these three totals since in theory they are identical.

Chapter Summary 11.1

- **A simplified model, to show the interrelationship between income, output and expenditure, involves studying a two-sector economy only, to identify the circular flow between businesses and households.**

- **The simple circular flow model highlights:**
  1. **that households sell factors of production in return for incomes**
  2. **that businesses sell goods and services to households**
  3. **that there is a significantly close relationship between income, expenditure and output.**

- **Economic activity can be measured in three different ways.**

National Income Accounting

This involves attaching monetary values to each of the main flows identified in figure 11.1. Indeed, in the UK an annual government exercise, executed by the **Central Statistical Office (CSO)**, involves adding up totals for all the expenditure, all the income and all the output that has occurred. As suggested above the three totals that are arrived at do not differ significantly from one another, in fact in most years there is less than 0.5 percent discrepancy between the three totals. This small discrepancy is due to each of the totals being calculated via different statistical methods.

To get a better idea of the magnitude of the numbers involved, students can do no better than look at the *United Kingdom National Accounts* which are published annually by HMSO and held for reference at most libraries. A question within the tutorial preparation section will encourage you to take the library route and consider some of these figures.

GDP and Growth

Before considering any national income figures, however, we must fully understand what they convey and the significance of any changes in their size.

National income can be looked at from many statistical perspectives; the most common nowadays is **Gross domestic product (GDP)**. GDP represents the total money value of all the production within a country during one year. **Gross national product (GNP)** is very similar but includes a net figure for property-type income flowing in and out of the nation's economy from overseas. (For a more accurate distinction between GDP and GNP, see the dictionary definitions.)

When the GDP figures have been adjusted for inflation and show an increase between one year and the next, 'real' economic growth is said to have taken place. This means that more economic activity has occurred and the **real value** of production has increased. If GDP falls this is described as a recession. In the majority of years during the last half century the recorded figures have been positive.

Chapter Summary 11.2

- UK national income accounts employ three methods of measurement (ie output, income and expenditure). Each national income table represents a flow of economic activity.

- GDP represents the total money value of all production created within a country during a year. (It is only slightly different from GNP.)

- Economic growth is measured by changes in the 'real' GDP.

The Circular Flow: From Model to Reality

From the presentation of the two-sector circular flow model in figure 11.1 it seems that the amount of money that flows around an economy's circuit never changes. The GDP figure remains constant. Economic growth is always equal to zero. This is because the diagram highlights that income levels are determined by expenditure levels and expenditure is in turn determined by income and so on. Therefore, in a theoretical two-

sector economy, income and expenditure levels are permanently static: there is no growth and no decline. Such an economy could be classed as being in **neutral equilibrium**.

Every economy in reality, however, experiences **leakages** (withdrawals) from the circular flow through the sectors we initially excluded, namely: overseas, financial and government. Simultaneously there may be **injections** of funds into the economy through the same sectors, for example, export earnings, as money expenditure flows in from abroad. The various leakages and injections are identified in figure 11.2.

Figure 11.2   The circular flow – model with injections and leakages
To make the circular diagram more realistic, we must recognise that households save, spend money on imports from abroad, and provide some funds to the government via taxes (ie leakages occur). In turn we need to also recognise that businesses experience investment funds, export earnings and spending from government sources (ie injections occur).

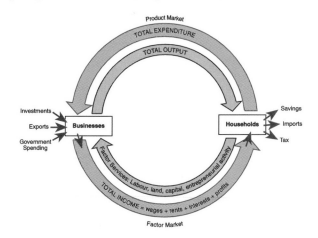

Leakages and Injections

In figure 11.2 we have identified three leakages from expenditure, namely savings, imports and tax. To counterbalance these there are three injections, namely investments, exports and government spending. The various decisions affecting these leakages and injections of funds are carried out by disparate groups of individuals with different motivations. It is most unlikely, therefore, that leakages and injections will be equal and cancel one another out.

If the total level of leakages is greater than the level of injections, the economy will become run down, thus raising unemployment and reducing standards of living. To take one extreme example, if every household decided to spend their money on imports from abroad then this would represent a major leakage of funds from our circular flow, and a significant boost to the total income and total output of other countries.

Conversely, if the total level of injections is greater than the level of leakages the economy will be boosted, thus increasing the employment opportunities and raising the amount of national income.

Equilibrium of the Macroeconomy

As implied in chapter 3, equilibrium means a 'balanced state'. In the macroeconomic context this means that income, expenditure and output levels continually adjust upwards and downwards to keep in tune with one another. For example, when leakages exceed injections expenditure on domestic output will be less than factor incomes. Consequently firms will not receive sufficient revenue to cover their output costs. Stocks will accumulate and firms will need to cut back output and income until they equal expenditure again. Indeed it is this fluctuation between leakages and injections that prompts changes in output from year to year. These changes lead to different levels of activity circulating within the economy—which represent different levels of national income. The important point to note, however, is that while all economies will tend towards an equilibrium the equilibrium point is not necessarily the point of full employment.

Chapter Summary 11.3

- All economies tend towards an equilibrium.

- The size of the injections (exports, investment and government spending) set against the leakages (imports, saving and tax) determines the annual level of economic activity within a specific economy.

- The equilibrium point is not necessarily a point of full employment.

Manipulating the Level of Economic Activity

If the government is faced with a situation of unemployment it can intervene in various ways to reflate the economy. The easiest option is to increase its own spending and thereby inject funds into the circular flow. This idea, known as **demand management**, was fashionable throughout Europe from 1945-75, especially as injections of government funds were seen to have a multiple effect on national income level. This forms the basis of J M Keynes' multiplier which is briefly reviewed at the close of this section.

The important point for us to acknowledge here, however, is that governments used to invest money into the economy to revive it to a full employment equilibrium. The monies that were invested were often invested into construction-related activity. This acknowledged the important role of the construction industry for the domestic economy and for the development of infrastructure. In fact, many post-war economists regarded the construction industry as a 'regulator'. The building of motorways during the early 1970s are an example. We shall deal with demand management more specifically in the next chapter.

Conversely, should the government wish to deflate the economy owing to rapidly rising prices, then it could pursue other policies such as reducing public spending or raising interest rates to encourage saving. Either of these policy manoeuvres would increase leakages and hence slow down the economy. These issues will be dealt with in subsequent chapters when we deal with the policies of the **supply-side** and **monetarists**.

Pump up the Volume

As a final illustration to the purpose of this chapter we shall briefly outline Keynes' **multiplier** as it highlights how the circular flow concept provides insight into government policy.

In figure 11.3 we show an amended version of the circular flow. It is clear that demand determines output, which generates income (indeed it may help if the price of output is regarded as bundles of income that have been paid out during the course of production). In turn the income facilitates expenditure. As the figures suggest, the economy is in a state of neutral equilibrium of £100 million. If this amount is insufficient to maintain full employment it may be advisable for the government to intervene to 'pump up the volume'.

Figure 11.3   A simplified flow-diagram showing expenditure, income and output relationships
Demand is measured in terms of expenditure. Expenditure determines the level of output and its associated income. In this diagram the economy is shown to be in a state of neutral equilibrium, since no leakages or injections occur to change the flow of income from £100 million.

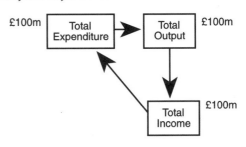

This is where Keynes' multiplier theory comes in, since he emphasised that an injection of funds would cause a more than proportionate increase in national income. To get an idea of how this works we shall follow the progress of a government injection of funds through several rounds of the circular flow.

In figure 11.4 (p 92) we have introduced some amendments to figure 11.3. These are shown in red. The important point is that any government investment, for a road or whatever, will cause expenditure and output to raise by the same amount. To increase output more labour will be taken on and more firms may develop. The additionally employed resources will be rewarded with incomes totalling the injection (£40 million in figure 11.4). We assume that some of this will leak out of the flow in the form of savings, imports or taxes. Economists refer to this as the **marginal propensity to leak (MPL)**. We have already discussed the concept of the margin in chapter 7, where we explained that the term focused on additional or incremental amounts. The marginal propensity to leak, therefore, represents the proportion of the 'additional' income that does not get used on consumption. If we assume an MPL of 0.25, we can quickly calculate that households will spend £30 million of their increased income on consumption. (This will certainly be the case if the recipients of the income were previously unemployed.) This additional spending will add a boost to total expenditure. In turn, firms producing consumer goods will need to increase output, they will take on more resources and have to pay out more in interest, wages and rent in order to earn more profit. Again incomes will increase. This will lead to successive rounds of further expenditure. If we continue to calculate the increase in additional expenditure occurring as a result of the initial government investment of £40 million, we quickly realise that national income is 'pumped up' by a significantly larger amount. In this example it would actually be £160 million. The determining factor is the size of the leakage; since the multiplier is equal to the reciprocal of the MPL. In developed European economies, the leakages are quite large, and accordingly the multiplier effect is significantly smaller than our example suggests.

Figure 11.4   A flow–diagram showing the multiplier effects of an injection of funds into an economy

The neutral equilibrium presented in figure 11.3 is now disturbed by a government injection of £40 million. In red we follow through the subsequent changes to output, income, and expenditure through two successive rounds. If we worked the figures through to conclusion, the initial injection of £40 million would have a multiplier effect of 4 on the national income, expenditure would increase by £160 million.

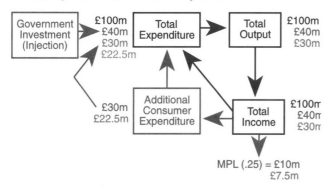

Chapter Summary 11.4

- If governments wish to slow down or speed up the rate of economic activity, they may use policy to affect the size of injections or leakages.

- Examples of policy affecting the circular flow of income will be dealt with under the headings of demand management, supply side and monetarism in subsequent chapters.

- Any change in government expenditure causes a multiplier effect on the level of national income.

- The larger the marginal propensity to leak, the smaller the multiplier effect.

Tutorial Preparation

1   Looking in different economic texts will show that circular flow diagrams are presented in differing formats, yet the principles they illustrate remain the same. With this in mind, copy the outline in figure 11.5 and complete it by following the questions below:

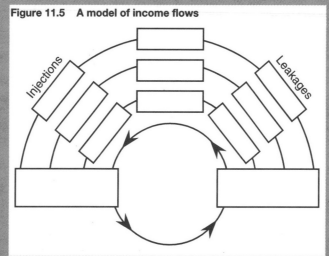

Figure 11.5   A model of income flows

a. Locate in the appropriate boxes the following five sectors: households, business, overseas, government and financial
b. Show the basic monetary flows between households and businesses
c. Distinguish the main injections relating to the other three sectors, by completing the appropriate boxes on the left-hand side of the diagram
d. Now distinguish the main leakages relating to the appropriate sectors in the remaining boxes
e. Which flow would commercial property development most affect?

2   Define in your own words
a. Gross domestic product
b. National income (net national product at factor cost)
c. Using the most up to date source, preferably official government statistics, find figures in current prices relating to (a) and (b)
d. What adjustments are made from GDP figures to arrive at national income?
e. Does GDP include export earnings?

3   Consider the table in figure 11.6 which gives details of monies relating to property developments during 1989, set in the broader context of related national income totals, and then answer the questions below.

Figure 11.6   The importance of construction and property development in the United Kingdom during 1989

		£ million
Gross Domestic Product		**515,317**
Gross Domestic Fixed Capital Formation		**103,262**
of which	New dwellings	20,986
	New buildings and works	31,189
	Transfer costs of land and buildings	4,381
Sub-total for land and buildings		**56,556**

Source: *The United Kingdom National Accounts* (1992 edition)

a. Calculate gross domestic fixed capital formation as a percentage of GDP.
b. Identify what gross domestic fixed capital formation includes (NB the dictionary section may help).
c. Calculate the construction industry's percentage contribution to GDP.
d. Repeat (c) but with data that relates to a recessionary year (for this you will need an edition of the *UK National Accounts*. Be careful to extract the relevant data, which is usually contained in the tables making up chapters 1 and 13).
e. The figure £56,556 million includes public and private sector activity. How does this figure break down in percentage terms? You may either estimate this or use the *United Kingdom National Accounts* again for actual figures.
f. What activities relating to property markets and/or construction does the figure £56,556 million exclude?

4   In a closed economy with no government sector, given that national income in year 1 is 1,000, and that the marginal propensity to leak is 0.2 what is the national income in year 2 if there is an additional investment of 100, assuming no time-lags?

A   500
B   1,125
C   1,225
D   1,500
E   5,100

5   The national income of a simple economy, in which there is neither government economic activity nor foreign trade is in equilibrium at £30,000 million. The full employment national product, however, is £35,000 million and the marginal propensity to save at banks is one-fifth. How large an injection of investment is required to bring the economy into equilibrium at full employment?

A   £500 million
B   £1,000 million
C   £2,000 million
D   £4,000 million
E   £5,000 million

Tutorial Reading

Housing Equity Withdrawal

The relationship between consumer spending and the housing market comes about through the practice of housing equity withdrawal (HEW). This is the tendency of individuals, when they move, to increase their mortgages by more than the difference in price between their old house and their new house. In other words they take advantage of their house move to remove some part of the equity, or value, that they have accumulated in their existing property. They might want to do this for very good reasons. Moving house costs a lot of money, in estate agents' fees, solicitors' fees, survey fees, removal costs and in stamp duty. In addition movers might wish to 'over-borrow' to finance

improvements to their new property, such as refitting the kitchen; or they may simply take the opportunity to finance additional spending on consumer durables such as carpets or household appliances at mortgage rates of interest. This is attractive to households because mortgage rates, secured by a charge on the consumer's property, are considerably below rates payable on bank overdrafts and credit card accounts...

Housing equity withdrawal serves to boost consumer income above that normally measured by the government's Central Statistical Office. Published total disposable income is estimated as the

total of income from employment or self-employment, earnings from investments pensions and rent etc. It has been estimated that HEW boosted consumer income by £12 billion in 1988 (ie nearly 5 percent of the total).

Economists have suggested that one way of reducing the impact of the housing boom on consumer spending and, therefore, on inflation, would be to tax **capital gains** from housing, but allow roll-over relief (so that you do not pay the tax if you reinvest in housing).

Source: Adapted from 'Spending, saving and the housing market' *Economic Review* September 1990

Questions

1   Define in your own words the following economic terms:
    a) Income
    b) Wealth
    c) Housing equity withdrawal

2   a) Would you categorise housing equity withdrawal as an injection or leakage?
    b) Using some of the ideas and terms developed in this chapter, explain why housing equity withdrawal is often regarded as an economic problem.

3   The potential equity value available to be withdrawn from owner-occupied housing doubled between 1982 and 1988. Identify at least two factors that would account for this rapid increase.

4   Suggest a way that the total amount available for housing equity withdrawal may be calculated. (NB the concept only relates to owner-occupied properties.)

5   Why is there less commentary on office equity withdrawal?

6   How may the amount raised by equity withdrawal affect the annual national income accounting process, and what problems may it cause?

7   Comment on one advantage and one disadvantage of the 'roll-over relief' idea discussed in the final paragraph.

8   What would housing equity injection involve and why is this a less common phenomenon?

Tutorial Reading

The Multiplier in Reverse

The much publicised £12 billion roads programme that followed the *Roads for Prosperity* White Paper in 1989 has become the worst casualty of the spending cuts that subsequently occurred.

The continuation of the programme requires annual expenditure on new road construction to be set at £1.2 billion-1.3 billion a year over the three years, 1992-95. In 1987/88—before the Government's conversion to the infrastructure cause—new road construction spending was just £750 million.

Contractors fear that new work will drop to previous spending levels, with by-pass contracts delayed but motorway widening schemes escaping cutbacks.

'It does not require much intellectual skill to cut capital programmes,' says Neil Ashley, chairman of the UK's sixth largest roadbuilder, Amey. 'The Government should look at far more wasteful areas of expenditure, like public sector salaries'.

'For the sake of saving a few hundred million, the Government risks having inadequate infrastructure when economic growth resumes', says British Aggregates and Material Industries economist Jerry McLoughlin. 'It is absolutely ludicrous to reduce the roads programme when we should be looking for ways to increase revenue to boost expenditure'.

Source: 'We're on a road to nowhere but traffic jams' *Building* 31 July 1992

Questions

1   a) State three other areas of public expenditure.
    b) Try to identify some up to date figures for the annual expenditure involved in these three areas.
    c) Could any of these be cut back if necessary?

2   Identify three arguments for and three against road building.

3   What economic concept is Jerry McLoughlin supporting in the final statement?

4   Describe how cut-backs to public spending may lead to a multiplier effect in reverse.

Tutorial Reading

Chaos Theory

A fad in the City during the early 1990s was the concept of chaos. This is thought-provoking because it provided analysts and economists with a theoretical basis for admitting that they don't know what is going to happen in the markets. In effect, **chaos theory** tells fund managers, foreign exchange dealers, and property developers that what they expect to take place in a rational market will not occur in the real world.

Source: Adapted from 'Chaos in the City' *The Independent on Sunday* 4 February 1990

Questions

1   Give an example of chaos theory operating in any property market.

2   Why was it apt for this theory to be a fad of the early 1990s?

3   Can you find evidence that supports its growth after 1993?

4   What arguments are there supporting economic theory?

5   How may continuation of chaos theory help to support the economic discipline?

12

From demand-side to supply-side

Chapter Summaries to Review

- *Demand and Supply Curves (3.3) and (5.3)*
- *Shifting Demand Schedule (4.2)*
- *Laffer Curve (9.3)*
- *National Income Accounting (11.2)*
- *Injections, Leakages and Equilibrium (11.3)*

As suggested in chapter 11, the consensus approach to manipulating economic activity from 1945 to 1975 was attributable to John Maynard Keynes. His basic idea was that any government could **fine-tune** the economy. Using the multiplier as a **demand management** technique, employment could be maintained at a full level. Indeed, judging by the historical record, unemployment remained exceptionally low throughout the 1945–75 period; this is clearly shown in figure 12.1.

Figure 12.1   Percentage of UK workforce unemployed 1931-91
A portrait of 60 years is given, so that the period of Keynesian consensus (1945-75) can be considered in a broad historical context. The reference line scanning across the graph at 3 percent highlights how near to an acceptable level of full employment the economy had been for many years.

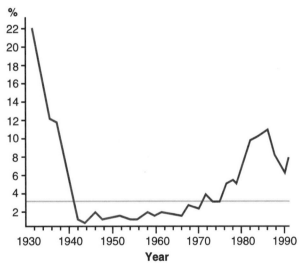

Source: *Abstract of Labour Statistics, Ministry of Labour and Economic Trends*

Unemployment levels below 3 percent are quite acceptable, as this allows for people changing jobs, weather fluctuations and economic conditions overseas. Each of these factors is expected to affect the employment levels of any dynamic economy.

Alongside this impressive employment record, a concern began to develop over the continuous increases in price levels — ie inflation. In fact, the problem became so dominant that, throughout the 1980s and early 1990s, the focus of government policy shifted and governments concerned themselves with squeezing inflation out of the system. Furthermore, during the same period, **supply-side economics** began to challenge the conventional wisdom of the **demand-side economics**.

In order to explain these transitions of policy, we will use the tools of supply and demand, as outlined in chapter 3, but with two major modifications. Instead of looking at the price of one commodity, on the vertical axis, we will look at the *price level* (an index of general prices) and on the horizontal axis, we shall consider how these relate to *total* (aggregate) quantities.

Aggregate Demand

The central focus of Keynesian analysis is **aggregate demand (AD)**. A definition of aggregate demand is the total spending on goods and services produced in a whole economy. At the beginning of chapter 11 we introduced total expenditures on a theoretical level in a two-sector economy. In such a model, aggregate demand would be equal to consumption expenditures (eg beer and chocolate) by households and investment expenditures (eg buildings and machinery) by businesses. In reality, however, we need to add government expenditures (eg on road construction) and export expenditures by foreigners on UK output (eg American purchases of Jaguar cars). Aggregate demand (AD) therefore, consists of four elements: consumer spending (C), investment spending (I), government spending (G) and the expenditure on exports (X). To be technically correct the spending on imports (M) that leak abroad need to be subtracted as they do not represent monies spent on UK products. It is traditional for the following shorthand notation to be allowed when summing up the components of aggregate demand.

$$AD = C + I + G + X - M$$

At this juncture you could be excused the feeling of *déjà vu*, as it was only a few pages ago that we discussed national income accounting and made it clear that this involved putting monetary value to economic activity. Aggregate demand can in fact, during a one year period, be regarded as analogous to GDP. Figure 12.2 shows the magnitude of the amounts involved for 1991 (rounding of the figures has caused the total GDP for that year to be £1 billion higher than the recorded amount).

Figure 12.2 Measuring aggregate demand in 1991 market prices (figures are rounded into billions)

Components of aggregate demand:	C + I + G + X - M = AD
Related amount in £bn. during 1991	368 + 90 + 121 + 135 - 140 = £575bn

Source: *United Kingdom National accounts (1992 Edition)*

The Aggregate Demand Curve

Clearly we no longer have in mind one specific product; we are not considering, as we did in chapter 4, the demand for naturally ventilated buildings. We are considering the demand for all products at once. This does not preclude us, however, from using a price/quantity graph. An aggregate demand curve, AD, shows the relationship between the total quantity purchased and the price level. In formal terms: on the horizontal axis we measure national income and on the vertical axis we measure the price level. From figure 12.3 it is quickly apparent that the higher the price level, the lower the total output that is demanded by the economy and vice versa, the lower the price level, the higher the total output.

Figure 12.3 The aggregate demand curve
On the horizontal axis we measure national income. On the vertical axis we measure the price level. At price level P_1 national income demanded will be 600 but when the price level increases to P_2 real national income decreases to 400, other things being equal.

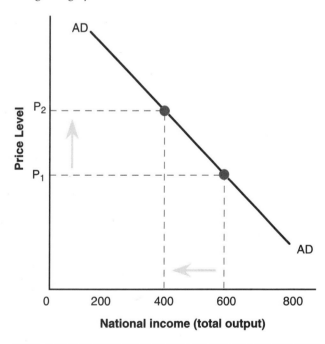

The explanations for a downward-sloping demand curve for *all* commodities are similar to those for individual commodities. For example, if domestic goods rise in price then home markets may accept cheaper substitutes from abroad and foreign markets will buy fewer exports. Similarly, when prices in general rise, the real wealth of those holding cash will fall and cause them to spend less. Prices and spending, therefore, continue to be inversely related.

The Aggregate Supply Curve

We shall consider **aggregate supply** more carefully at a later juncture in this chapter. For the moment we simply need to be able to discuss full employment equilibriums; therefore we shall derive an aggregate supply curve (AS) and leave it at that.

The aggregate supply curve displays the same relationships as the aggregate demand curve—but from the producers' perspective. Some interesting points, however, arise according to the level of economic activity experienced during the time-period.

Firstly, if the economy has many factories operating at less than capacity, it is possible to increase output without there being any pressure on prices. In these circumstances the aggregate supply curve would be a horizontal line (perfectly elastic) at the current price level; this is shown in figure 12.4. Next, consider the other extreme where there is no excess capacity. The economy is working at full employment; machines are operating 24 hours per day. It is impossible therefore to produce any more units of output; the only thing that can happen in the short-term is price increases. (In such a situation supply can be regarded as perfectly inelastic.) This stage is shown in figure 12.4 by a vertical line at output rate Y_2. Finally, between these two extremes one can envisage a situation where there is excess capacity in some sectors of the economy, but no excess in others. Consequently, as production is increased, the price of some goods and services will be pushed up (but not all prices). As these supply constraints develop, successive increases in spending will lead to smaller increases in production. Again this stage is shown in figure 12.4 as the phase between Y_1 and Y_2.

Figure 12.4 The aggregate supply curve
There are three stages to this curve's shape. At a price level of P_1 the AS curve is a horizontal line up to the point where output is marked Y_1. Secondly, there is an intermediate stage where some sectors of the economy are experiencing excess capacity but others do not. In those sectors that are near full capacity, producers find their unit costs rising. At Y_2 there is no excess capacity in any sector of the economy. The only thing that producers can do is raise prices.

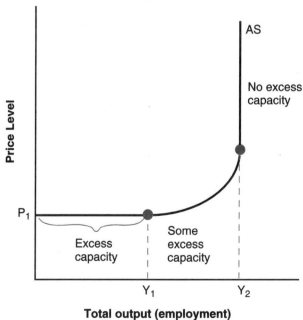

We have now reached a point where we can represent aggregate demand and aggregate supply simultaneously on one graph. This will enable us to consider demand management problems and the possible remedies.

- Full employment involves an acceptable level of unemployment. During much of the post-war period, 3 percent unemployment was the target.

- Aggregate demand is the sum of all expenditures in an economy. It is usually considered in four categories; using the standard notation these are $C + I + G + (X–M)$.

- The aggregate demand curve (and aggregate supply curve) show relationships between the price level and total output. (See figures 12.3 and 12.4)

- The aggregate supply curve highlights three stages related to capacity. These basically emphasise that the nearer the economy gets towards full capacity, the more likely price increases become.

The Problem of Demand Management

Any government policy that desires to influence the comprising elements of aggregate demand will meet with problems. There are, for instance, over 20 million households involved in consumer expenditure and no one can be sure how each will react to government changes or how long their reaction will take. These quantitative and qualitative problems, however, seem to pale into insignificance when economists consider the related problem of inflation.

Into the Inflationary Gap

In figure 12.5 we use shifts of the aggregate demand curve (AD) to represent the results of government injections into the economy, 'to pump up the volume', to bring us towards full employment.

Remember that shifts to the right of demand, or aggregate demand, represent increases at each and every price. When dealing with total demand it is very difficult to shift the aggregate demand curve to the precise point of full employment (as represented by AD_3). In fact government economists have often been accused of overshooting and causing the economy to overheat. The resultant excess demand achieves nothing except continually increasing prices—inflation.

Obviously, as firms compete for scarce resources in order to raise output that is related, directly or indirectly, to government injections, price levels will begin to increase. This is the situation between AD_1 and AD_3. Once demand exceeds the full employment equilibrium, nothing can be done to increase output, since all resources are being used. In terms of figure 12.5, once the aggregate demand curve shifts beyond AD_3 the price level increases rapidly but output remains static. Indeed in 'real' terms, output (national income) cannot physically exceed Y_2. In monetary terms, however, national income can increase. This rather special circumstance is known as the **inflationary gap** and is shown by P_2, P_3 in figure 12.5. The inflationary gap highlights the excess between aggregate monetary demand and full employment output. The caption to figure 12.5 will help clarify how we got into this situation.

Figure 12.5   Demand-management inflation

When the economy is at a point of equilibrium represented by AD_1, the output rate is Y_1, some resources within the economy are unemployed and prices are stable. Any increase in demand, thereafter, will lead to a rise in price level. Thus a shift from AD_1 to AD_2 will cause the price level to increase slightly, from P_0 to P_1. Beyond output rate Y_2, any increase in demand will simply result in a higher price level since, by definition, at full employment, no more output is physically possible. An increase in demand from AD_3 to AD_4 will increase the price level from P_2 to P_3, with no corresponding increase in output. This problem is highlighted by the inflationary gap—a situation of price rises and nothing else..

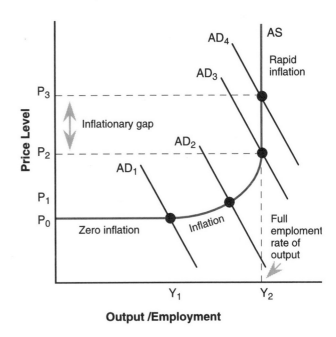

Out of the Inflationary Gap?

How may these inflationary tendencies be eliminated; how may the gap between accelerating price increases and unchanged output levels be closed? This is the type of question that economists have concerned themselves with since the mid-1970s.

Professor Frank Paish, when he was lecturing at the LSE during the 1960s, suggested that the problem with Keynesian demand management techniques lay with the concepts of productive capacity and actual output. As he understood it, adding to productive capacity generates income before it generates actual output. Therefore, to achieve stability, he recommended maintaining a margin of unused productive capacity.

Since then the focus has shifted to discussions relating to potential output and actual output. Once spare capacity has been used up, once full employment of resources has been achieved, actual output will be restricted in the short term.

The answers to the problem, therefore, seem to rotate around ensuring an amount of unused productive capacity and/or increasing the potential output of an economy. In short, to improve the efficiency of the resources that are used; to generate more capacity. Technically speaking, economists became concerned about the supply side, about ways of shifting the aggregate supply curve to the right. In other words, about ways of increasing the potential level of output at the full employment point. These supply-side ideas will be considered next.

- Demand management techniques become closely associated with the problem of inflation.

- The inflationary gap highlights the situation in which aggregate monetary demand exceeds full capacity output.

- If resources are used more efficiently, the aggregate supply curve will shift to the right, and potential output increase. Inflationary pressure will thus be reduced.

Aggregate Supply

One of the hallmarks of economic policy since 1979 has been concern over the supply side of the economy. That is, the focus on spending and aggregate demand has shifted to production and aggregate supply.

Aggregate supply can be regarded as total production and clearly many factors will influence its size. For example, the level of profits, ease of movement into and out of markets, the level of wages, the efficiency of capital and labour, the level of fixed costs etc. In fact, the kind of factors that we discussed within the context of microeconomics. Consequently economists concerned with this perspective seem to place more trust in market forces than government intervention.

Supply-side policy, therefore, has been geared to making markets work more efficiently. This may be achieved by reducing the structural rigidities that clutter many markets. For example, 67 **wage councils** have been abolished since 1979, trade union activities have been restricted and market competition has been opened up via the processes of privatisation and deregulation. Similarly, broad reductions in rates of income tax (from 33 percent to 25 percent at the basic rate and from 83 percent to 40 percent for the top rate) have been enforced to induce people to work harder (this concept was already explored in chapter 9 when we discussed the Laffer curve). Indeed, there seems to be no market that has escaped from the plethora of supply-side measures, to take just two detailed examples.

The Housing Market

The spirit of market liberalisation promoted through supply-side measures is well illustrated by the way house purchase has become easier since 1980. For example, council tenants have been encouraged to buy their houses at a discounted rate, stamp duty has been reduced, financial intermediaries have been deregulated creating a more competitive mortgage market and conveyancing is no longer the solicitors' monopoly.

The Commercial Property Market

The amount of red tape and related barriers to business have been reduced within this sector. For example, various planning controls have been simplified, specific tax allowances have been increased for industrial buildings and properties built for letting, and the **business expansion scheme** has been extended to companies specialising in letting residential property.

Why Supply-side Measures?

By devising methods to promote as many competitive markets as possible, the government believes it is saving money on intervention and encouraging the

entrepreneurial spirit that drives production. In technical terms, it is aiming to shift the aggregate supply curve to the right. If we consider figure 12.6, we can see how over a fairly long time period the equilibrium level of national income can significantly increase from Y_1 to Y_2. More importantly, as the aggregate supply curve moves outwards, the equilibrium price can fall; in figure 12.6 the fall is from P_1 to P_2. Consequently, in theory, we have devised a system that increases the potential output and lowers the rate of inflation.

Figure 12.6   Increasing aggregate supply over time
The equilibrium in 1985 is given by the intersection of the aggregate demand curve and the aggregate supply curve; the price level is P_1 and national income is Y_1. Subsequent to incentives to strengthen market forces and increase productivity, the aggregate supply curve can eventually shift to the right, shown by AS 1995. The new equilibrium is at an increased output of Y_2 and a reduced price level P_2.

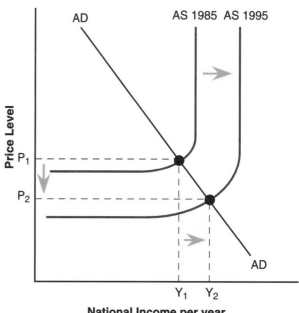

Postscript

The historical evidence is not overwhelmingly supportive of this supply-side argument as, although inflation has fallen since the mid-1980s, the rate of output in recent years has not increased significantly. However, the problem of time-lag is recurrent within any government economic policy be it demand side or supply side in orientation. Consequently, post-war governments have often placed emphasis on **intermediate macroeconomic targets** to gauge how their policies are progressing. We shall deal with one such target—the housing market—as a tutorial reading to this chapter.

- Economists have become concerned with the microeconomics that underpins aggregate supply.

- Supply-side economics revolves around the freeing up of markets, mainly by taking the government 'off the backs' of the people and the economy.

- If people can be encouraged to work more efficiently the aggregate supply curve will shift to the right.

Tutorial Preparation

1 a. Complete the following statement.
   Consumer expenditure + government expenditure + investment expenditure + ... minus ... = ...
   b. In your own words explain the significance of the statement just completed in (a).
   c. What relevance do the two missing links (before the equals sign) have for property markets in the UK?

2 a. The caption to figure 12.1 (p 93) implies that a full employment target of 3 percent unemployment was acceptable during much of the post-war period. With technological developments and less occupational mobility, this target level has risen. Discuss what may be considered as an acceptable level of unemployment in the 1990s.
   b. Use the *Department of Employment Gazette* to see how many regions in the UK have an unemployment problem according to your revised target figure.

3 A multiple-choice question. When aggregate demand rises, output will not increase if
   A   there is spare capacity
   B   there are some planning stages to consider
   C   real national income is increasing
   D   the aggregate supply curve is vertical

4 a. Study the flow diagram in figure 12.7 and insert the appropriate time-spans for the development of a large office block (approximately 30,000 sq ft of floor space)

Figure 12.7   The time-lag in commercial property development

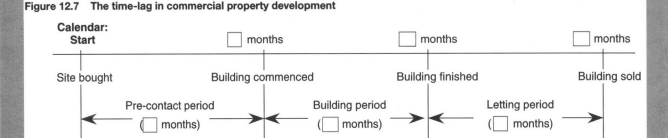

Source: (Adapted from) *Industrial and Business Space Development*, Morley et.al. Spons 1989

   b. Explain how the development of a prestigious office block would affect aggregate demand.
   c. Explain how the same development would affect aggregate supply.
   d. Use an inflationary gap-type diagram to explain the problem that may occur between aggregate demand and aggregate supply, especially when we consider the existing office market.
   e. How may economic problems such as that outlined in (d) above be avoided within the commercial property market?

Tutorial Reading

The Housing Market: An Intermediate Macroeconomic Target

The concept of intermediate macroeconomic targets became popularised when the control of inflation was understood to be related to money supply (there is coverage of this in chapter 13). Other intermediate targets, however, also exist. A recent one is the housing market. The recurring idea is that a chosen target (the housing market, money supply, or whatever) is *not* the final objective, but an important step along the way.

Given that something like 70 percent of the housing stock in the UK is owner-occupied, changes within the market will have significant repercussions on the broader economy. To take just a few examples: expenditure on consumer durables, such as fridges and carpets, occurs most frequently when people buy houses. Changes in interest rates affect the number of houses being bought and sold, or even repossessed. When unemployment increases, income and confidence decrease and the housing market slows down.

As a consequence, forecasting models of the economy now incorporate housing market behaviour. For example, a recent development of the Treasury model involves following the impact of changes in housing wealth and consumer expenditure. This proceeds along the following lines: an increased level of demand in the economy produces a rise in real house prices and the resulting increase in housing wealth stimulates consumer expenditure and hence boosts the multiplier. We have already considered some of this process in a previous reading entitled 'housing equity withdrawal'.

Questions

1   Complete the diagram in figure 12.8 (p 100) by filling in examples for each of the three stages.

Figure 12.8   The housing market—an intermediate macroeconomic target

Three stages of controlling an economy	Examples
Policy instruments	
Intermediate macroeconomic target	
Government objective	

2   State examples to prove that the government considers the housing market an area of economic activity that needs to be controlled.

3   Name four other possible targets that the government could aim for; categorise two as final and two as intermediate.

4   a) List some of the causes of the housing market recession 1990-92.
    b) List some of the consequences of the housing market recession 1990-92.
    c) State some arguments in favour of the housing market being used as an intermediate macroeconomic target.

Tutorial Reading

Commercial Property and the Construction Sector

The following paragraphs (written in the middle of 1992) are taken from a Bank of England commentary on the domestic economy.

'Oversupply remains the principal feature of the commercial property market. **Rental values** and **capital values** have continued to fall in many locations although conditions vary quite widely between centres. In some areas, the supply of unlet property is sufficiently large that many, less well-equipped offices are unlikely to be brought back into active use at current rental values, remaining as a constraint on the market for the foreseeable future. Lower rentals have, on the other hand, meant that the flow of lettings has remained broadly in line with averages for the past decade—although below those seen in recent years. In London, for example, there are indications that rentals are becoming attractive relative to those of other European capitals.

Since its peak in the first quarter of 1990, output of the construction industry has fallen by 14 percent. The decline persisted into the first quarter of this year and may be continuing. Total new construction orders fell by 16 percent in the three months to May, with all major sectors affected: private commercial and industrial orders fell by 9 percent and 24 percent respectively, and private residential orders dropped by 11 percent.

Accordingly, immediate prospects for the sector remain depressed. The Building Employers' Confederation expects output to decline by 4-5 percent during 1992 with only a modest pick-up next year. The National Economic Development Office's forecast is even more pessimistic, seeing new work falling by 7.5 percent this year and not recovering until 1994. Commercial construction, held back by the large overhang of empty offices, is not expected to recover until later still.'

(Reviews such as this are a regular feature of the Bank's bulletin and it may be worth comparing these statements with a recent issue.)

Source: 'The domestic economy' *Bank of England Quarterly Bulletin* August 1992

Questions

1   In your own words distinguish between rental and capital values.

2   a) Did the commercial property sector experience excess capacity or supply constraints during 1992?
    b) What are the implications of this setting for the broader economy?

3   Listed below are some sectors of an economy. Rank them in numerical order according to their response to any economic recovery post-1992.

Commercial construction sector, retail sector, housing construction sector, financial services sector

4   List some arguments for and against the commercial property market being regarded as an intermediate macroeconomic target.

5   a) Using some of the terms and ideas introduced in this chapter, write an account of what has happened to the general economy since 1992.
    b) As a result of these changes to the general economy, what has happened to the sectors concerned with commercial property and construction?

6   Using examples from the extract consider whether the construction industry is a 'leading' or 'lagging' indicator to the general pattern of economic activity.

13

Inflation and expectations

Chapter Summaries to Review
- *Macroeconomic Objectives (10.1)*
- *The Inflationary Gap (12.2)*

UK governments, since the mid-1970s, have considered the control of inflation as their number one objective. The monthly press releases relating to the official measurement always make news and often appear on the front page. In fact, we shall distinguish in this chapter the difference between the **headline inflation rate** and other possible inflation rates. We shall also consider why inflation is regarded as a problem, what may cause it and how it can possibly be resolved. But first of all we start with some descriptive matter that puts the problem into a historical context.

Inflation: In a Historical Context

Inflation may be defined as: a *sustained* (or *persistent*) increase in the general price level. The italicised words in the definition are important as a one-off increase in the price level would not be categorised as an inflationary situation. Continuous annual price rises, however, such as those experienced in the UK, can definitely be categorised as inflation.

In figure 13.1 we show the annual average inflation rate for the period 1970–89. Clearly the 1970s witnessed the highest levels in fact, during 1975 alone, prices rose by 24 percent. The 1980s, relative to the 1970s, could be classed as a decade of **disinflation**, that is prices continued to rise each year but the overall rate began to slow down. The 1990s, judging from recent trends, may become known as the decade of **low inflation** with figures below 5 percent being the norm. In December 1992 the annual rate of inflation was 2.6 percent. (The rare occasions when prices fall are known as negative inflation or deflation, but this has not been experienced since the period 1925–33).

Figure 13.1 Inflation rates in the UK 1970-89

Years	Annual average change in price
1970 - 1975	12 %
1976 - 1979	13.5 %
1980 - 1985	9 %
1986 - 1989	5 %

Why Price Increases Matter

Fluctuating prices affect existing contracts, influence business confidence and alter exchange rates.

If prices are continually changing, entrepreneurs are hesitant to enter into contracts as they cannot work out the long-run results of their investments. This is often compounded further by the problems of changing exchange rates and interest rates which often accompany inflation. A stable economic environment is easiest to work within. Indeed economists often discuss **menu costs** as the associated effects of inflation on business. These costs consist of aspects such as vending machine alterations, the costs of printing revised price lists, the time spent renegotiating and so on.

Similarly, inflation affects those that are not economically active. If price changes are not monitored, pensioners, students and those reliant on state benefits suffer, unless their fixed incomes are revised to be kept in line with price increases.

In consequence many aspects of economic activity today are index-linked to allow for inflation. For example, savings, business contracts and pensions can all be adjusted in the light of inflation. All that is needed is a reliable price index.

How Inflation is Measured

Any measure of inflation involves representing changes in price over a period of time. The statistical device best suited for this purpose are **index numbers**. Index numbers are a means of expressing data relative to a given **base year**. They enable the cost of a certain product(s) to be expressed as a percentage of the cost for the same product(s) during a base year. The basic principle is shown in figure 13.2.

Figure 13.2 Calculating a price index
In this example there are two identical baskets of goods. The base year is 1987. The price index of 1993 compared to 1987 ends up as 116. In other words, the basket of goods has increased 16 percent in price during the period 1987-93.

$$\text{Price Index} = \frac{1993}{1987} \times 100$$

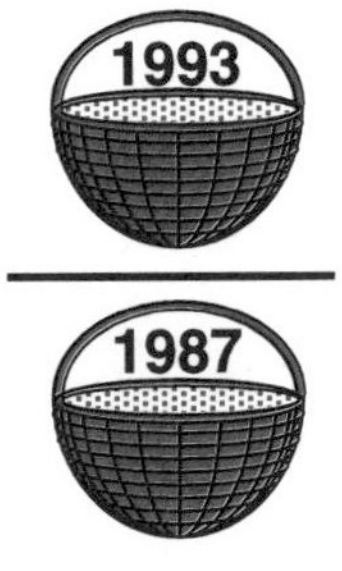

$$\text{Price Index} = \frac{£35.60}{£30.48} \times 100$$

$$\text{Price Index} = 116$$

What one actually puts in the basket for the base year and comparative year must be consistent. That is, the system is dependent on comparing the price of the *same* good or service. For example, the property consultants, Richard Ellis, compile a commercial property price index by comparing capital and rental values for the same types of property in London on a regular basis. Their data goes back to a base year in 1979. The index reached a peak during the third quarter of 1989 with an index number around 320 and declined to around 160 in the first quarter of 1992. This represents a decline in value from 1989 to 1992 of around 50 percent—but an increase of 60 percent since 1979.

Similarly, Nationwide Anglia (and other building societies) regularly publish a house price index. The Nationwide Anglia index involves comparing each month the price of four different house types across 13 regions of the UK. This allows them to present detailed information and an average picture for the UK as a whole. According to their June 1993 bulletin, the average house in the UK cost £52,866. The monthly index number had fallen from 201.70 in May 1992 to 190.67 in May 1993, this represented a 5.47 percentage fall in price over the year (ie 201.70 − 190.67 = 11.03 ÷ 201.70 × 100). Many other institutions and professional bodies also construct specialised indices. A relevant example is the RICS **Building Cost & Information Service (BCIS)** which is briefly examined in the tutorial preparation section at the end of this chapter.

The Retail Price Index

In the UK the most popularised of all price indices is the **Retail Price Index (RPI)**. As the name suggests, this is an index of the prices of goods and services purchased by the typical household. It includes everything from food and housing to entertainment. Movements in this index therefore reflect changes in the cost of living. Indeed, the annual percentage increase in the RPI is the way inflation is measured.

To be precise the RPI is based on the regular price comparison of about 600 items. These are 'priced' in various retail outlets in 180 different regions of the UK. In comprising this monthly index, therefore, over 100,000 prices are recorded (180 × 600), however, only the national averages are published. For example, on the 13 November 1990, 686 prices were collected for a pint of draught bitter. The average used for the RPI was £1.14 per pint. The price quotations, however, had ranged from under 98p to over £1.26.

The various items in the basket are given a 'statistical weighting' to take account of their importance to the typical household. That is, the items that take more of people's incomes are given a higher weighting. For example, the statistical weight for food is higher than that for tobacco, as changes in food prices affect everybody, whereas tobacco prices only affect smokers. The statistical weight attached to items comprising housing is even higher, since this type of expenditure takes the largest percentage of most people's income. In fact, as owner-occupied housing has increased during the last decade, the statistical weight on mortgage interest payments has been revised upwards, to the extent that commentators on RPI movements often discuss an underlying rate which excludes mortgage interest payments. (It is sometimes abbreviated as RPIX.) We consider in more detail the debate on how best to measure inflation in the tutorial reading entitled 'Core Inflation'.

The Causes of Inflation

There are many different explanations for inflation. Here we shall just consider the two most common categories. According to these, inflation either occurs because an increase in demand pulls up prices or because an increase in the cost of production pushes up the price of final products. Let us take each category in turn.

Demand-pull Inflation

As we have already explained in figure 12.5 (p 97) when aggregate demand in an economy is rising inflation may occur. The severity of the problem depends on how near the economy is to its full capacity level (eg full employment). As previously detailed in the caption to figure 12.5, there is, during any specific time period, a fixed output rate and if demand increases beyond that point the only way businesses can respond is by increasing their prices. Hence, beyond a full employment level no more output is physically possible, the pressures of excess demand can only be countered by price increases. To put it in other words: when total demand in the economy is rising and the capacity available to produce goods is limited, **demand-pull inflation** may occur.

Cost-push Inflation

Prices also rise when the economy is nowhere near full employment, for example, during the recession in the mid-1970s. Consequently other explanations of inflation have developed. A common feature of these explanations relates to changes in business costs owing to wage rises, widening profit margins or increased import prices for raw materials.

To develop just one of these possibilities: following the action by **OPEC**, oil prices quadrupled during the 1973 to 1974 period. As a result, during 1975, most oil-importing countries experienced inflation above 12 percent. In fact, in the UK inflation rates went as high as 25 percent. Oil is a major energy source for business vehicles and office heating, consequently the costs of production were pushed up, and, in turn, passed on to the consumer in the form of higher prices; hence the term **cost-push inflation**.

Two closing anecdotes to this scenario put the problem of cost-push inflation into a sharper focus. The mid-1970s saw energy efficiency become an important criterion when designing buildings, and experiments such as **passive solar** design now exist. Secondly, alongside the search for alternative energy sources, the 1973 oil crisis also provided the necessary impetus to develop the North Sea oilfields, which protected the UK economy during the 1980s.

Other solutions to the inflationary problem are more government-orientated in strategy and some of the possibilities will be reviewed next.

Cures for Inflation

Taking a broad chronological overview we will briefly explain three cures that seem to typify the decades since 1970.

Prices and Incomes Policies

During the 1970s the favoured device of stopping, or at least slowing down, cost-push inflation involved various versions of wage and price controls. In generalised terms, these involved employers, unions and governments getting together to agree an annual 'norm' for wage increases. The negotiations, however, proved difficult to manage and even the policies that were enforced effectively only restrained cost-push inflation for a temporary period.

Control of Money Supply

The 1980s witnessed a shift in emphasis, and the control of inflation, especially demand-pull inflation, seemed to be inextricably related to the size of a nation's **money supply**. 'Too many pounds chasing too few goods' was the glib explanation that the press popularised, as their news stories explained variants of money supply. Indeed, it is difficult to appreciate fully the money supply argument until the various forms of money that exist in a modern society are acknowledged. We shall briefly review this analysis in the next chapter but need not be too concerned with the intricacies, since explicit money-supply control has dropped from favour.

Interest Rate Manoeuvres

The early part of the 1990s experienced the 'one (golf) club' approach which involved using only interest rate manoeuvres to achieve many government targets, including that of controlling inflation. Again this is a theme of the next chapter.

Conclusion

The problem with these cures is that each of them is a response to a different perceived cause of inflation. For example, the militant trade union activity of the 1970s and the excess demand of Keynesian policy, resulting in inflation during the 1980s, and so on. Yet, no one can be sure that different causes exist as historical eras change from one decade to the next. Therefore, in the next two sections we develop a more subtle and broader approach, one that seems to have found favour with politicians during the 1990s.

Chapter Summary 13.2

- **Demand-pull inflation occurs when the total demand for goods and services rises faster than the rate of growth of supply.**

- **Cost-push inflation is due to one or more of the following: (1) union power; (2) widening profit margins; and/or (3) raw materials price increases.**

- **Price and incomes policies, control of money supply and interest rate manoeuvres have all been used as attempts to reduce inflationary pressures.**

Expectations

Nowadays, economists and politicians believe that expectations influence all types of economic variables, including inflation. In the past these expectations had been considered as external influences that were beyond control. In formal terms they represented an example of an exogenous variable.

Modern economic theory, however, seeks to understand the behaviour based on expectations. Initially, during the 1970s, the **adaptive expectations hypothesis** was accepted.

Adaptive Expectations

The basic idea here was that people gauged what happened in the past as the best indicator of what will happen in the future. Look at figure 13.3. Here we represent the actual rate of inflation by a black dashed line. It is rising. In year one it is 6 percent per annum, during the second year it is 8 percent, during the third year it jumps to 12 percent. Thereafter it stays at 12 percent.

According to the theory of adaptive expectations, the expected rate of inflation this year is whatever the rate of inflation was last year. This is represented by the red dashed line in figure 13.3. During the second year, workers believed inflation would be 6 percent because that is what it was the year before. During the third year they believed it would be 8 percent (because that is what is was the year before). In this simplified model, workers are always behind in their expectations. When the rate of inflation is rising, they will always believe it is going to be less than it actually turns out to be; when the rate of inflation is falling, they will always believe it is going to be more than it actually turns out to be. Only when the rate of inflation remains constant for a period of time do expectations come into line with reality.

Figure 13.3   Adaptive expectations theory
According to this hypothesis, individuals formulate their expectation of inflation according to the rate in the previous year. Here we show the actual rate of inflation via a black dashed line. The expected rate of inflation is shown in red and clearly lags one year behind in pattern. For example in year 2 people expect inflation to be 6 percent because that is what it actually was in year one.

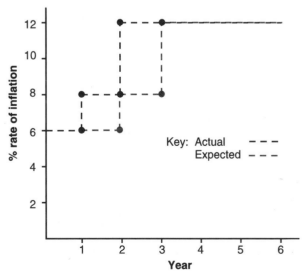

A more sophisticated model of expectations would not allow people to be proved consistently wrong. It would recognise that opinions are based on a whole range of available data of which historical trends form just one part.

Rational Expectations

The **rational expectations hypothesis** is the logical development, since it is more concerned with human behaviour; it allows for the sifting and weighing of all available information.

Within this theoretical framework, people do not simply look at what has happened in the previous year. They consider what has happened in the past and combine it with their knowledge of current government policies, and those that are likely to be introduced. Rational expectations, therefore, require judgement about current and future policies combined with lessons from the past.

For example, the shrewd forecaster dealing with property prices during the late 1980s, would have recognised from previous episodes that prices do not continue to rise forever, especially when the current government policy was to increase interest rates.

Rational Expectations and the Built Environment

Clearly rational expectations take on more importance in some spheres of economics than others. For example, City stockbrokers, investment managers, property developers, institutionally based fund managers, estate agents, and those involved in the various fields of valuations will depend upon their specialist and skilled knowledge of a specific sector to make shrewd judgements. It is debatable, however, whether managers, workers and consumers within the general economic scene can be expected to have developed the same level of expertise. Consequently, it is often the case that the expectations of the professionals are adopted by the general public. Although this may appear better than the 'blind leading the blind', it can lead to scenarios where power psychology seems to generate interesting outcomes. A detailed example will be considered next.

Chapter Summary 13.3

- The adaptive expectations hypothesis argues that people make predictions of this year's rate of inflation, based on what the rate of inflation was last year.

- The rational expectations hypothesis suggests that individuals form judgements by examining all information. That means that economic forecasters will not only look at past data, but also at current and future government policy.

The Wage-price Spiral

Expectations can be regarded as the driving force that underlies the beginning and end of a **wage-price spiral**. If we consider figure 13.4, it is evident that, regardless of the initial cause of inflation, workers eventually obtain a wage increase which subsequently leads to prices being marked up. The interesting point, however, is that what perpetuates and accelerates this spiral-type behaviour is expectations; most notably the expectations of those in charge of governments, trade unions or employer confederations.

We shall develop the explanation from box 5 onwards. By this stage in the proceedings it is most likely that labour correctly anticipates further rounds of inflation. Hence they do not only negotiate a wage increase to restore their purchasing power, they also incorporate a 'hedge' against future inflation. For example, if there has been a period of inflation at 15 percent, workers will demand pay increases of a greater amount, say 30 percent. This would allow 15 percent for the previous inflation, 10 percent for unanticipated events and 5 percent which can be given up during negotiations. Next in the proceedings we can see, in box 6, that entrepreneurs employ a similar rationale and increase prices sufficiently to cover the total increase in their wage bill plus a precautionary amount to avoid further price increases having to occur too soon. In both cases, the claims relating to wage and price increases are being made on the basis of judgements about the future. By box 7, therefore, it should be evident that judgements anticipating inflation create a self-fulfilling prophecy. In other words, it is rational expectations that drive the wage–price spiral.

Figure 13.4   The wage-price spiral

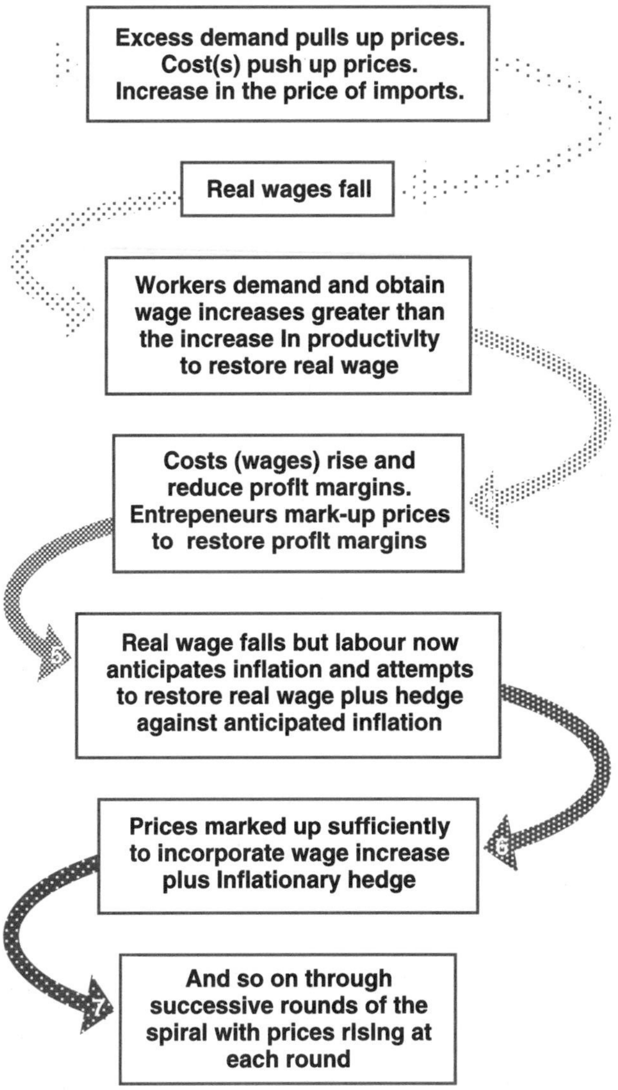

Likewise, during the late 1980s and early 1990s, Conservative government leaders tried to convince society that their policies would slowly eradicate inflation, providing that judgements were adjusted in the light of future expectations. Indeed, this is why the government during the 1990s was distressed whenever the downward trend of inflation changed course. Any 'blips' in the monthly RPI figures were carefully accounted for, as people's expectations should not be allowed to change. The problem with all economic forecasting, however, is that unforeseen events occur, 'blips' can turn into 'blots' and prices can easily start to rise again. Once this occurs, rational expectations will see the wage–price spiral accelerate upwards with a vengeance. Consequently, we can begin to appreciate that the psychology of expectations play a crucial part in determining all economic destiny, especially that of inflation.

Chapter Summary 13.4

- The wage-price spiral represents the inflationary process as one where incomes and prices continually chase each other in an upwards direction. (See figure 13.4)

- Employers and employees strive to cover themselves against expected and unexpected inflation.

- It is rational expectations that determine the speed and direction of price changes.

Tutorial Preparation

1 What is wrong with the following definition of inflation? 'Inflation is caused by too much money chasing too few goods'.

2 From the five themes listed below, link up two causes of inflation with two appropriate cures:
demand-pull inflation, prices and incomes policy, cost-push inflation, interest rate manoeuvres, money supply control.

3 a. Define each of the following terms:
Disinflation
Low inflation
Deflation
Inflation
b. Match each of the above terms to the appropriate historical era: 1930, 1970, 1980, 1990

4 Using the *Department of Employment Gazette* and/or a newspaper article, find the annual rate of inflation for the current year.

5 The RPI is not necessarily the best indicator to use when index-linking a builder's contract'.
a. Explain this statement.
b. Name some indices that a builder may use.

6 a. What can you find out about the BCIS?
b. Define in your own words what you think a tender price index measures.
c. Define in your own words what you think a general building cost index measures.
d. Consider the data in figure 13.5 and answer the three questions on p 106.

Figure 13.5

Year	Quarters	Tender price index (Base 1985 = 100)	General Building Cost Index (Base 1985 = 100)
1989	1st	134	120
	2nd	134	122
	3rd	138	126
	4th	134	127
1990	1st	135	128
	2nd	131	131
	3rd	126	135
	4th	123	136
1991	1st	117	138
	2nd	114	139
	3rd	114	141
	4th	112	142
1992	1st	112	142
	2nd	107	143
	3rd	106	146
	4th	105	147
Forecast			
1993	1st	103	147
	2nd	103	148
	3rd	102	149
	4th	102	149
1994	1st	102	150
	2nd	102	151
	3rd	104	153
	4th	104	154

Source: *BCIS Quarterly Review March 1993*

i. Explain what the forecast figures for 1993 and 1994 for each index suggest.
ii. What actually happened during 1993 and 1994?
iii. What implications do the two sets of index numbers alongside each other have for profits in the construction industry?

e. The BCIS market condition index is calculated as follows:

$$\text{Market condition index} = \frac{\text{Tender price index}}{\text{General building cost index}}$$

Describe as accurately as possible what this is trying to indicate. Use data from figure 13.5 to give examples to illustrate our answer.

7 Calculate the percentage change between the following index numbers.
a. 100 to 160 = percent
b. 120 to 160 = percent
c. 200 to 150 = percent

8 Index numbers enable comparisons to be made. The table presented in figure 13.6 shows data dating back to 1914. This will be used as the basis for the following historical cost analysis.

Figure 13.6

Year	Craftsman rate	Labourer rate	Fletton bricks	Cement	Total building cost	Retail price index
1914	100	100	100	100	100	100
1923	169	197	157	158	110	175
1933	165	190	151	124	98	140
1943	222	267	167	138	180	266
1953	382	513	318	257	330	377
1963	613	804	394	327	430	486
1973	1419	1856	548	662	1000	842
1983	4888	6662	3417	2636	4800	3016
1992	8393	10983	5882	3285	5950	4880

Source: *Building 150th Anniversary Supplement February 1993*

a. Since 1973 what has increased at a faster rate, total building cost or the retail price index?
b. Account for the rates of a labourer increasing faster than a craftsman's.
c. What do figures which portray such long historical periods fail to measure?
d. Can you calculate from these indices what the most expensive component of a building is?

9 On the basis of adaptive expectations (and figure 13.6) what general themes may emerge relating to costs during the 21st century?

10 State two examples when your future profession may require you to employ the rational expectations hypothesis.

Tutorial Reading

Core Inflation

Some countries—including the United States and Canada—prefer to assess the degree of inflationary pressure by reference to a measure of 'core' inflation. The construction of a 'core' rate of inflation involves stripping out of the RPI items which are volatile and might obscure the underlying trend in inflation. At first sight such an approach appears attractive, and there is a case for excluding certain components, such as mortgage interest payments, on a consistent basis. The argument for excluding other items from the index on *a priori* grounds is less strong ...

The danger in stripping out too many items from the RPI—housing, food, energy, indirect taxes, administered prices, and so on—is that the resulting index is not representative of movements in the average price level. For this reason the Bank has constructed an RPI-based measure of inflation—the 'housing-adjusted' RPI (or HARP index)—which replaces the mortgage interest payments component of the RPI with an alternative measure of owner-occupied housing costs. This may be useful as an addition to, not a replacement for, existing measures of inflation. The alternative measure is based on a user-cost approach which attempts to adjust for the degree to which house purchase is both a consumption and an investment decision.

Source: Inflation 'report' *Bank of England Quarterly Bulletin* February 1993

Questions

1 a) What does the retail price index in the UK try to measure?
   b) What uses do you think the retail price index has?

2 Each 1 percent rise in the mortgage interest rate lifts the RPI by approx. 0.4 percent. This effect has been referred to as 'perverse'. Can you explain why?

3 Why do you think the UK includes mortgage interest payments in the 'basket' of goods comprising the retail price index?

4 What arguments can be made in favour of removing mortgage interest payments from the retail price index?

5 a) What is an administered price?
   b) What arguments would there be for stripping these out of an RPI?

6 The HARP index (housing-adjusted retail prices) was one attempt to measure housing costs in a different way.
   a) What has happened to the HARP index since 1993, and what do you understand to be its distinctive quality?
   b) How else can housing cost be measured in a price index?
   c) Find out how another nation treats housing costs when compiling its retail price index.

Tutorial Reading

The 'Upward Only' Rent-review Clause

Not least of the effects of the commercial property market recession of the early 1990s has been to throw into question some of the most basic assumptions on which the market is built. In particular, the structure of the typical 'institutional' lease has come under attack.

To see what has happened, and why, we need to go back to basics. Take London offices as a convenient example. The developers of the immediate post-war period usually attempted to negotiate a lease as long as possible with the tenant. Inflation was not perceived as an important factor, and leases of 99 years without rent review or with only one review at the half-way point were not unknown.

The developer reckoned to create a value for himself from the difference between his development costs and the value of the building on completion. And, in the days when borrowing costs were close to, or below, the yields on which offices were valued, the developer who chose to hang on to his completed development as an investment looked forward to a continuing income surplus from the difference between the rent he received and the interest he paid on his long-term fixed-rate finance. Subsequent increases in capital value were not at the forefront of his mind.

As inflation gradually asserted its grip, and the shortage of central London offices forced rents up in an expanding economy, the position changed. The property development and investment companies wanted to benefit from the subsequent increase in rents as well as from the initial development surplus. Typical rent review periods came down first to 21 years, then to 14 years, then to seven years and finally to today's usual five years.

Until the 1990s the 'upward only' clause built into the rent review (which meant that rents could rise but never fall) was not perceived as a great problem by tenants. Rental levels fluctuated a certain amount, but the overall trend was strongly upwards and it was considered very unlikely that rental levels at any point would be lower than they had been five years earlier. It therefore cost tenants very little to concede the 'upward only' clause.

A property investor, however, was doubly protected under the typical 25-year 'institutional' lease with five-yearly upward only rent reviews that had evolved by the 1980s. He had the security offered by the property itself and generally reckoned that he would have little problem in reletting it if the existing tenant went bust. And, in addition, he had the undertaking by the tenant to pay for 25 years a rent that would never fall below the starting level—in practice, of course, the landlord expected it to increase at five-yearly intervals.

This structure had always assisted considerably in property financing in Britain. With a virtually guaranteed income for at least 25 years, it was possible to finance property investment with very long-term borrowings—a 25 year mortgage being typical.

Source: 'Beginner's guide: the shortening lease'
Estates Gazette 27 June 1992

Questions

1 What do you understand by the phrase 'the typical institutional lease'?

2 Explain the relationship between inflation and the development of the 'upward only' rent review clause.

3 Name two characteristics of the property market during the early 1990s that made the 'upward only' rent review clause problematic.

4 Identify at least three differences between the contract relating to a commercial property and a student's privately rented accommodation.

5 How may tenants negotiate around the problem of the 'upwards only' clause during a phase of deflation?

6 The thrust of government policy is intended to make the 'upward only' clause obsolete. (See the *BEQB* February 1993 extract, in chapter 9 tutorial readings, p 81.)

   a) Explain this statement, making it clear why the government would not support the clause.
   b) What has happened to the upward only clause since 1993?

Tutorial Reading

Inflation and Some Effects on Property

It is generally accepted that high and fluctuating rates of inflation hamper decisions about business investment and make business more risk averse. In the property market of the 1970s inflation had the effect of disguising the cyclical nature of both commercial and residential property investment. People came to see real estate as a store of value; the yield structure became distorted by over-optimistic multiples which then collapsed in the 1980s where investors looked more carefully at rental trends in **real terms**.

Perhaps the most deceptive feature of inflation is the way it drives a wedge between nominal and real interest rates. Uncertainty about inflation and the level of **real interest rates** creates huge difficulties in asset valuation.

There is no better illustration of this than the housing market in the second half of the 1980s. Most people who bought in the boom thought that the increase in house prices would cover the interest rate on their mortgage—that is, the long-run real rate of interest in housing would be negative. Since 1990 the real rate, expressed in terms of the mortgage rate adjusted for the decrease in house prices, has been positive to the tune of 15-20 percent.

Source: Adapted from 'Plender's perspective'
Estates Gazette 8 August 1992

Questions

1 Explain why 'high and fluctuating rates of inflation hamper (property investment) decisions'.

2 Explain the phrase 'people came to see real estate as a store of value'.

3 Consider figure 13.7 and answer the following multiple choice question.

Using the data presented in the graph select the year when a house would have proved to be the most effective hedge against inflation.

A 1979

B 1981

C 1984

D 1988

E 1985

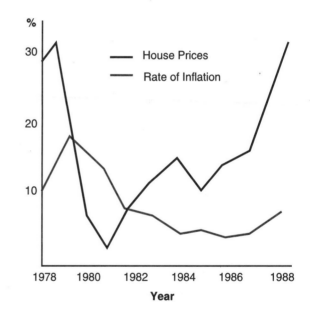

Figure 13.7   Year on year growth in the fourth quarter

4 a) Define in your own words the term 'real rate of interest'.
   b) Define in your own words the term 'nominal rate of interest'.
   c) What is the basic difference between the nominal and real rates of interest?
   d) Explain the full implications of a positive real rate of interest and give an example.

14

Money, financial institutions and interest rates

Chapter Summaries to Review
- Supply and Demand Graphs (3.2)
- Government Policy Instruments (10.2)
- Inflationary Gap (12.2)
- Cures for Inflation (13.2)
- Expectations (13.3)

As the song goes 'money makes the world go around...', and it has since civilization began. Throughout the history of the world money has taken on many forms in different societies: from the bill-hooks, knives, shirts and spades of ancient China to the plastic cards of today. Indeed, we will begin by briefly studying the nature of money to enable us to understand the world of finance and the related structure of interest rates that comprise the bulk of this chapter. Ultimately these aspects have a strong bearing on property investment as will be emphasised in the tutorial readings.

Functions of Money

Money is anything that acts as a **medium of exchange, a store of value, a unit of account** and a **standard of deferred payment**. In today's society direct debits, cheques and credit cards serve these purposes. Therefore, it is important to recognise that when we talk about money we must not just think about cash. In fact, a nation's money supply will be defined in many ways and in most the percentage of cash will be particularly small.

Some Definitions of Money Supply

Monetarists acknowledge that one of their theoretical concerns relates to the size of a nation's monetary stock. Consequently central banks try to measure its size and across the world a number of monetary aggregates are published. For example, the OECD published a table during 1977 showing how its 24 member states were using 23 different definitions of money supply. In the UK, we have experimented with various possibilities since 1963, ranging from broad to narrow definitions. The broad measures include various types of money on which interest is paid. The narrow measures focus more specifically on money held primarily for transactions. In other words, the broad measures stress the role of money as store of value and the narrow measures the role of money as a means of payment (medium of exchange).

In the UK today there are four main measures on which data are published regularly, namely M0, M2, M4 and M5. As the numbers increase in size the range of monetary assets included become broader. M0, therefore, is the narrowest measure, and the only one in which cash is the dominant percentage. In figure 14.1 we present a spectrum of assets which could form a check list of items

definable as money, and we categorise the components of M0, M4 and M5. M2 is slightly more difficult to portray in this format, since it is M0 plus interest-bearing bank and building society deposits which are withdrawable in one month. For our purposes, however, we need not be concerned with the finer detail. The important point to recognise is that the money supply definitions consist largely of products created by the financial institutions. The nature of these products will change as financial institutions develop and new formats of money are created. Consequently, we should not be surprised to discover, as this chapter proceeds, that governments throughout the world have experienced difficulty in targeting and controlling the money supply.

Figure 14.1   A range of assets defined as money
Money is not just cash; it can take many forms in a sophisticated modern society, and several possible examples have been listed below. The assets we have chosen to list have been presented in order of liquidity, as this is something we wish to refer back to later in the chapter. To emphasise the formative nature of this topic we have also chosen to identify assets that are not at present defined in any category of money supply. Indeed, each of the three official measures listed have probably been developed during your lifetime. For example, M0 is the oldest measure shown and it dates back to 1981.

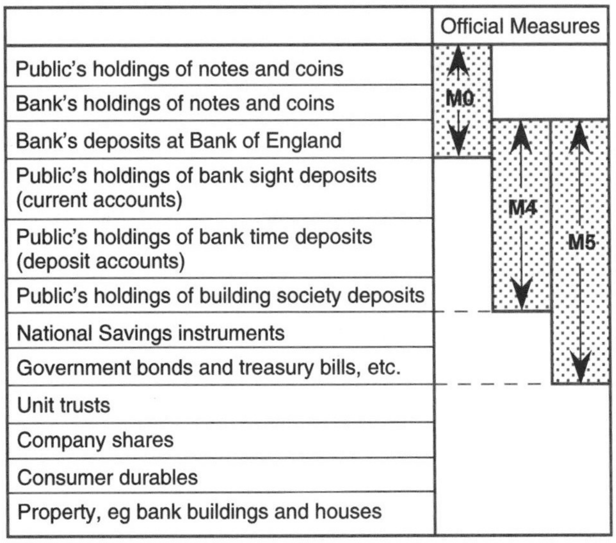

	Official Measures
Public's holdings of notes and coins	M0
Bank's holdings of notes and coins	M0
Bank's deposits at Bank of England	
Public's holdings of bank sight deposits (current accounts)	M4
Public's holdings of bank time deposits (deposit accounts)	M4 M5
Public's holdings of building society deposits	
National Savings instruments	M5
Government bonds and treasury bills, etc.	
Unit trusts	
Company shares	
Consumer durables	
Property, eg bank buildings and houses	

Source: Adapted from *British Economy Survey* Spring 1993

Why Controlling the Money Supply Matters

Recognition that the size of a nation's money supply is important dates back to classical economic thought. Already at the beginning of this century the medium of exchange (as money supply was then termed) was acknowledged as a key variable in an economy. This became formalised via the **Fisher equation** which represented the **quantity theory of money**. Details of Fisher's contribution can be reviewed in any mainstream text (or briefly in our dictionary). The important point, for our purposes, is that Fisher's four-part equation enabled economists to suggest a correlation between monetary stock and price level.

More recently during the 1970s, these ideas were popularised once more by the empirical work of Milton Friedman. His research seemed to prove that an increase in the money supply was invariably followed, albeit after a time-lag of approximately 18 months, by an increase in prices. The data he presented proved this again and again across different historical periods and nations of varying political structure. As he put it 'Inflation is always and everywhere a monetary phenomenon... and can be produced only by a more rapid increase in the quantity of money than in output'.

It seems evident, therefore, that there is some relationship between output, prices and money supply. Obviously, if economic growth occurs the money supply must increase to facilitate the increased amount of exchanges that will take place. If the growth of the money supply, however, outstrips the economic growth then there will be more money flowing around the economy and inflation would be a strong possibility.

The limitation to this seemingly straightforward analysis is what do we mean when we refer to money supply. As pointed out above, there are many possible definitions. Controlling inflation, therefore, via money supply targets may be problematic. The experience of the Conservative Government during the 1980s seems to bear this out, as they consistently failed to achieve the money supply targets that should have reduced inflation. In fact, the problem caused so much political embarrassment, that money supply data was dropped from being a high-profile monthly indicator. During the 1990s it has become a low-profile indicator, but one that is still respected academically; for example, it certainly affects business expectations and general economic forecasting.

Chapter Summary 14.1

● **Money is defined by its functions which are a medium of exchange, a unit of account, a store of value and a standard of deferred payment.**

● **When we think money we must not just think cash.**

● **There are various definitions of money supply, for example: M0, M2, M4 and M5 (see figure 14.1 for details).**

● **Monetarists believe that changes in the rate of growth of the money supply can affect the rate of inflation.**

Financial Intermediaries

Most students would expect us to discuss banks here, and they are not wrong. It is important, however, right at the start, to recognise that saving and borrowing is carried out by many specialist institutions. Of these the high street banks have the highest profile. The important point is that we are dealing with any institution that mediates between those that supply funds and those that demand them. This position is reinforced by the diagram in figure 14.2.

Figure 14.2   Financial intermediaries
These are institutions that link up those that can supply funds with those that demand them.

The Functions of Financial Intermediaries

The **high street banks** are often referred to as the **joint-stock banks** or **commercial banks**. Each of these terms emphasises an important function of all financial intermediaries, namely to make a profit for their shareholders. In order to achieve this main aim, various other functions are undertaken, for example:

● Deposits are accepted for safekeeping (in time accounts and sight accounts).

● Loans are made to customers (usually called advances).

● Funds are invested in government securities and company shares.

● Support services are provided.

Profitability Versus Liquidity

In executing each of the above functions it must be remembered that the underlying motive is to achieve a profit. This creates a dilemma for all **financial intermediaries**, since there is an inverse relationship between liquidity and profitability. That is, the more money they keep as liquid funds in their tills to meet customers' requests to withdraw deposits, the less funds are available to invest in money-gaining ventures. In figure 14.1 we listed the assets that could be defined as money in order of liquidity. At one extreme we showed notes and coins and sight deposits which are assets that are quickly recognisable as highly liquid, since they can be instantly used as a means of payment; and at the other extreme we put property and shares which potentially could yield high profits but involve more stages to switch back into funds.

Chapter Summary 14.2

● **Financial intermediaries are institutions that link up savers who have extra funds and borrowers who need funds.**

● **The profit motive underpins all the activities of financial intermediaries.**

● **The basic dilemma that all financial intermediaries face is that there is an inverse relationship between profitability and liquidity.**

A Bank's Balance Sheet

In common with other private (joint-stock) companies, banks must keep an account of their **assets** and **liabilities**. Broadly speaking, assets are what a firm owns and liabilities are what it owes to others. In a bank's case these differ considerably from other companies.

Assets

We have suggested above that banks, and all other financial intermediaries, try to use the funds deposited with them to yield as great a profit as possible, while also maintaining the confidence of their customers by allowing them to withdraw their money whenever they wish. The financial institutions' assets, therefore, include a range of items: some are highly liquid but have a low profit yield, and others are less liquid and more profitable.

In figure 14.3 we present an amalgamation of all commercial banks' sterling assets for February 1992 in order of decreasing liquidity.

Figure 14.3   Sterling assets of all commercial banks in the UK (February 1992)

	£ Million	Percentage
(1) Notes and coins	2,999	0.5
(2) Balances with Bank of England	1,510	0.3
(3) Money at call	107,346	18.4
(4) Bills (mainly treasury and commercial)	9,961	1.7
(5) Advances	380,548	65.0
(6) Investments	31,738	5.4
(7) Miscellaneous	50,666	8.7
Total Assets (Sterling)	**584,768**	**100**

Source: Adapted from *BEQB May 1992* (Table 3)

One or two of the assets in figure 14.3 may need clarifying, and for this purpose they have been numbered in brackets. Items three and four are explained below.

(3) **Money at call**, this represents the funds lent out to other financial intermediaries. These loans, made to alleviate short-term cash problems, may be overnight or just for a few days. Most of the funds involved in this category are processed through a small group of London-based institutions known as **discount houses** who specialise in the movement of short-term funds. The rates of return (or discount) on these very secure and short loans form an important reference point for all other loans placed out in advances. This will be developed further in the section on interest rates.

(4) **Bills**, these represent debts ('paper') issued by the Treasury, local authority or commercial enterprises. In our dictionary we define them all under **commercial bills** as these form the broadest relevant category. For example, of the £9961 million shown in figure 14.3, approximately 25 percent represent bills originating from the Treasury or local authority, the remaining 75 percent derive from some form of commercial enterprise.* It is probably easiest to envisage all these bills as post-dated cheques with a unique feature, namely, they may be redeemed before their maturity date, which is usually 91 days after they are issued. The 'commercial banks', therefore, regard these bills as a secure asset, since they are redeemed quickly and can be passed on again, for example to a discount house, at a slight loss if need be. In fact, much of the borrowing and lending that occurs between financial intermediaries is operated using these bills, and the rates of discount offered affect the other interest rates operating in the economy.

Liabilities

In figure 14.4 we present the other side of the commercial banks' balance sheet, namely the liabilities. As the table shows the largest portion of these is taken up by customers' accounts. Miscellaneous includes the loans made to the bank, especially those represented

*Other items in figure 14.3 are also defined in the dictionary.

by share capital. **Certificates of deposit (CD)**, are another form of promissory note (similar to bills) but ultimately payable by the bank with whom the appropriate deposit was originally made. Indeed, all the liabilities represent items that the banks may ultimately have to pay.

Figure 14.4   Sterling liabilities of all commercial banks in the UK (February 1992)

	£ Million	Percentage
Deposits (Time & sight accounts)	455,290	78.4
Certificates of deposit	51,199	8.8
Miscellaneous*	74,218	12.8
Total liabilities (sterling)	**580,707**	**100.0**

* *Items not yet in customers name, notes issued by Scottish banks and Shareholders funds etc.*

Source: Adapted from: *BEBQ May 1992* (Table 3)

The Credit Multiplier

The important point to recognise from this overall balance sheet analysis is that banks are using the money deposited with them to create profits. As a consequence, their non-interest bearing assets (lines (1) and (2) in figure 14.3) are kept to a minimum and stand at £4,509 million. These highly liquid funds are available to meet the claims that theoretically could be made for all the customers' deposits, ie £455,290 million (see figure 14.4). In other words, there is approximately only 1 percent of liquid sterling funds to cover the total deposit liabilities. The banks, however, are not particularly worried by this situation, since most funds are transferred in response to a written instruction (eg a cheque or direct debit). Instructions such as these do not involve a corresponding movement of notes and coins. Nowadays, funds transfer from one account to another via computer.

With this knowledge, banks are able to create credit. Bank account holders are permitted, in return for interest payment, to draw more money than is available; deposits are created on their behalf on computer. In turn these loans lead to further deposits and a process known as the **credit multiplier** occurs. The amount of credit that is created is determined by the amounts deposited and the bank's attitude to reserves. For example, if banks operate a 10 percent cash ratio a deposit of £1 million would enable them to lend out £10 million.

The worrying thing is that this process also operates in reverse: reductions to the monetary base result in a multiple contraction of deposits. For example, bankruptcies lead to bad debts, such as bank advances being left outstanding; as a result, the banks' assets-to-liabilities ratio becomes suspect and further advances are not permitted. Ultimately this could lead to a downward spiral, a loss of confidence and a run on banks.

Central banks, therefore, employ supervisory teams to prevent financial intermediaries, within their monetary sector, from allowing themselves into vulnerable positions. Obviously this centralised supervision is also justified on the basis that the money supply of today cannot be controlled via the mint, it must be controlled via a nation's banking system.

- A balance sheet shows what a company owes set against what it owns. In a bank's case the loans to their various customers represent assets and accounts represent liabilities.

- Banks use customers' deposits to create credit (allow loans) for others. This process, known as the credit multiplier, is motivated by the search for profits since interest is charged on every loan.

- The credit multiplier can also operate in reverse; this would lead to a multiple contraction of deposits.

Central Bank Supervision

Every nation has a **central bank** to supervise its monetary sector. In America it is called the Federal Reserve Bank, in Germany it is the Bundesbank. In most other nations the central bank is more explicitly titled, for example, the 'Central Bank of Ireland' and the 'Bank of England'.

During the last decade, the Bank of England has become increasingly liberal. A term that epitomises the supervisory regime throughout the 1980s is deregulation; a term that we have already introduced in chapter 9.

By 1993 most of the levers that had existed to regulate financial intermediaries had been removed. Specific credit controls were no longer in force; the cash requirements and reserve ratios previously imposed on banks had faded into insignificance. The credit squeezes created by the calling of **special deposits** had also stopped. Journalists expressed this very colourfully when they coined the phrase 'the removal of the corset' as this portrayed the previously constrained financial intermediaries being able to flow naturally into new territory. In the mid-1980s this financial liberalisation was extended to building societies and the distinction between these institutions and other financial intermediaries became blurred.

Financial Intermediaries and Property Markets

Within the housing market, the effect of the above changes was most evident. Mortgages became easily available from many competing sources (see the tutorial reading at the end of this chapter for details) to the extent that 100 percent first-time mortgages were not uncommon. In fact, people even found it easy to extend their existing mortgage loans on the strength of rising house prices; this process is referred to as **equity withdrawal**. Equity withdrawal involves the house owner liquidating some of the funds locked up in the property's value. It is possible that this process helped to fuel the consumer boom of the late 1980s. (A version of equity withdrawal was considered in a tutorial reading to chapter 11.)

In the commercial property sector, funds also became easier to obtain, this is clearly portrayed in figure 14.5. The loans represent money provided for construction and commercial property purchase. The bulk of the funds are from British commercial banks, although approximately 40 percent represents overseas banks, especially Japanese and American. The worrying thing about this trend is that property is affected by any recession; rents decline, offices are not let and so on. Consequently, as developers go into receivership, banks assets become bad debts. To take just one example, Barclays Bank provided £2.6 billion to cover bad debts during 1992. Of this amount approximately

£800 million was to cover losses relating explicitly to property and construction (eg £100 million related to Olympia and York's Canary Wharf failure). Furthermore, of the remaining £1.8 billion, the majority will be backed by some form of property asset as **collateral**. As the value of this collateral will fall during a recession, many other debts that a bank has may turn sour. For example, the market value of a property acquired as collateral for a firm's borrowing may no longer be sufficient to cover the value of the loan if the client goes bankrupt. Through this type of scenario one can begin to sense that declining values in the property world quickly lead to a contraction of deposits, which in turn affect other sectors seeking to invest.

Figure 14.5 Bank lending to the property sector 1972-92
The figures portrayed in the graph represent the outstanding loans made to property developers by British and overseas banks; the British banks account for approximately 60 percent of the funds. The figures are expressed in current prices, and a thousand million is taken to represent 1 billion.

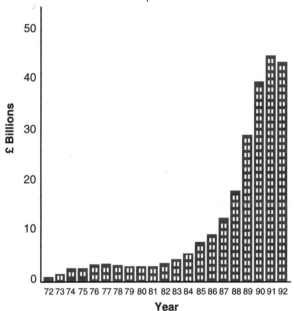

Source: Bank of England and Debenham, Tewson & Chinnocks February 1992

- Every nation has a central bank.

- The central bank of the UK, the Bank of England, has become increasingly liberal during the 1980s, allowing market forces to dominate in a deregulated system.

- More financial intermediaries have competed within the property sectors as evidenced by equity withdrawal in the late 1980s and bad debts in the early 1990s. Some idea of the size of the loans involved is shown in figure 14.5.

Introducing Interest Rates

Interest rates may be defined very simply as the price of money. (The price is expressed as a percentage of the sum involved.) Like all other prices the principal determinants will relate to supply and demand. Consequently, one sees explanations of interest rates employing supply and demand graphs. A very generalised representation is shown in figure 14.6. The important point to notice is, that on the axis where price is traditionally shown we now have interest rate, and on the other axis we have the amount of funds.

Figure 14.6 The supply and demand of funds
The amount of funds supplied in any one market, set against the demand for those funds, will determine the interest rates charged to borrowers and paid to savers in that specific market.

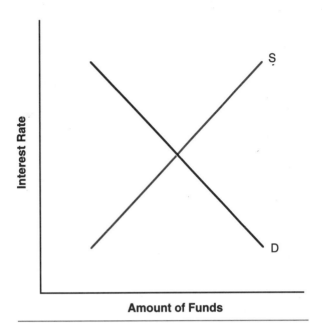

Figure 14.6 The supply and demand of funds
The amount of funds supplied in any one market, set against the demand for those funds, will determine the interest rates charged to borrowers and paid to savers in that specific market.

In more technical texts the supply curve may be presented as a straight vertical line, since it is assumed that within the general economy, in the short run, money is inelastic, ie it does not change size due to price movements.

For our purposes, however, it is very important to view the supply and demand of funds as differing from market to market. For example, there is a supply and demand of interbank funds moving around the City at one rate of interest, and a supply and demand of funds moving in and out of building societies at other rates of interest. The supply and demand of funds, represented in figure 14.6, therefore, must be seen as happening simultaneously in many markets at slightly differing rates.

A Spectrum of Interest Rates

All the rates of interest operating in our economy at any one time stem from the dealings between the financial intermediaries and the discount houses, as outlined above. That is, the rates of return on the funds moving between the City institutions determine most other rates. For instance, if interbank loans between trusted and respected financial intermediaries, such as the Bank of England, can earn 10 percent interest, then corporate and individual clients will have to pay more.

In general terms, there are three qualities that will determine a position on the spectrum of interest rates. These qualities are liquidity, risk and expectations.

Liquidity

Normally speaking, financial intermediaries will quote lower rates of interest on short-term finance. If the funds can be recalled quickly then the necessary price for their release will not be as high, as longer term funds. Consequently, in the table showing the assets of a bank

(figure 14.3), the rates of return increase as we progress from lines (2) to (6). Lines (1) and (2) earn no interest as no funds are lent out. This position of loans in terms of liquidity is summarised in figure 14.7.

Figure 14.7 Liquidity and costs
Short-term finance ranges from loans made overnight to those for anything up to two or three years. Long-term finance refers to loans made for more than ten years. (These time periods are not rigid, the distinctions are arbitrary.)

Type of Finance	Liquidity	Interest Cost
short-term	highly liquid	relatively low interest rates
long-term	illiquid	relatively high interest rates

Risk

The more collateral supporting a loan the less risk is involved for the financial intermediary. Consequently, although credit card funds are normally charged for every month, the interest rate is high since the funds are provided without question to anybody who has a card. Conversely in the property market, interest rates will not be so extortionate, as although the funds may be tied-up for a very long time, the security of the property means that the funder is not taking too big a risk. It should be evident, therefore, that in some markets, such as those relating to property, the effect of risk more than offsets the effect of liquidity.

Expectations

It is common within the financial markets that, over time, the whole structure of interest rates will change in response to government policy at both home and abroad. In fact, finance is now very much an international affair. For example, as the caption to figure 14.5 suggested, much of the lending to the property sector originates overseas. As a consequence, expectations relating to foreign interest rates, exchange rates and inflation rates will all play a major part on funding and investment decisions.

Monetary Policy

Another factor that affects the spectrum of interest rates is monetary policy. This policy, executed by the Bank of England on the government's behalf, determines the 'anchor' rate from which the spectrum stems. This is because a significant rate of interest is the rate at which the Bank of England deals with the City institutions, especially the discount houses. To some extent this specific rate of interest is not solely determined by supply and demand; it is an 'administered rate' reflecting government policy. Consequently, throughout 1988 to 1990 the base rate, the starting point of the spectrum, was kept deliberately high as the government made an attempt to reduce inflation and maintain the exchange rate (we shall return to this briefly in the concluding section).

Interest Rates and Property Markets

The **CBI (Confederation of British Industry)**, estimated that during 1991 every 1 percent added to interest rates increased business costs in the UK by £500 million. Similarly a 1 percent increase in mortgage rates adds a still larger amount to repayments. As a result property markets are sensitive to interest rate changes.

In figure 14.8 we show the impact of interest rates on some of the smaller property developers during the recession of the early 1990s. Column 2 shows the companies' annual rental income, column 3 shows the associated annual interest changes, and in the final column a ratio of the two previous columns is expressed by dividing rent into interest.

Figure 14.8   Annual rent and interest flows of six property development companies (January 1991)

Name of Company	Rental Income £mn	Interest Charges £mn	Rent/ Interest cover
Allied London	13.22	10.03	1.30
Asda Properties	7.35	11.82	0.60
Erostin	00.00	2.03	0.00
Helical Bar	14.17	18.70	0.80
Rosehaugh	3.50	41.50	0.08
Speyhawk	4.10	13.06	0.30

Source: *Smith New Court* January 1991

Clearly, Allied London had no real problem since income covered their costs. According to some commentators, there is not even a problem if the rent:interest ratio falls below one.

Presumably, this is because commercial property development involves a high initial capital outlay, which generates an income stream over a long period, say 25 years at least. Consequently, in the early years of a project, rental income is likely to be zero or lower than the related interest charges.

The following example illustrates this situation by explaining a concept known as the **reverse yield gap**. Let us assume that a property developer borrows £1 million at 13 percent on a long-term basis. This is used to finance a development which is let to tenants at an annual rent of £80,000 net, with five-yearly rent reviews. The yield on the asset in the first instance is only 8 percent. In other words there is a reverse yield gap of 5 percent (13 percent minus 8 percent), implying a loss of £50,000 per annum for the first five years.

However, some of the situations listed in figure 14.8 seem less tenable; indeed Rosehaugh went into receivership. In fact, during the period 1990-92, over 1,500 insolvencies occurred in the construction sector. Many of these were the smaller firms. Banks are hesitant, however, to foreclose on uncompleted developments as all they get is an unsaleable mess of concrete pillars which in their terms is a liability, not an asset. The normal course of action, in such cases, would be to fund the developments until completion and then turn on the pressure and/or possibly call in the receivers. This is what happened with Speyhawk.

Interest Rates and Macroeconomics

Regardless of the problems that high interest charges cause to business enterprise, they were maintained as a dominant policy tool from the mid-1980s, to the extent that British macroeconomic government policy was likened to a golf player who uses just one club to the exclusion of all other available instruments.

The interest rate emphasis was certainly a change, as during the Keynesian era it had been assumed that investment and consumption were interest-inelastic at certain levels. Monetary theory was, therefore, somewhat overshadowed during the immediate post-war years.

With the steady increase of owner-occupation and the development of an **enterprise culture**, responses to interest rates manoeuvres may have heightened. A rise in interest rates will affect demand, especially in those areas where funding is important, such as property development and house purchase.

The drawback with interest rate policy, however, is time-lag, as people take a while to adjust and are hesitant to shelve ventures that are still being completed. Professor F Paish, when lecturing at the LSE, expressed the problem via an entertaining analogy; he likened a monetary tightening to pulling a brick across a rough table top with a piece of elastic. You pull and pull and nothing happens. Then suddenly, the brick hits you in the eye.

Chapter Summary 14.5

- Interest rates represent a 'price' paid for borrowing or a 'price' given as a reward to saving.

- Different rates of interest prevail in different markets.

- Four important factors that determine the positions within a spectrum of possible rates are: liquidity, risk, expectations, and last but not least, monetary policy.

- High interest rates were maintained as a government policy throughout the late 1980s. Many property developers began to experience difficulties as a result during the early 1990s.

Tutorial Preparation

1 Make notes about another group of financial intermediaries, and compare their functions and importance with those of the commercial banks.

2 State three functions of a central bank.

3 Following bank balance sheet procedures, list the following items under the headings liabilities and assets.
   a. Interest-bearing current account
   b. Deposit account
   c. Bank's balances with Bank of England
   d. Loans to commercial property developer
   e. Mortgages
   f. Share capital
   g. Bank buildings

4 Read the following set of definitions relating to bonds and guarantees, which were first published in *Building* magazine 5 March 1993, and then consider the following questions.

> **Building Magazine: Four Definitions of Bonds and Guarantees**
>
> 1. **On-demand bonds**
>   Contractors are required to arrange a bond with their banks. The amount is typically 10 percent, but can be as high as 20 percent of the value of their contract. The bond is held by the firm employing the contractor and can be presented to the bank for immediate payment without any cause or reason.
>
> 2. **Performance bonds**
>   These are normally 10-20 percent of the contract sum and are used as the stick to make contractors perform to the programme, and also put right defects. Justification for calling in the bond is usually required. However, some performance bonds are being doctored to include on-demand clauses.
>
> 3. **Design warranties**
>   A new development whereby specialists who are responsible for design, such as M & E contractors, are required to give a warranty, typically 10 percent of contract. The warranty can be for up to 15 years. It can be a time bomb because if the building is sold on, the new owner can claim that a component, say air-conditioning, is not fit for the purpose.
>
> 4. **Parent company guarantees**
>   Where a firm is part of a group, the parent company may be asked to provide a guarantee against defects or failure to perform by the subsidiary.

   a. What are the main differences between the bonds (1 & 2) and the guarantees (3 & 4) listed above?
   b. Why did *on-demand bonds* increase during the early 1990s?
   c. Identify the main differences between the bonds defined above and the bills discussed in this chapter.
   d. How may on-demand bonds affect the loan collateral of the contractor?

5 a. Complete the following flow diagram .

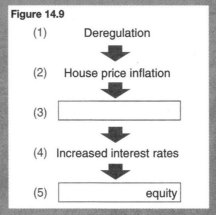

Figure 14.9

(1) Deregulation

(2) House price inflation

(3) ☐

(4) Increased interest rates

(5) ☐ equity

   b. Explain each of the five stages in your own words.

Tutorial Reading

Deregulation of Financial Intermediaries

Scatter-gun expansion, devilish competition and skin-thin profit margins. Sounds familiar? Right. Everything that happened, in fact, from the mid-1980s as banks, building societies and insurance companies began to compete in each other's territory.

Everybody is now fighting for a slice of Britain's mortgage market, worth £40 billion a year in new lending. Financial firms believe that once hooked with a mortgage, customers can be persuaded to buy their other services in particular the profitable life assurance policies which are tied to most British mortgages. This explains the extraordinary £2 billion swoop, over the past two years, by banks, insurance companies and building societies on Britain's estate agents ...

For building societies, worried by their declining share of the mortgage market, estate agents are a defensive purchase. In fact, estate agents, once purchased, achieve a 'conversion rate' of around 20 percent ie that proportion of house-buyers get their mortgage from the same firm.

Source: Adapted from 'Big bang in Britain's high street' *The Economist* 15 October 1988

Questions

1 a) Name a bank that is associated with a chain of estate agents.
   b) Name a building society that is associated with a chain of estate agents.

2 Name a building society that offers bank services.

3 Since the mid-1980s how have building societies affected the services of banks?

4 What are the implications of financial deregulation for the consumer?

5 State at least three economic changes that have occurred due to financial deregulation since this article was written in October 1988.

Tutorial Reading

Negative Equity 1988 to 19??

One of the most distinctive features of the downturn in the housing market since the second half of 1988, is that prices have fallen in both real and **nominal terms**. In some regions, most notably the South East, nominal house prices have been falling for nearly four years. This situation has left many households with a home worth less than the value of their mortgage, a phenomenon that has been termed **negative equity**.

Negative equity is most prevalent among first-time buyers who bought in the South in the late 1980s on high loan-to-value ratios, and have since seen the value of their properties fall substantially. For such home-owners, the presence of negative equity represents a considerable constraint on their ability to move.

Of interest is the value of negative equity. That is, the shortfall which must be financed if affected households are to move home. An example helps to explain.

A first-time buyer in the South East who took out a 100 percent endowment mortgage on a house costing £80,000 in the fourth quarter of 1988 has since seen the price drop to £60,000 while the value of the mortgage has remained at £80,000. Hence, this household faces a shortfall of £20,000. Applying similar calculations to the 876,000 people caught in this trap leads to an estimated aggregate national shortfall of around £3.6 billion for first-time buyers and £2.3 billion for former owner-occupiers, a total of around £6 billion, and an average of £6,000 per affected household.

Source: Adapted from 'Negative equity in the housing market' *Bank of England Quarterly Bulletin* August 1992

Questions

1 Distinguish between the terms 'nominal' and 'real'.

2 Define in your words the meaning of negative equity.

3 What is the relationship between this reading and the one on deregulation that precedes it?

4 How come the commentary and calculations relating to negative equity commence from the second half of 1988?

5 Why are the first-time buyers the main victims of negative equity?

6 Does negative equity continue today? If so, by how much, and if not, why not?

7 State at least two consequences of negative equity.

8 Is it yet possible to complete the title of this reading?

Tutorial Reading

Aspects of Property Finance

The fundamental characteristics of commercial property are clearly the same as they were four years ago. It is a type of investment requiring more management than, say, bonds or equities. It is a relatively illiquid investment (more so than usual in the depressed conditions of 1992). And so on. The real changes in perception revolve around two main factors: security and growth.

For much of the post-war period, property was regarded as a growth investment and an alternative to equities in institutional portfolios. Because planning restrictions kept most types of property in relatively short supply, the demand from prospective tenants kept rents moving ahead. And, over the long term, capital values moved up to reflect the rental growth. Investors in commercial property were prepared to accept low yields at the outset — occasionally even below 4 percent for the very best property — because of the growth in income and capital values that they expected to collect later ...

Indeed property income in Britain was generally exceptionally secure. Tenants had to pay rent before they could consider paying a dividend on their shares. And while dividends usually grew over a long period, they could go down (or disappear) if the company hit a bad patch. If a company went bust, an investment in its shares would probably be worthless. If a tenant went bust, the landlord still had the building, which he could almost certainly let to someone else.

Property income was also secure because of the nature of leases on most good quality commercial property in Britain. The form of the 'institutional' lease which became pretty standard in the 1980s usually specified a term of 25 years with upwards-only rent reviews every five years, and the tenant was responsible for insuring and repairing the building. The rent could thus rise but never fall (provided the tenant remained solvent) during the term of the lease. The five-yearly rent reviews ratcheted the rent up to a new base, which then became the minimum the tenant would pay the remainder of the term.

And under the 'privity of contract' principle, in English (though not Scottish) property law, even if the original tenant of the building assigned the lease before the 25-year term was up, he still remained responsible for the rent if the new tenant defaulted.

Most of these characteristics of property investment in Britain were little challenged until the end of the 1980s. Rising rents and property values meant that the 'upwards-only' clause in rent reviews was of little practical consequence to the tenant. The rental value of the building was almost always higher at each review than it had been five years earlier, so the tenant's rent would have gone up even without the upwards-only clause, which thus seemed irrelevant (though it was a comfort for the property owner or provider of finance).

Source: Adapted from 'Beginners guide' *Estates Gazette* 28 November 1992

Questions

1   a) Describe either a 'bond' or 'equity'.

  b) What makes a bond or equity less problematic to manage than property as an investment?

2   Why did property investment begin to look different between 1985 and 1993?

3   Identify the main characteristics of property as an investment today.

Tutorial Reading

Discounted Cash Flow (DCF)

A basic principle involved in investment appraisal is that of **discounting**, which is the opposite process to compound interest. Discounting may be defined as: calculating the present value of flows of money, which are expected to arise at some time in the future. The main reason for such a calculation is that any capital outlay has an opportunity cost: this may be the cost of borrowing or the returns to an alternative investment. We shall concentrate, for the time being, on the cost of borrowing angle.

Let us see how this works in practice. To start with, it is important to acknowledge that £1 in the pocket today is worth more than £1 receivable in the future because, if you had the £1 today, you could be putting it to work to earn interest. And remember that it follows from this that £1 receivable in the future has to be 'discounted' to find what it is worth today. The crucial factor is the rate of interest at which you choose to discount. If you thought you could currently put £1 to work to earn 10 percent interest, you might discount £1 receivable in the future at a 10 percent rate of interest.

At a 10 percent rate of interest, £1 receivable in three years is worth about £0.7513 today. This is the same thing as saying that £0.7513 is the sum which will grow to £1 in three years, at 10 percent a year compound interest. You do not have to work these figures out for yourself — there are plenty of compound interest tables available, or programmes for computers or pocket calculators.

So £0.7513 is the 'present value' of £1 receivable in three years, at a 10 percent rate of interest. In the same way, you can calculate the present value of a whole series of receipts and expenditures involved in a property investment, by discounting each for the appropriate period. The aggregate of these discounted values will be the 'total present value' of the property, at the interest rate you have chosen and on the assumptions you have made. The total present value may then be compared with the price of the property. If it is greater, the property is a 'buy'. If lower, the property is overvalued from your viewpoint. An example makes the process clearer.

Suppose the asking price for an office building just let at a rent of £60,000 a year is £1 million. By the first rent review in five years time, you reckon that the capital value will be approx. £1,500,000. Should you, therefore, buy it at the asking price?

The next stage is to work out your receipts from the building, including the actual or hypothetical sales proceeds after five years. For simplicity we are ignoring purchase and sales costs — though they would in practice be allowed for in the calculation — and we are also assuming that rents are paid annually in arrear, although in practice they are paid quarterly in advance.

The picture looks like this:

Figure 14.10

Receipts	£
End of year 1	60,000 (rent)
End of year 2	60,000 (rent)
End of year 3	60,000 (rent)
End of year 4	60,000 (rent)
End of year 5	60,000 (rent)
End of year 5	1,500,000 (sales proceeds)

Now each of the receipts from the property has to be discounted back for the appropriate period to reach a present value. At what rate of interest do you discount? Let us assume your target is a 14 percent rate of return. At a 14 percent discount rate, a pound receivable in a year's time is worth £0.877, in two years' time £0.769 and so on. So £60,000 receivable in a year is worth £60,000 x 0.877, or £52,632. (As suggested previously these calculations can be taken from present value tables for £1. The relevant figures are presented in figure 14.11.)

Figure 14.11

	Receipts £	Discount factor (at 14%)	Present value £
Year 1	60,000	0.877	52,632
Year 2	60,000	0.769	46,168
Year 3	60,000	0.675	40,498
Year 4	60,000	0.592	35,525
Year 5	60,000	0.519	31,162
Year 5	1,500,000	0.519	779,053
Total Asking Price			**985,038** 1,000,000
Difference			**-14,962**

In this case the present value of all the receipts from the investment, including actual or hypothetical sales proceeds of £1.5 million at the end of the day, is £985,037 at your chosen target rate of return of 14 percent. This means that if you bought the building at £985,037 and your assumptions on growth and end value turned out to be correct, you would receive a return — an **internal rate of return** or **IRR** — of 14 percent on your outlay.

Source: Adapted from *Property and Money*, M Brett, Estates Gazette 1990

Questions

1   Describe in your own words why a property investment appraisal may be subjected to a discounted cash flow analysis.

2   State a source where you could find the present value calculations for £1 at various rates of interest.

3   a) At the beginning of our example we state the asking price for the office building as £1 million. What does the discounting exercise suggest we should do with this deal?
   • leave it
   • buy it
   • negotiate
   Select one option and explain your decision.
   b) If the target rate of return was revised to 12 percent how would the deal look?

4   In our example, for simplicity, we ignored purchase and sale costs, what do these involve?

5   Time is an important feature of any discounting type process. For instance if rent payments are made in arrears or advance then through compounding the effective rates change. This is shown for a nominal interest rate of 5 percent in figure 14.12.

Figure 14.12

Nominal Rate		Effective rate
5%	annually in arrear	5%
5%	annually in advance	5.26%
5%	half-yearly in arrear	5.06%
5%	half-yearly in advance	5.19%
5%	quarterly in arrear	5.09%
5%	quarterly in advance	5.16%

   a) How does this affect the example we presented?
   b) If a fixed-interest government bond yielded the same annual return as a property being considered which would be a better investment and why?

6   Identify at least two limitations of DCF analysis.

Tutorial Reading

The Relationship Between Mortgage Rates and Other Rates in the Spectrum

Mortgage lenders cannot simply decide to set interest rates at any level they choose. They have to operate within three main constraints which, in practice, leave them little room for manoeuvre.

Firstly, most mortgage lenders are permanently in the mortgage market and can make new loans only if they can raise the necessary funds from investors, and on-lend them at a profit. Building societies raise most of their funds (as they are required to by law) from the **retail money markets** while centralised mortgage lenders raise all of their funds on the **wholesale money market**. Other lenders use wholesale and retail funds to varying degrees.

Secondly, mortgage lenders must have some regard to notions of equity and fairness, however hard these might to define, because of the size of mortgage repayments in relation to incomes. The past record clearly shows that at times of rising or high interest rates mortgage lenders try to shield their borrowers from the full effects knowing that to do otherwise could cause unnecessary hardship. Conversely, at times of falling rates, or when rates generally are low, mortgage lenders need to have due regard to the interests of their investors. Well over 50 percent of the funds in building societies are held by those over the age of 55, many of whom are reliant on the interest on their savings to maintain their living standards. Media attention tends to be focused on the financial position of borrowers (perhaps because most commentators are borrowers) but building societies in particular must pay equal regard to the interests of their investors. Balancing these interests is more difficult when interest rates are rising for which reason margins are narrowed when this occurs, conversely widening when rates fall.

Finally, there are regulatory issues. The past five or so years have seen unprecedented turmoil in the banking industry around the world. In many countries there has been systemic failure. Nowhere is this more true than in the USA where the equivalent of the building society industry has encountered massive bad debts and the government deposit insurance scheme has meant that taxpayers have had to find over $150 billion to meet the liabilities of institutions which have failed. In Britain no building society has failed in the last five years (and for many years before), and the industry has come through a very difficult market healthy and with strong and rising capital. This can be achieved only by operating on a profitable basis, and making up for any bad debts with increased profitability on existing business. In addition the Building Societies Commission has increased the capital adequacy requirements for societies and is requiring higher loan loss provisions, factors that necessitate a widening of margins.

Source: Adapted from a paper distributed to the House of Commons Select Committee on the relationship between mortgage rates and interest rates generally. *Housing Finance No. 17*, Council of Mortgage Lenders February 1993

Questions

1   Study the rates of interest in figure 14.13 and answer the following questions.

Figure 14.13   Base rates and mortgage rates, 1982-92

	Base rate percent	Mortgage rate percent	Margin
1982	11.93	13.30	1.37
1983	9.93	11.03	1.20
1984	9.68	11.84	2.16
1985	12.25	13.21	0.96
1986	10.90	11.83	0.93
1987	9.74	11.54	1.80
1988	10.09	10.97	0.88
1989	13.85	13.65	-0.20
1990	14.77	15.12	0.35
1991	11.70	12.95	1.25
1992 H1	10.33	11.04	0.71

Source: Council of Mortgage Lenders

a) Define base rate and mortgage rate.
b) Why is the margin between the mortgage rate and base rate not constant?
c) Find some more up to date figures for each of the columns and comment on the reason for the 'margin' narrowing or widening.

2   Although building societies have not failed for many years, banks based in the UK have. Name one of these banks, outline the circumstances and state the Bank of England's actions.

3   a) Distinguish between the wholesale money market and retail money market.
b) Distinguish between borrowers and investors at a building society.
c) Why must mortgage lenders, especially building societies, be careful about setting interest rates to investors?

4   State the factors that determine the average mortgage rate.

Tutorial Reading

A Pension Fund Case Study: The Church Commissioners

The Commissioners, who manage a £2.3 billion fund, warned that investment income increased only 1 percent last year to £167 million — not enough to meet growing demands from pensioners, an 11 percent hike in clergy stipends and an inflation rate of 5.4 percent. First Church Estates Commissioner Sir Douglas Lovelock is forecasting no further income growth for a few years.

The fund has 45 percent of its assets in property which contributed only £54.8 million in rents last year. Stock market investments — shares and bonds — make up 41 percent of the fund and did rather better with a total return of 20.5 percent, but not enough to make up the shortfall.

The Church saw the writing on the wall last year and announced its intention to sell off £500 million of real estate — almost half the portfolio. So far it has generated £237 million, targeting central London properties such as the £20 million — plus Angel Centre in Islington. However, a major slug of the portfolio is agricultural - some 400 farms valued at £211 million and yielding only £8 million. That market is currently in the doldrums and likely to stay there for some time. And succession rules mean that tenanted farms are passed on from father to son, making sale with vacant possession difficult.

The Church's exposure to property is larger than any other pension fund. According to the W M Co, average holdings by pension funds were 8 percent in 1991.

Source: 'Property crash hits church funds'
Estates Gazette 20 June 1992

Questions

1   a) Calculate the general yield from property rents to the Commissioners' fund.
b) Calculate the specific yield earned on farms.
c) How do you account for these low property yields?

2   What other assets would pension fund managers invest in?

3   In the light of these results the First Commissioner, Sir Douglas Lovelock, appealed to Church members to donate more generously.
a) Does this make commercial sense?
b) Is it right to judge Church funds in the same light as pension funds?

4   How, and why, do the Church Commissioners differ from other pension funds?

15

The public-private sector debate

Chapter Summaries to Review
- Types of Economic System (2.1)
- Mixed Economies (2.3)
- Market Failure (9.1)
- Correcting Market Failure (9.2)
- Government Failure (9.4)
- Macroeconomic Objectives (10.1)
- Deregulated System (14.4)

Congratulations on reaching the final chapter. If you have read all the preceding pages then you should appreciate more fully the issues we tried to raise in the introductory chapters. Indeed, it is our intention to use this last chapter as a means of revisiting some of the central issues.

What we review will impinge on your future careers, and the intention is to close with a larger number of readings to emphasise one final time that economics is relevant to many of the areas and debates that should concern you as professionals within the built environment.

When the Conservatives came to office in 1979, there was much discussion of how the public sector had been **crowding out** private enterprise. Ten years later, private enterprise was more significant. The state sector had been 'rolled back'. To some extent, this transition between sectors should remind us of the spectrum of economic systems that was discussed in chapter 2. In fact, it may be worth considering a modified version of figure 2.1, in order to focus the central debate of this chapter; this has been done in figure 15.1.

Figure 15.1   The public—private sector spectrum
On the extreme left-hand side of the diagram is the public sector and on the extreme right-hand side the private sector. From one political era to the next the UK economy shifts between these extremes; the mix of public and private sector, therefore, changes from time to time.

No one would argue for a totally extreme position on this spectrum but there is much debate relating to the appropriate mix.

Much of the debate relates to attitudes about the market mechanism. Even in these days of *perestroika*, privatisation and deregulation, there are those who agonise over problems of market failure. At the other extreme, there is a developing literature of public choice theory which emphasises the limitation of government, or government failure.

Marketed and Non-marketed Output

The debate we are considering here was encapsulated in the work of Bacon and Eltis published in 1975. Their title, *Britain's Economic Problem: Too Few Producers* caught the imagination and alluded to an important part of their argument. The crux of their work, however, lay in some new classifications: marketed and non-marketed output. These classifications correspond very roughly to what we understand to be the distinctions between the public and private sector, but they developed two important features. Firstly, that the public sector also produced marketed output and secondly, that non-marketed output depends largely on the wealth creation of the marketed output.

The implications of this argument caused successive governments to begin a major transition. Hence, much of the public sector's marketed output has subsequently been privatised; for instance Bacon and Eltis used to refer to British Airways as marketed output, and this was privatised in 1987.

To understand these developments in more depth an historical perspective helps. We shall begin to consider the public sector/private sector shifts, therefore, by going back to 1945. In a strict economic sense nationalisation dates back to the Labour government of 1945–51.

Nationalisation

Nationalised industries, although owned and controlled by the state, produce private goods which are charged for through the market; British Rail and British Coal are examples.

During the post-war period, nationalised industries represented a significant part of the economy. At their peak, during the 1970s, nationalised industries contributed approximately 10 percent of GDP, 17 percent of investment in fixed capital and 8 percent of the nation's employment.

The commanding heights of the economy were in government control, in so far as energy, communications and transport were all nationalised. Interestingly, in the mid-1970s, there was even an official report to consider adding the construction industry to the list.

The industries had come under national ownership for various political and economic reasons. The arguments for nationalisation included: a **natural monopoly** argument; the control aspects, as government could thereby manipulate prices and employment; the internalising of various externalities; and the advance of technology. In fact, the arguments in favour of nationalisation were expressed concisely in the Labour party manifesto of 1945, as follows:

'Amalgamation under public ownership will bring great economies in operation and make it possible to modernise production methods... Public ownership... will lower charges, prevent competitive waste, open the way for co-ordinated research and development... Only if public ownership replaces private monopoly can industry become efficient'.

Public Sector

As well as the nationalised industries, the public sector includes the output of goods and services provided by central and local government. In fact, you may remember in chapter 9 that we described some goods called public goods and merit goods. These items were provided by government because of limitations within the market system. As a consequence, even with nationalised industries being sold off, the public sector still contributes a significant part of our nation's economic activity.

In fact today's government provides the road networks, the education and health systems, law and order, etc. Consequently, as we entered the 1990s, the public sector employed over 6 million people. The spending undertaken by government was equivalent to almost 40 percent of GDP (even though approximately half of this involved transfer payments, such as grants and pensions).

Chapter Summary 15.1

- Bacon and Eltis helped to focus the debate between the public sector and private sector by considering two classifications: marketed and non-marketed output.

- Nationalised industries are state owned and produce goods which are charged for through the market; these industries were important to post-war Britain.

- The public sector comprises central government, local authorities and public corporations, such as nationalised industries. In 1993 it was an important sector of the UK economy.

Privatisation

Privatisation involves the transfer of assets and opportunities from the public sector to the private sector. This can take many forms: from the **contracting out** of local authority 'in-house' activities to selling off entire nationalised industries. In fact, approximately 50 state corporations have been sold off since the programme began in 1979. The main sales are listed in figure 15.2.

The industries that were privatised first were not particularly controversial. Since the mid-1980s, however, the process has become more radical involving the sale of natural monopolies and other 'key' industries, such as gas, water, electricity and telecommunications. In the foreseeable future, the government intends to add British Rail and British Coal to this list.

Obviously, such large transfers of activity from the public to private sector have several consequences. For example, six million people own shares in privatised companies, the cumulative proceeds in today's terms exceed £40 billion (this sum excludes the money from council house sales, which are dealt with below) and over one million jobs have been transferred out of the public sector.

The arguments supporting the privitisation programme include: the need to expose all production to market forces and thereby increase efficiency; to raise revenue for the government and hence reduce the public sector borrowing requirement; to widen share ownership; and to avoid the diseconomies of scale that centralised

Figure 15.2   The privatisation programme
The list is presented chronologically according to the first time each specific industry was offered for sale. That is, the asterisked items were sold in tranches, the date shown is of the first share issue.

Date	Company
1979	British Petroleum* ICL
1981	Cable and Wireless British Aerospace*
1982	Britoil* Amersham International* National Freight Corporation
1983	Associated British Ports British Rail Hotels
1984	Enterprise Oil Sealink Jaguar British Telecom*
1985	British Shipbuilders
1986	British Gas National Bus Company
1987	British Airways Rolls-Royce British Airports Authority
1988	Rover Group British Steel
1989	Water/sewerage companies
1990	Girobank Regional electricity companies
1991	Generating companies
1992	Trust ports

Source: HM Treasury: *"Guide to the UK privatisation programme"*, June 1992

government control may have created. In fact, the arguments in favour of privatisation were reiterated in the 1992 Conservative Party manifesto, as follows: 'Competition and private ownership are the most powerful engines of economic efficiency, innovation and choice. They lead to the creation of world-class companies ...'

Private Sector

By 1992, two-thirds of the companies previously owned by the state had been returned to the private sector. This enlargement made the private sector by far the most significant sector in the UK economy. By definition, the private sector involves any activity not within the control of government. In most of the chapters of this book, where we have studied the allocation of economic resources, we have been considering the private sector. The private sector constitutes the households and businesses discussed in figure 11.1, the financial intermediaries covered in the previous chapter, and the firms theorised about in chapters 7 and 8. The motives of maximising profit and satisfaction are also central interests of the private sector, and they were discussed in our analysis of the market mechanism in chapters 3, 4 and 5. In fact, in the UK today, the private sector is responsible for approximately 80 percent of the nation's economic activity.

Does the Private Sector Need Regulating?

The virtues of the private sector seem to dominate the press and political debate of the 1990s. The more ink that is spilt on the subject, the plainer the irony becomes that, the simple idea of privatised companies being able to operate independently of government, is incorrect. To paraphrase several journalists: it is becoming blatantly obvious that the government cannot simply wash its hands of huge businesses.

If a company is operating in a market over which it has substantial control, owing to the lack of competition, then the government needs to regulate. This has been proven by the busy existence of the Office of Fair Trading and Monopolies and Mergers Commission. Consequently, when utilities have been transferred from the public sector to the private sector with a monopoly position still intact, then this change in status has been associated with the development of a regulatory office. The major regulatory offices set up to date are: **OFGAS** (for gas), **OFTEL** (for telecommunications), **OFWAT** (for water) and **OFFER** (for electricity generation). The choice of public or private sector, therefore, is not always entirely black or white, since, if a government chooses not to own a business, it may still have to regulate. (This will be considered further in the tutorial readings.)

Chapter Summary 15.2

- Privatisation has been a government programme since 1979. It involves the transfer of assets from the public sector to the private sector (see figure 15.2 for examples).

- The arguments supporting the privatisation programme include those relating to market forces, PSBR, share ownership and diseconomies of scale.

- Although the private sector accounts for approximately 80 percent of the UK's GDP, governments still take an important regulatory role.

Council Housing: a Case Study

Local authority accommodation developed from 1919, following the Town and Country Planning Act which obliged local authorities to meet housing needs. The objective was to provide subsidised housing for rent to low-income families. Council property, therefore, represents an example of a public sector good, since central government subsidies were provided to local authorities who provided houses for accommodation at a reasonable rent. By 1979, six and a half million dwellings existed for rent from local councils. This meant that 31.5 percent of all households in Great Britain were housed by the public sector.

The idea of transferring the ownership of these assets to the tenants, predates all other forms of privatisation. In fact, in legal terms councils could sell their property to the tenants from 1936 onwards. The Conservative Government of the early seventies (1970-73) promoted these sales by discounting the market value by 20 percent and, as a result, over 100,000 tenants transferred to owner-occupiers.

Throughout the period of successive Conservative governments from 1979 onwards, privatisation grew in importance. Again, housing was high on the agenda. In fact, the **Right to Buy Act of 1980** actively encouraged tenants to purchase their rented property by offering substantial discounts below the market price. Nowadays, these discounts may be as high as 70 percent depending on a tenant's rental history. The average discount, however, taking all council purchased property to date, is around 40 percent.

Since 1980, one and a half million households have transferred from being public sector tenants to private sector owners. The total monies from these sales, net of discount, represent more revenue to the government than most of the other privatisation schemes added together. For example, during the period 1979–90, proceeds from the sale of council housing represented £33 billion (at 1990/91 prices) compared with £36 billion (1990/91 prices) accumulated from all the other schemes of privatisation.

These monies epitomise the belief in the virtues of ownership and free markets. The Conservative manifesto of 1992 actually stated that: 'The opportunity to own a home and pass it on, is one of the most important rights an individual has in a free society. Conservatives have extended that right ... We want to see wealth and security being passed down from generation to generation'.

The problems of providing homes for low-income families and homelessness have still not been resolved. All that has happened is that the threat of repossession now hangs over more people's heads. These are some of the limitations of markets driven by the private sector and we shall consider the broader implications in the tutorial readings.

Chapter Summary 15.3

- Council house sales commenced from 1970, ie before the major privatisation programme got under way.

- Following the Right to Buy Act in 1980, the privatisation of council property represented the biggest set of transfers from the public to private sector, 1.5 million households took advantage of the discount incentives.

- The limitations of this scheme will be considered in the tutorial readings.

Macroeconomic Criteria

In dealing with the broad backcloth of the economy, is the public sector or private sector more important? This is the type of question we wish to examine in this final main section. Clive Lewis suggested in his presidential address to the RICS, in July 1993, that 'clients are asking surveyors to evaluate both local and national economic trends, to take into account demographic factors ... and unemployment ratios in order to be able to forecast ...

The Treasury follows a number of economic indicators which steer their policy, including target ranges for money supply and inflation among others. The results of our research showed ... the impact of house prices and commercial real estate values on the economy as a whole ...'.

Lewis' words suggest a need for future professionals within the built environment to recognise the significance of the macro scene.

Macroeconomic issues often involve accepting the need for government policy. Below, we discuss briefly three areas to exemplify how managing an economy necessitates an active public sector. The areas we will consider are **regional policy, research and development policy**, and **environmental policy**.

Regional Policy

If the private sector were left to its own devices, a decline in one particular region should lead to a downward adjustment in the prices of the factors of production which, in turn, should attract new industries into the area. At the same time, labour may move to other more prosperous regions to avoid the threat of unemployment or lower wages. The model is self-adjusting. Simple observations, however, show regional imbalance. For example, consider the distribution of unemployment across the UK as presented in figure 15.3.

Figure 15.3   Regional unemployment

Unemployment statistics are traditionally presented as comprising 11 regions making up the UK. These standard regional classifications are set out alongside the UK average below.

Region	Percentage of workforce unemployed (June 1993)
South East	10.1
East Anglia	8.3
South West	9.5
West Midlands	10.9
East Midlands	9.4
Yorkshire and Humberside	10.1
North West	10.6
North	12.0
Wales	9.9
Scotland	9.5
Northern Ireland	13.7
Average United Kingdom	**10.2**

Source: *Employment Gazette August 1993*

The market-driven private sector does not adjust. Regional unemployment is a recurrent and long-term problem owing to market imperfections. For example, labour tends to be **geographically and occupationally immobile** and prices, especially factor prices, are not likely to decrease. Consequently, public policy has had a long history of intervening in the regional distribution of resources.

Regional policy, in fact, dates back to 1934, when the Special Areas Act identified certain depressed towns as being in need of incentives to promote industrial diversification. That is, certain areas became able to offer firms financial assistance to entice them into their locality. If this was not done, whole areas would remain depressed. The areas that have benefited as a result of this policy have tended to experience higher levels of unemployment than the national average. In fact, during its peak, 1960s-70s, regional selective assistance seemed to apply in one form or another to the whole of the UK, apart from the South and South-East.

Through the 1980s and into the 1990s, however, the assistance has declined. Since 1980, expenditure on these policies has decreased by about 50 percent in real terms. A new map for assisted areas was redrawn in July 1993 and it shows very few locations but, interestingly, it now includes parts of London and several seaside towns. The table in figure 15.4 gives an idea of how the map has changed.

Figure 15.4   Regional selective assistance

The areas benefiting from public sector grants to entice firms into their localities change from time to time. The table presented below shows the revised position for July 1993 onwards.

Towns that have been deleted	Towns added to the list
Accrington and Rossendale	Alfreton and Ashfield
Badenoch	Chesterfield
Bradford	Clacton
Cardiff (centre)	Dover and Deal
Corby	East Thames Corridor
Cinderford and Ross on Wye	Folkestone
Darlington	Harwich
Kidderminster	Hastings
Lampeter and Aberaeron	Lea Valley (NE London)
Manchester (except Trafford Park)	Mansfield
Newport	Park Royal (NW London)
Scunthorpe	Sittingbourne and Sheerness
Shotton, Flint and Rhyl	Skegness
Stewartry	Wakefield and Dewsbury
Telford and Bridgnorth	Weymouth and Portland
Wrexham (west)	Wrexham (east)

Source: *Estates Gazette 31.07.93*

Research and Development Policy

Research and development (R and D) is undertaken by both public-sector and private-sector organisations. Public-sector institutions, such as universities, tend to concentrate on research to extend knowledge and private-sector institutions tend to concentrate on development, which involves applications of knowledge. Various government laboratories and agencies, such as the **Building Research Establishment (BRE)**, act as catalyst to the processes and try to link up the sectors. It was estimated that, during the 1980s, the government funded about 50 percent of these activities but during the 1990s, it is more interested in devising self-funding mechanisms for these activities. This is, however, easier said than done. Research and development by nature is a risk-laden activity. The monies spent may lead nowhere or the monies spent may carry external benefits to other companies. As a result, governments across Europe, America and Japan are involved in R and D funding.

Environmental Policy

Maintaining a stable environment is a developing, international, public-sector responsibility. As detailed in chapter 9, whenever externalities cannot be absorbed by the market mechanism, the government may step in. Environmental issues represent an example of such intervention. Left to the private sector, would energy-saving buildings develop, would recycling be on the agenda and would carbon dioxide emissions be controlled? There may be some hesitation to answer each of these in the affirmative, but the present UK government does not accept full responsibility either.

In fact, in each of the macroeconomic areas discussed, the government seeks to liaise with the private sector; its aim is certainly not to increase the public sector.

Conclusion

For the time being, let us remind you that we are not in the right subject area to list definite answers—even though we are in our concluding section. As you have seen throughout this book, economics has many schools of thought and the topics studied have many variables. The value of the subject area has more to do with analysis and insight. For example, to understand residential and commercial development, changing land values, strategic town plans, property cycles, technological change and social issues—aspects of public and private sector economics within both macro and micro contexts are important; but they will not enable you to be 100 percent certain. Indeed, the initial idea behind a text such as this is not to provide definite theories but to enable students of the built environment to understand the nature of economic circumstances.

Economics provides a way of thinking. The reason for introducing so many students to its methodology is so that we educate broad-based professionals; not narrow-minded technicians. All buildings and their related issues need to be seen in the context of society as a whole. Hopefully, therefore, those that successfully complete this course will be in a better position to lead the market when they graduate,

rather than merely react to it; or, as they say in modern business parlance, to be proactive rather than reactive.

Chapter Summary 15.4

- Macroeconomic issues often require a public-sector policy response.

- The public sector can be seen to play a part in many areas of an economy, for example, regional policy, research and development policy and environmental policy.

- Economics is an open-ended subject which complements many professional fields, especially those within the built environment.

Tutorial Preparation: Essay Questions

Many courses conclude with an essay exam paper. In preparation for these, we suggest that you revise a topic and then try your hand at an unseen question. For this purpose we have listed below 15 essay questions broadly relating to each chapter. Take 10 minutes to plan each answer and then use 30 minutes to write up the essay. The important thing is to practise with unseen questions, not to learn answers off by heart. For more sample questions, you will probably find that your department keeps past papers.

1 Using examples from the built environment show how the concept of opportunity cost is fundamental to economic analysis. (25 marks)

2 Discuss the proposition that UK government housing policy during the last decade has displayed qualities of equity and efficiency. (25 marks)

3 a. Explain and draw a supply and demand diagram to illustrate why increases in interest rates are likely to depress house prices. (17 marks)
b. To what extent is this theoretical explanation supported by the history of the last decade? (8 marks)

4 a. Explain the difference between a movement along, and a shift in, a demand curve. (5 marks)
b. Account for the change (shift) in demand for owner-occupied housing in the UK since World War II. (20 marks)

5 Discuss the factors which would be expected to determine the price of commercial office property. (25 marks)

6 'The property market is typified by price inelastic supply'.
Discuss this statement and explain how the concept of price elasticity of supply helps to account for economic behaviour within this sector of the economy. (25 marks)

7 a. Explain what you understand by the term 'the construction industry' and outline its importance in the UK economy. (5 marks)
b. Describe the two following economic concepts and explain how they provide insight and understanding into the performance of the construction industry:
The law of diminishing returns
Economies of scale (20 marks)

8 The commercial property market, based on traditional institutional leases, is an imperfect market. Explain and discuss this statement. (25 marks)

9 a. Outline the causes of market failure. (9 marks)
b. Discuss whether rent controls and planning gains enable governments to correct some of these market failures effectively. (16 marks)

10 a. Explain how certain economic indicators can be used for forecasting the performance of property markets. (20 marks)
b. What problems face the economic forecasters? (5 marks)

11 'Changes to fiscal instruments will influence the economy and the performance of the property markets'.
Explain and discuss. (25 marks)

12 a. Distinguish between demand-side and supply-side economics. (8 marks)
b. Explain how monetary policy may be used to promote *one* of these sides, and how the economy and property market may be affected as a result. (17 marks)

13 'For the successful management of any property-related contract and the economy generally, the retail price index must be referred to'. Explain and discuss. (25 marks)

14 a. What has caused the development of negative equity in the UK in the 1990s? (15 marks)
   b. What effects has it had on the housing market? (10 marks)

15 a. Why is a council house regarded as a merit good? (7 marks)
   b. Discuss the arguments for selling council accommodation since 1979. (18 marks)

Concluding Note: Useful Publications

In a lot of instances, you will find it beneficial to state up-to-date examples. Therefore further reading of journals, magazines and newspapers would be worthwhile, as well as engaging you more in this area of study. The following annotated list of sources used to compile the readings in this book should help you find your way through the broad choice of options.

Building	A weekly journal, covering business, construction and design, available from newsagents and/or libraries.
Bank of England Quarterly Bulletin (BEQB)	As the title suggests this publication appears every three months. It provides authoritative coverage on a broad range of economic issues. Most academic libraries will subscribe.
Economic Review	The five issues per academic year cover a broad range of introductory ideas in a magazine format. The target audience is 'A' level and first year undergraduate economists. Most libraries in further and higher education subscribe.
Estates Gazette	A weekly journal providing property information and analysis. Available from newsagents and/or libraries.
Housing Finance	A quarterly publication, produced by the Council of Mortgage Lenders, detailing economic issues and statistics relating to the residential market. Academic libraries subscribe.
The Economist	A weekly magazine, containing a broad range of national and international business articles. Available from newsagents and stocked by libraries.
The Guardian, The Independent, The Financial Times	Daily broadsheet newspapers that always carry a general economics and business section. Available from newsagents.

Tutorial Reading

Design Away Problems in Inner City Estates

You are a tenant on a council estate. People dump rubbish on pavements and walkways. It maddens you, but it's the council's job to clear up, isn't it?

Eighteen months later, same estate. All the ground floor flats have enclosed gardens attached. Someone does the usual trick of chucking refuse over the walkway and it lands on your patch. Ignore it? Like hell. You go upstairs and sort your neighbour out.

That's what John and Nora Tavener did. They have lived in a ground floor flat on the Rogers Estate in east London for 18 years and, for the past six months

or so, have been proud possessors of a verdant back garden.

The Taverners are guinea pigs in a social experiment—and have behaved just as one academic predicted they would. The theory is that, given their own space, tenants in former problem areas will begin to police their own 'defensible space'. Therefore, communal rubbish chutes are out and rows of dustbin kennels are in.

The academic in question is controversial 70-year-old Alice Coleman. She first promoted her theories in her book *Utopia on Trial*, published in 1985. It was based on a simple premise: if her 16

design guidelines were rigidly applied to problem estates, anti-social behaviour could be reduced or even eradicated.

A direct appeal to then prime minister Margaret Thatcher led to a £50 million grant from DOE for a five-year trial of her theories.

Seven estates were to be refurbished and then closely monitored and analyzed by accountant Price Waterhouse. The first of these was the Rogers Estate. Its £3.5m refurbishment programme was finished last September.

Source: 'Alice proves wonders of looking through glass' *Building* 30 July 1993

Questions

1 How do Alice Coleman's ideas fit into the public sector–private sector debate?

2 Discuss whether the public expenditure on refurbishing problem estates is worthwhile.

3 As suggested in the extract, forming private gardens and making defensible space represent an important sum part of the 16 guidelines. Suggest two other guidelines that Coleman may have laid down.

4 'Anti-social behaviour is best policed by the public sector'. Discuss.

Tutorial Reading

Government Housing Initiatives

Do-it-yourself shared ownership is being promoted by the government as a means of breaking down the barrier between the tenanted sector and owner-occupation.

Conventional shared ownership involves the acquisition by a housing association of a suitable property which is then offered to the homebuyer on shared ownership terms. The association chooses the property and may well develop it itself. But, under DIYSO, the homebuyer himself chooses the property just as other homebuyers do. DIYSO tenants can go out and—with the support of a housing association—find a suitable property on the open market. They then buy it in conjunction with the association.

This year the Housing Corporation plans to spend £80 million on DIYSO schemes, on top of a similar allocation for conventional shared ownership. Together, these programmes are expected to help 6,600 families to become homeowners this year.

Another way in which both local authority and housing association tenants can be helped into home ownership is through cash grants to buy homes on the open market. Their former home is then released for

reletting to a homeless family. It is estimated that some 7,000 local authority and housing association tenants benefited from these incentives in 1991-92.

Then there are the 'rents to mortgages' schemes. These are directed at council tenants who would like to own the house or flat in which they live, but cannot afford the full cost of exercising their right to buy. There are estimated to be some 1.5 million such tenants paying their rent without the help of housing benefit. Many of these are likely to be interested in rents to mortgages, the government believes. Tenants purchasing under this scheme will have to make payments no greater, initially, than their current rent. They will use this rent to service the repayments on a mortgage from a building society which will finance their payment of a deposit. They will receive a discount—related to the length of time that they have been a tenant—which, with their deposit, will give them a sizeable stake in their home. Tenants will be allowed to leave the rest of the price of purchasing their home outstanding until they can afford it, at which point they will be entitled to a further flat rate discount.

Pilot rents-to-mortgages schemes in Milton Keynes and Basildon have attracted some 100 sales in seven months. Legislation is to be introduced to extend the scheme to all local authority tenants...

Sir George Young, minister of state responsible for housing, contrasted the current excess supply in the owner-occupied sector, where demand is now weak and the excess demand in the social rented sector, where supply cannot keep pace. There are two obvious—if not necessarily complete—answers to this problem, Sir George said. Houses can switch from one sector to another, from private to public. And so can people, but in the opposite direction, from public to private. Builders whose housing developments started during the 1980s boom have found the first to be a good solution for developments which failed to sell. Properties which are not selling in the depressed owner-occupied market can perhaps be sold to a housing association for letting to people in housing need. A total of 3,000 dwellings were sold to associations in this way in 1990-91.

Source: 'Housing initiatives' *Estates Gazette* 23 May 1992

Questions

1 Define public sector housing.

2 List four ways that the government is encouraging the trend towards owner-occupation.

3 Explain why the government is keen to support policy that increases the proportion of owner-occupiers.

4 Are the housing associations a private sector or public sector responsibility?

5 What problems may present themselves if the government policy outlined is followed successfully?

6 One of the Labour Party's responses to the policies outlined is to encourage shared ownership schemes to be offered as of right by social landlords, with purchasers able to 'staircase up' to full ownership or to 'staircase down' by reducing the mortgage element if financial difficulties occur.
a) How does this differ from the Conservative policy outlined in the extract?
b) What are the advantages and disadvantages of this proposal?
c) What do you think the Labour Party would do with regard to local authority accommodation?

7 The table in figure 15.5 shows the distribution of tenure in Great Britain at the end of 1991.

Figure 15.5   Housing stock in Great Britain, December 1991

Tenure	000s	%
Owner-occupied	15,601	67.7
Public sector rented	5,017	21.8
Private sector rented	1,704	7.4
Rented from housing association	724	3.1
Total number of dwellings	23,046	100.0

Source: Department of Environment, *Housing and Construction Statistics* HMSO 1992 (Also published in *Housing Finance*).

a) Using the same source, look up more recent data to discover how the distribution has changed.
b) Identify two trends and comment on the implications.

8 Will owner-occupation ever exceed 75 percent of the tenure in Great Britain? Explain your answer.

Tutorial Reading

Market Housing Initiatives

The market system is the main means of allocating housing in Britain today, with over 70 percent of the dwellings allocated by the market system. Of course, there are numerous forms of government intervention within the private market, including regulation and tax/subsidy policies and different types of private property ownership but, in essence, most housing is provided through the market system. As described in chapter 2 the market system has several distinct advantages, and a number of serious shortcomings. In the case of housing, these shortcomings have often manifested themselves in the failure to meet society's minimum standards and the failure to produce an efficient quantity of housing. Next we shall examine some of the reasons for this failure.

There is no reason to expect a market system to achieve the aim of a guaranteed minimum standard. This is because many families simply do not have sufficient purchasing power to buy, or even rent, good quality accommodation. Thus one of the main reasons for the persistence of substandard dwellings is the poverty of the families that occupy them. Recognition of this correlation between poor housing conditions and low-income households has led some economists to argue that the problem is not really a *housing* problem at all. For them it is just one other manifestation of general poverty: just as, without assistance, the poor would not be able to afford adequate food or clothing so they cannot afford adequate housing.

According to this view, slum housing may be inequitable but it is not necessarily inefficient. Indeed, some writers have argued that, given low-income demand for housing, slum housing represents an efficient supply response. But is this claim correct? Can a market system in housing be expected to produce efficiency? Other economists have argued that while general poverty is certainly an important contributory factor towards the persistence of substandard housing, it is not the only one. They point, in addition, to certain special features that can be expected to produce an inefficient allocation of resources. These are capital market imperfections, imperfect information, discrimination, and the existence of externalities ...

Source: Adapted from *The Economics of Social Problems* By J Le Grand et al. Macmillan 1989

Questions

1 a) Identify four or five features of the market system that may lead to inefficient housing allocation.
   b) Give an example how each of these features may affect housing markets.
   c) How has legislation since 1980 changed these features?

2 Explain the argument 'that, given low-income demand for housing, slum housing represents an efficient supply response'.

3 Describe two of the ways the state intervenes into the private housing market.

Tutorial Reading

A Case for Housing Tenure Reform?

Our system of housing tenure is as big an obstacle to labour market efficiency as is our wages system. Economists of all political colours agree on this. Patrick Minford and others have calculated that the immobility of unskilled labour induced by the Rents Act and council house subsidies adds two percentage points to the natural rate of unemployment, say, 500,000 workers.

The government has been far too timid in its approach to housing deregulation. At present, 30 per cent of households are locked into tenancies, private and public, that cannot be traded—bought and sold. Samuel Brittan and Martin Ricketts have argued that tenants' rights in rent-controlled property—whether owned by local authorities or private landlords—should be specified and then made tradeable. An active market in secondary letting would arise. Leases in regulated private tenancies could be granted for between five and 10 years, with council tenants retaining rights to lifetime occupancy. Decontrol of the private rented sector would take place as the leases ran out, rather than through 'natural wastage', as the government seems to want.

A country's system of housing tenure has a major impact on the performance of its economy. Low levels of private rented accommodation in the UK not only hinder labour market mobility but also mean young people get locked into mortgages, and are thus less likely to accept the delay in income represented by adequate training than their continental counterparts. While training will address the problem of *occupational* mobility, the reform of housing tenure will increase *geographic* mobility.

Gearing up our society to the challenge of flexible specialisation requires a revolution in the mind. Co-operation and trust must work upwards from the firm, not downwards from 'the economy'. Governments can play their part by decollectivising and deregulating wage and housing systems wherever possible, but also by encouraging new forms of partnership within firms, as well as the growth of more balanced kinds of income earning and wealth holding.

Source: 'Factory bargains and mobile homes' *Independent* 30 June 1993

Questions

1 The author of the extract suggests that 'the government has been far too timid in its approach to housing deregulation'. Explain and discuss.

2 What happens in other sectors of the UK property market and/or abroad that may help to alleviate problems of immobility?

3 There are various incentives in the UK towards owner-occupation. Explain and discuss how some of these incentives affect labour efficiency.

4 What measures could a government take to increase private accommodation available for rent?

5 How would a situation where people used information technology at home and went to the office infrequently affect the arguments discussed?

6 Can you think of other reasons to support a case for housing tenure reform?

Tutorial Reading

Research into Occupiers' Requirements: The Customer is King

For a so-called 'people' business, the property industry seems to be remarkably poor at listening to its paying customers, according to the findings of a survey of **warehouse** occupiers conducted by Fuller Peiser (investment consultants) and materials-handling equipment manufacturer Lansing Linde. More than half of the 109 companies interviewed were of the opinion that developers lacked specific working knowledge of warehouse operations, while a frightening 80 percent of companies felt that landlords had taken no real interest in their modes of operation. This communication gap may explain why about three-quarters of the UK stock of warehousing has an **eaves height** of 6 metres when 73 percent of the consumers questioned would prefer 7 metres or more. Cost does not appear to be the issue, since the added expense of extra height is relatively small when weighed against the increased cubic capacity. From the investor's point of view, increased flexibility in the way in which the building can be used by a tenant must be a selling point.

This is by no means the first time that providers of real estate have been charged with falling disastrously short of fulfilling the reasonable expectations of its consumers. Almost exactly three years ago Vail Williams published an innovative report looking at the needs of business space users. The results were very similar: a disturbing number of business space users felt that developers, architects and agents all failed to pay adequate attention to their occupancy needs. Complaints about their buildings and the service provided by property professionals not surprisingly followed hard on the heels of this sentiment. At the time Vail Williams argued that a much greater interest in the most important link in the development chain—the occupier— was essential and advocated that **post-occupancy evaluations** be adopted as standard practice in order to ensure that practitioners were truly in tune with their clients: by returning to buildings and talking to occupants, vital lessons could be learned and quickly translated into improved buildings and services...

Occupiers represent an invaluable database of knowledge which is currently not being exploited to its full potential by those providing them with accommodation. This is an unnecessary waste and one which could ultimately prove expensive. He who puts the right product in the right place at the right time will profit. Listening to the needs and concerns of the end-user is the best way of finding out what and where. The firms that will be a force in the next upswing will be those which best understand the businesses of their clients.

Source: 'Listen and learn' *Estates Gazette* 12 June 1993

Questions

1 The cost of a warehouse does not increase pro rata as it increases in height. For example, doubling the eaves height of a building, from 6 metres to 12 metres would only increase costs by approximately 12 percent.
   a) Explain this cost pattern using economic terms, as far as possible.
   b) What significance does this costing exercise have for the warehouse market of the early 1990s?

2 Who in the following list is best located to undertake research relating to the occupiers requirements for warehouse design and construction?
      The funding institution
      The government
      Equipment manufacturers
      Warehouse tenants
      The developer
   Choose your preferred option and detail the economic arguments that would support your case.

3 Research relating to occupiers' requirements can clearly help to enhance profits and lettings. Design a questionnaire that would help a speculative investor to construct an office block.

4 a) Describe in your words what a post-occupancy survey involves.
   b) Identify professionals within the built environment that might find post-occupancy evaluations useful.
   c) What circumstances might prevent post-occupancy evaluations being carried out.

5 Should research relating to occupancy needs be a public or private sector responsibility?

Tutorial Reading

Building Regulations in a Deregulated Britain?

For too long Britain has lagged behind other North European countries in terms of energy efficiency in the home. This isn't to say that we haven't produced imaginative and original energy-saving initiatives and designs. We have, but sadly these have tended to remain the exception rather than the rule.

The truth of this was brought forcibly home to me when reading a description of one recent scheme involving low-energy cottages, built for North Sheffield Housing Association. A combination of good design incorporating high insulation specifications on top of conventional construction methods and a mechanical heat recovery system has achieved a staggering 83 percent energy reduction compared with the same design built to current **Building Regulations**. What's more, all this was achieved within the far from generous Housing Corporation cost yardstick.

The advantages are obvious. In the first place, cutting energy costs will help many low-income households who simply do not have enough money to keep warm in winter, particularly when fuel costs are being forced up disproportionately by the imposition of VAT.

The government's justification for imposing VAT on fuel bills is the need to cut carbon dioxide emissions. This is entirely understandable given Britain's commitment to reducing greenhouse gas emissions to 1990 levels by the year 2000—a commitment which will be difficult to achieve without far more effective policies to curb domestic fuel consumption.

However, the imposition of VAT without measures to extend energy efficiency in the home is a recipe for large numbers of low-income households going cold.

So the publication of the government's consultative paper on the new building regulations might well have been expected to set the agenda with ambitious targets for improving insulation standards and home energy efficiency. Sadly, it fails this test, proposing no improvements in U-values for roofs, walls or floors.

Even more shocking is the provision for increased flexibility which will allow even lower standards than permitted in the 1976 regulations in some respects if

improvements are achieved in others...

Source: 'Energy saving measures left out in the cold' *Building* 26 March 1993

Questions

1 What is a 'U' value?

2 Which North European countries are more energy-efficient than Britain and why?

3 Why are housing associations more likely to experiment with energy-saving designs?

4 Explain the reasons for the government being so hesitant to extend its building regulations.

5 'The imposition of VAT without measures to extend energy efficiency in the home is a recipe for large numbers of low-income households going cold'. Explain and discuss.

6 Should greenhouse gas emissions be controlled by the public or private sector? Fully explain your answer.

Tutorial Reading

Funding Infrastructure in the 1990s

The Conservative Party in its post-Thatcher mode has become a late convert to infrastructure spending. Among the predicted £28 billion public sector borrowing requirement is £5 billion for infrastructure investment, which includes £1 billion a year to sustain the British Rail modernisation programme and £750 million for 24 road schemes announced by transport secretary Malcolm Rifkind.

These are in addition to the £200 million bill for the cost of turning the 120-mile stretch of the A1 linking Newcastle upon Tyne with Edinburgh into dual carriageway...

If the Tories have indeed made a U-turn on infrastructure spending, it creates difficulties for the Labour Party.

Labour's proposed freeze on new road construction while carrying out a six-month review of national road strategy would mean the delay or cancellation of bypasses and other improvements. This could lead to more deaths and casualties on the roads. It has been estimated that 100 deaths and 4,500 casualties have been saved over 30 years for every £100 million invested in trunk road improvements.

The idea that expenditure on infrastructure improvements is somehow a luxury only to be entertained in the occasional boom year when the government shows a surplus can now be shown to be the economic logic of a sweet shop.

In an important report, *Urban Infrastructure: finance and management* commissioned by the OECD and

published in 1991 the authors suggest: 'The quality of the environment and the basic infrastructure, as well as the provision of cultural and social facilities, are no longer viewed merely as objects of consumer demand or social concern, but also as instruments of economic growth and survival'.

What is needed, as the OECD paper recommends, is a shopping list of infrastructure projects which can show the best social, environmental and financial return. Also as advised by OECD, the projects should be capable of attracting private finance.

Source: Adapted from 'French polish for economy kick start' *Building* 27 March 1992

Questions

1 Make out a case for one infrastructure improvement or development in your home town, and describe how this project may attract private finance.

2 Select another infrastructure project and outline the problems that would have to be tackled if private finance was involved.

3 What do the authors of the OECD report mean by saying that infrastructure equals 'growth and survival'?

4 Why did the government intend to fund British Rail more heavily than all road schemes totalled together?

Tutorial Reading

A Letter Against the Privatisation of BRE

The following extract from Dr Andrew Short (a former president of the European Concrete Commission) appeared on the letters page of *Building* 30 July 1993 ...

Dear Sir

One only needs to look at the effects of other privatisation exercises to foresee the consequences of privatising the Building Research Establishment's essential services.

The Cement and Concrete Association was a privately financed, fruitful and necessary research and education body. It was in fact destroyed because the cement barons were unwilling or unable to continue funding it. This is what would happen to the BRE.

The Government is in need of an objective and professionally highly qualified body to advise them in cases such as Ronan Point or the use of high alumina cement. Such problems may well increase in number and cost because of the complex character of modern construction practice.

The answer is not privatisation. The answer is proper staffing, adequate funding and continuing strict public accountability.

Yours faithfully
Dr A Short

Questions

1 What are the functions of the BRE?

2 What arguments can you list in favour of the BRE's privatisation?

3 What arguments can you list in favour of the BRE remaining 100 percent within the public sector?

4 Try to find out the percentage of the BRE's work that is funded by the private sector today.

5 a) State at least two other examples of privatisation (including contracting-out) that have occurred within the building or property industries.
   b) Describe one of these examples in detail and comment on the process that the transfer involved.

Tutorial Reading

Problems of Valuation and Privatisation

As privatisation gathers pace more public sector assets will come under the valuations spotlight. Inevitably this will point out some anomalies in the way assets are assessed.

The normal basis of valuation is the **open market value** of the asset, assuming the continued use and occupation of the company. Many public sector assets, however, are rarely, if ever, sold in the open market; hence, there is a paucity of comparable market evidence. These specialist properties have to be valued on a **depreciated replacement cost (DRC)** basis.

A DRC valuation involves first assessing the cost of building a modern substitute building, including the cost of professional fees and financing. This replacement cost is then depreciated to reflect physical, functional and locational obsolescence.

The depreciated replacement cost is added to the open market value of the land in its existing use to give the total DRC valuation. This rather esoteric and unworldly valuation method was workable at a time when building costs were rising. However, the slump in building tender prices since their peak in 1990 is causing severe problems and undermining the logical basis of this method.

Given that many specialist buildings are of a substantial size and may take two to three years to develop, valuers are being directed to use building cost data from 1990 to assess depreciated replacement cost values in 1993. Not surprisingly, this gives an artificially inflated costing.

The scale of the problem is illustrated by reference to the Building Cost Information Services Index. This shows an estimated 25 percent drop from its peak in the third quarter of 1989 to the quarter ended March 1993.

To highlight the discrepancies in the current DRC valuation method two calculations are shown in figure 15.6. One set of calculations shows the value of a specialist building when 1990 construction costs are applied, the other set of calculations shows the value using tender prices for March 1993.

Source: 'Overvaluation of specialist buildings' *Estates Gazette* 7 August 1993

Figure 15.6 A case study

This example involves a 100,000 sq.ft. specialist building occupying a town-centre site, which would take three years to build. Two calculations are shown.

First Calculation: Adhering to the DRC convention

Construction costs, contract commencing March '90	10,000,000
Professional fees @ 12%	1,200,000
Finance during construction period, say	1,800,000
(average, say, 12%)	
Replacement cost	13,000,000
Depreciation, say	50%
Depreciated replacement cost	6,500,000
Land value in existing use	750,000
Existing use value	7,250,000

Second Calculation: Reworking the calculation off March 1993 tender prices

Construction costs, contract commencing March '93	7,600,000
Professional fees @ 12%	912,000
Finance during construction period, say	784,000
(expected average, say, 7%)	
Replacement cost	9,296,000
Depreciation, say	50%
Depreciated replacement cost	4,650,000
Land value in existing use	750,000
Existing use value	5,400,000

Questions

1 a) Distinguish between the following two types of valuation:
   Open market valuation
   Depreciated replacement cost
   b) How could the following assets be sensibly valued?
   A water tower
   A printing press
   A modern office block
   An old brewery
   A hospital

2 State some examples of public assets that may need to be valued in the near future.

3 In a few years' time when valuers are directed to look back at construction costs in 1993, what problem will a DRC calculation present?

4 Identify two economic concepts that underlie the DRC problems described in the extract.

5 Do you think that public sector assets may be sold off at the wrong value for any other reasons?

6 How does 'contracting out' avoid the problems discussed?

Tutorial Reading

Research and Development or Science Fiction?

A stone's throw from Helsinki's orbital motorway, on a patch of weed-ridden land, is the Finnish Technical Research Centre's (**VTT**) version of the energy-efficient office of the future. The VTT is keen to show off the prototype, part of a government drive to reduce energy consumption.

Built in 1991 and on trial until 1992, the concrete shell structure was designed to meet the greenest criteria. It only requires heating when the outside temperature drops below -15°C. Innovative devices minimise heat gain from equipment inside the building to make CFC-based cooling systems redundant, even when temperatures exceed 30°C.

To achieve its aims, VTT has heavily insulated the office and equipped it with low-energy lighting, direct heat extraction systems for office equipment and a variable air volume air-conditioning system which can be adjusted to individual requirements for each room.

The interior looks different from the typical office. First you notice the incandescent bulbs dangling from the ceiling. These are not part of a lighting system but simulate the typical heat load generated by office workers.

They are switched on and off by computer at the beginning and end of office hours to simulate the comings and goings of the workforce.

Just as striking are heating vents that look like giant cigarettes. Sticking up through the floor, these tubes with perforated caps deliver air from the air-conditioning system which is fitted in voids in the compartmentalised hollow slab floor construction.

The wall and ground slabs are a precast concrete sandwich construction with 120 mm of polyurethane insulation, produced without CFCs, as a central layer. The roof is stacked with 350 mm of loose fill insulation. The designers paid particular attention to sealing gaps which could let in draughts.

To minimise the cooling load when outside temperatures peak during summer, heat from computers is removed via an exhaust air system before it can enter the office environment.

VDU units are sealed beneath a glass desk top and the processors concealed in a vented cupboard resulting in furniture that looks like it was borrowed from a low-budget science fiction film set.

Source: 'Evening jacket' *Building* 10 July 1992

Questions

1 Is there a UK equivalent to VTT?

2 Are there any low-energy offices in the UK?

3 State any two features that might characterise a building designed to meet environmental criteria.

4 Why do government agencies involve themselves in this type of research?

5 a) Identify other building-related technologies that require development.
   b) Discuss in detail one of these technologies and make a case for it being publicly or privately funded.

Tutorial Reading

Demographic Data

Local planning authorities are an example of a public-sector agency needing a broad spectrum of population information. They have become adept, particularly at the county level, in monitoring population change and producing forecasts of future changes. In many cases, therefore, the planning departments provide a service not only to the whole authority for its demographic information needs but also to agencies in the private sector.

With the continuing publication of the results of the 1991 census, these authorities have an opportunity to appraise the quality of their monitoring systems following a period of very rapid social and economic change, and to provide new base data for continuing and improving their monitoring the forecasting systems. This also provides an opportunity for bodies and agencies which do not have access to primary demographic monitoring work to have population information which is up to date, reliable and consistent across the whole country.

The most recent Census of Population was undertaken on 21 April 1991, since then the **Office of Populations, Censuses & Surveys (OPCS)** has been collating and manipulating the data in order to publish a wide range of information. The first publications were the Preliminary Reports, which gave initial information on population in England, Wales and Scotland.

Currently the County Reports are being published. These are probably the best-known of the census publications and provide substantial demographic information for each county. These will be followed, towards the end of 1993, by summary tables and further specialist tables, concerning, for example, manpower,

migration and employment by workplace. Finally, OPCS will prepare special statistical abstracts to meet customer requirements following direct inquiries to their office.

Source: Adapted from 'Surveyors and information: population & the census' *Estates Gazette* 20 February 1993

Questions

1   State some uses that population census data may provide for your future profession.

2   In what other ways, apart from the 10-yearly census can demographic information be gathered?

3   Outline what may happen to the work of the OPCS as more services are privatised.

or

Make a case for keeping the OPCS supported by the public sector.

4   a) How should a university identify future student accommodation requirements?
     b) Make an argument in favour of the public or private sector providing student accommodation.

5   According to the OPCS there are 6.5 million disabled people living in Britain, and the number is expected to rise as the population ages. What use can your profession make of this specific information?

Tutorial Reading

Changes of Law: a Public or Private Sector Responsibility?

Retail giant Sainsbury this week took the running dogfight on Sunday trading between retailers and councils one step further: the company announced that, in selected areas where the local authorities are actively enforcing the existing rules, it will comply—but will still open. This means that this weekend cash registers will be ringing at stores in Cambridge, Chelmsford, Huddersfield, Norwich and Solihull, but only on selected goods. Only half the products normally available will be for sale, with those not legal under the Shops Act being covered by plastic sheeting. Banned items include detergent

and soap, fresh and frozen butchers' meat, hardware, nappies, pharmaceuticals and toiletries.

The store group's action graphically illustrates the anomalies of the existing law, the difficulties involved in enforcing it and the uncertainty that continues to prevail in the run-up to new legislation due to be decided in the next session of Parliament.

Despite these as yet unanswered questions, the retail property market is moving in favour of total deregulation. Supporters of this option point north of the border for supporting evidence. The

system is quietly working in Scotland where the moral problems appear to have been largely worked out, as have the patterns of trading. Retailers open when it is practical—and profitable—to do so. Some of the worries over deregulation should be compared to the ones which preceded the relaxation of the licensing laws in England and Wales. Mass drunkenness, lost working days and truancy, and staff exploitation were predicted, but in the event did not occur.

Source: 'Trade War' *Estates Gazette* 7 August 1993

Questions

1   If laws exist, is it correct for market forces to change them? Discuss this question fully, and consider any other examples that may seem relevant.

2   What arguments can you think of against Sunday trading?

3   How does Sunday trading affect the public sector?

4   How does Sunday trading affect shopping malls?

5   Where do the public and private sectors now stand with regard to Sunday trading?

Dictionary

adaptive expectations hypothesis A theory of behaviour which states that people's expectations of the future rate of inflation are formed primarily on the basis of what the rate of inflation has been in the immediate past. This process is also known as extrapolative expectations, and can be applied to many economic variables.

Advance Building Information Service Is funded by subscribers to collate data relating to contracts, planning and tenders, in order to provide leads in the building industry. A similar service is available via computer (ABI infoline). The organisation's offices are based in Kent.

aggregate demand (AD) All planned expenditures for the entire economy summed together.

aggregate supply (AS) All planned production for the entire economy summed together.

allocative efficiency The use of resources that generate the highest possible value of output as determined in the market economy by consumers. Also referred to as 'economic efficiency'.

appreciation The increasing of the value of a domestic currency in terms of other currencies. This occurs in a freely floating exchange market when the quantity demanded for the domestic currency exceeds the quantity supplied at the current price. In a fixed exchange rate market, appreciation cannot occur spontaneously; it must be done officially. Then it is called *revaluation*.

asset Anything of value that is owned.

average fixed costs Total fixed costs divided by the number of units produced.

average total costs Total costs divided by the number of units produced.

average variable costs Total variable costs divided by the number of units produced.

balance of payments A summary of monetary transactions with overseas nations. It is compiled as an account of inflows and outflows recording visible and invisible trade, investment earnings, transfers, and financial assets.

balances with the Bank of England The deposits that commercial banks keep with the central bank; they are also referred to, at times, as *operational accounts*, since they are basically the commercial banks' bank accounts.

barriers to entry Conditions in the market place that make it either impossible or difficult for firms to enter an existing industry and offer competition to existing producers or suppliers. Examples of these conditions include government restrictions and legislation.

base year The year which is chosen as the point of reference for comparison to other years.

bills *see* **commercial bills**

Black Wednesday Journalists coined this term to represent the day that Britain was forced to suspend its membership of the Exchange Rate Mechanism; the date was 16 September 1992.

boom A period of time during which overall business activity is rising at a more rapid rate than its long-term trend.

Building Cost and Information Service (BCIS) This was set up by the Royal Institution of Chartered Surveyors in 1962 to facilitate the exchange of detailed construction costs. The information is taken from a wide range of differing contracts and traders. Originally this data analysis was only available to quantity surveyors, but now the service is provided to those of any discipline. (There should be copies of the BCIS Quarterly in your library.)

Building Regulations A code of practice which specifies the type and minimum quality of materials to be used in a building. These regulations are legally enforced by district councils, eg via the building controls officer.

Building Research Establishment (BRE) A set of government laboratories based in Garston, Watford. They research developments that relate to construction of all types, eg those concerning the control of fire, energy and the environment.

building societies A group of financial institutions that specialise in providing long-term loans for house purchase (ie mortgages).

business cycles The fluctuations in overall economic activity, as evidenced by changes in national income, employment and prices. Sometimes referred to as trade cycles.

Business Expansion Scheme (BES) This is a government scheme aimed at supporting initiatives within the small firm sector; it operates by providing tax relief on invested funds.

capital All manufactured resources, including buildings, equipment, machines and improvements to land.

capital consumption *see* **depreciation** which is another name for the same concept.

capital gains The positive difference between the purchase price and the sale of an asset.

capital goods Equipment used in the production of other goods. Examples include cranes, factories and foundries. Consumers do not consume capital goods for production purposes.

capital value The monetary worth of an asset, for example the price it could be purchased for.

cartel Any arrangement made by a number of independent producers to coordinate their buying or selling decisions. The members of a cartel agree, in effect, to operate as if they were a monopoly.

central bank The official institution that monitors and supervises commercial banks, on the government's behalf. It normally acts as banker to the banks and other nationally important institutions.

centrally planned model A theoretical system in which the government controls the factors of production and makes all decisions about their use and about the distribution of income. This type of government is often associated with communist states and may also be termed a pure 'command system'.

certificate of deposit (CD) These are issued by banks to customers for large deposits, they have an agreed interest rate and fixed maturity date. An extraordinary feature of these deposits is that the holder can sell the certificate to someone else.

ceteris paribus The assumption that all other things are held equal, or constant, except those under study.

chaos theory This suggests that the natural order of things is stormy and erratic rather than efficient and predictable.

circular flow model A model of the flows of resources, goods and services, and the corresponding payments for them in the economy.

cobweb theorem A dynamic model which tries to explain why cyclical fluctuations in output and prices can occur, such as in the property sector.

collateral Security which is provided to cover a loan. For example, property is often used to back up a bank loan.

collusion Price determination by oligopolists which is coordinated and aims to avoid the danger of price wars breaking out.

commercial bank This is a privately owned profit-seeking institution, sometimes referred to as a *joint stock bank* to highlight the fact that it has shareholders. Most *high street banks*, such as National Westminster and Barclays have thousands of branches.

commercial bills A debt which will be honoured at a stated date in the future (usually 91 days). These are designed to alleviate cash flow problems, as the seller (eg an exporter) is effectively giving a period of 'grace' before payment. A distinguishing feature of these instruments is that they may be passed on for cash to another party (at a discounted rate, ie below face value) before the pay due date. The final holder then presents it for payment on maturity. Similar bills may be drawn up by local authorities and the Treasury .

competition policy Government attempts to maintain a healthy rivalry between buyers and sellers. For example, since the Monopolies and Mergers Acts of 1965 the government has made attempts to prevent mergers that are not in the buyer's interest.

complementary goods Two goods are considered complementary if both are used together. The more you buy of one, the more you buy of the other—and vice versa. For example, bricks and cement.

Confederation of British Industry (CBI) An organisation that was founded in 1965 to represent the interests of British firms. Membership, therefore, consists of thousands of companies, hundreds of trade associations and employers' federations. Its main aim is to express views to government.

constant returns to scale A situation in which the long-run average cost curve of a firm remains horizontal as output increases.

Construction Industry Council (CIC) This is a coordinating body, representing the various professional groups operating within the built environment. Therefore, it represents a broad set of interests from architects to engineers. The comprising separate chartered organisations have a total membership exceeding 300,000.

consumer (or consumption) goods Goods that are used directly by households to generate satisfaction. To be contrasted with capital goods.

consumer sovereignty The concept implies that the consumer is king, that is: the one who ultimately determines which goods and services will be produced in the economy. This idea may be out of date in markets which are dominated by very large firms.

contracting out When this term is used in the context of privatisation it refers to the transfer of publicly provided activities to private contractors. For example, a county council may employ a private sector surveying firm to manage its property portfolio.

cost benefit analysis (CBA) This is a way of appraising an investment proposal. It is normally undertaken by government departments, since it involves adding the external costs and benefits to the conventional private costs and benefits. This is done by estimating monetary values for aspects such as health, time, leisure and pollution.

cost-push inflation A rise in price level associated with a rise in production costs, eg the price of raw materials.

credit multiplier The amount by which a new deposit into a bank is multiplied as it is loaned out, redeposited and reloaned etc. In a simple world, the reciprocal of the cash/liquidity ratio, provides a numeric value of the credit multiplier, or *money multiplier* as it also known.

crowding out A term popularised since the mid-1970s to suggest that increased public sector expenditure had reduced the possibilities of private sector spending.

CSO The recognised abbreviation for the Central Statistical Office. This office is responsible for the government's statistical services.

demand function A symbolised representation of the relationship between the quantity demanded of a good and its various determinants. It looks like an algebraic equation but it is actually just shorthand notation.

demand management Government policies designed to control the level of total demand in an economy. These policy manoeuvres are closely associated with Keynesian economics.

demand-pull inflation An increase in price level caused by total demand exceeding the current level of supply. This problem is often associated with Keynesian policy which is aimed at achieving full employment.

demand schedule A set of pairs of numbers showing various possible prices and the quantities demanded at each price. This is a schedule showing the rate of planned purchase per time-period at different prices of the good.

demand-side economics This term generally refers to government attempts to alter the level of aggregate demand.

depreciated replacement cost (DRC) A method of valuing properties of unusual character or location for which evidence of comparable transactions does not exist. The valuer, therefore, chooses to focus on what it would have cost if work had commenced at the appropriate time so as to have the building available for occupation at the valuation date. This valuation technique requires an estimate of the open market value of the land in its existing use and an estimate of the new replacement cost of the building, from which deductions are then made for factors such as the age and condition. (*See example case study calculation in figure 15.6*)

depreciation Reduction in the value of capital goods owing to physical wear and tear and obsolescence.

deregulation A term popularised since 1979 in the UK when state monopolies began to be opened up to competition. Its general meaning now relates to any industry where official barriers to competition are liberalised or removed.

design and build An all-embracing agreement whereby a contractor agrees to undertake building, engineering work, design and cost estimating as part of a coherent package on behalf of a client. Frequently contractors develop a specialism of creating buildings for specific client groups.

design warranty A legally enforceable undertaking that the specifications meet with an agreed standard.

developer's profit The amount which covers the risk element between start and completion of a project plus an element of profit on the venture. A developer's profit therefore has two elements: the return for undertaking a project and a compensation for the risk involved.

direct relationship A relationship between two variables that is positive, such that an increase in one is associated with an increase in the other and a decrease in one is associated with a decrease in the other.

discount houses A group of eight specialised City-based institutions who borrow for very short periods of time from the banks (*see* **money at call**) and invest in 'bills' (*see* **commercial bills**) and other short-term assets. These institutions are therefore specialists in the movement of short-term funds between financial institutions. For instance, they often act as a middle-man between the Bank of England and commercial banks.

discounting A mathematical procedure by which the future value of a sum or a stream of sums due to be received at specific forthcoming dates are brought to their current value.

diseconomies of scale When increases in output lead to increases in long-run average costs.

disinflation A term coined in the early 1980s to describe the process that saw high rates of inflation begin to reduce.

eaves height This can be defined as an internal or external measurement. Internally, it refers to the height between the floor surface and the underside of the roof covering (ie up to the support purlins). Externally, it is the distance between the ground surface and the exterior of the roof covering.

economic goods Any good or service that is scarce.

economic growth An increase in an economy's real level of output over time; normally measured by the rate of change of national income from one year to the next.

economics A social science studying human behaviour and, in particular, the way in which individuals and societies choose among the alternative uses of scarce resources to satisfy wants.

economic system The institutional means through which resources are used to satisfy human wants.

economies of scale When increases in output lead to decreases in long-run average costs.

effective demand Demand that involves desire and ability to pay. In other words, it is the demand that can be measured by actual spending.

efficiency *see* **allocative efficiency** *and* **productive efficiency**

endogenous variables These are economic factors which affect other aspects of a theory or model from within. For example the level of unemployment will determine the amount of income tax collected.

enterprise culture A term used to represent Britain since 1979. It describes a hard-working, efficient society driven forward by the profit motive, in freely competitive markets, geared towards wealth accumulation.

entrepreneurship A factor of production involving human resources that perform the functions of raising capital, organising, managing, assembling other factors of production and making basic business policy decisions. The entrepreneur is a risk-taker.

environmental policy Governments across the world have taken on responsibility for global and local issues, as somebody needs to be concerned with the externalities that markets may overlook. The UK's White Paper, *This Common Inheritance*, stated the environmental strategy for the 1990s. It was broad-ranging and has led to a series of subsequent reports monitoring the progress of environmental targets.

equilibrium A situation in which the plans of buyers and sellers exactly coincide so that there is neither excess supply nor excess demand.

equilibrium price The price that clears the market where there is no excess quantity demanded or supplied. The price at which the demand curve intersects the supply curve. Also known as the market clearing price.

equity *see* **horizontal equity** *and* **vertical equity**

equity withdrawal In property parlance the term equity can be used to represent the owner's fund. Therefore, if you buy a £100,000 house of which £60,000 is borrowed, potentially you may be able to organise the release of the £40,000 that you own. This process would be termed equity withdrawal.

European Monetary Fund (EMF) Supervises the support systems of the Exchange Rate Mechanism. Member states pay a quota and can request credit if necessary.

Exchange Rate Mechanism (ERM) A coordinated system designed to stabilise exchange rates among the currencies of the European Community. It was set up in 1979; during 1991 there were ten members: Germany, France, Italy, Netherlands, Denmark, Belgium, Luxembourg, Ireland, Spain and UK.

excludability *see* **principle of exclusion**

exogenous variables these are economic factors which impinge upon a theory or model from the outside, eg the weather. They are sometimes referred to as autonomous variables and they contrast with endogenous variables.

external economies These are the savings a firm can achieve, per unit of output, due to increases in the size of the *whole* industry in which it is based. For example, state-funded training.

externalities The external benefits or costs that are experienced by parties other than the immediate seller and buyer in a transaction.

factor markets In this market, households are the sellers; they sell resources such as labour, land, capital and entrepreneurial ability. Businesses are the buyers of these resources to generate output (*see figure 11.1*).

factors of production Often grouped under four headings. *see* **resources**

financial intermediaries Those institutions that link up groups of savers who have extra funds and groups of borrowers who need funds, eg building societies.

fine tune A term used in economics to suggest that an economy has an engine like a car and this can be set up to run at different levels of efficiency by adjusting various flows.

Fisher's equation of exchange The number of monetary units multiplied by the number of times each unit is spent on final goods and services is identical to the prices multiplied by the number of transactions. Formally written as: $M \times V = P \times T$.

fixed costs The costs that do not vary with output. Fixed costs include such things as rent on a building and the price of machinery. These costs are fixed for a certain period of time; in the long run they are variable.

foreign exchange market The market for buying and selling foreign currencies.

free enterprise A system in which private business firms are able to obtain resources, to organise those resources and to sell the finished product in any way they choose.

free good Any good or service that is available in quantities larger than are desired at a zero price.

free market model A theoretical economic system in which individuals privately own productive resources and can use these resources in whatever manner they choose. Other terms for this type of system are a 'pure market' or 'pure capitalist economy'.

full repairing and insuring lease Rental terms under which the tenant bears most of the running and maintenance cost. Institutional investors favour these kind of leases, which are also referred to as an FRI lease.

geographically and occupationally immobile *see* **mobility of labour**

government failure This term has developed in recent years to highlight that intervention via policy may not necessarily improve economic efficiency.

gross domestic fixed capital formation This national income accounting category represents the expenditure on fixed assets (eg buildings, vehicles, plant and machinery). It is more common to refer to this expenditure as investment. The monies spent on maintenance and repairs, however, are officially excluded.

gross domestic product (GDP) The most common measurement of a nation's income generated from resources *within* its own boundaries; the value of its output of goods and services.

gross national product (GNP) Another measurement of the wealth of a country. It represents the total output of goods and services produced by the country in a year, in terms of residence of the owners of productive resources. In the case of the UK there is little difference between GDP and GNP. For example, in 1990 GDP was recorded as approximately £550bn and GNP was £552bn.

guarantee An agreement to rectify failure.

headline inflation rate The change in the Retail Price Index that is announced via the monthly press release. It contrasts to the *underlying rate of inflation*, which is adjusted to exclude mortgage interest payments.

high street bank *see* **commercial bank**

horizontal equity is concerned with identical treatment for identical people.

hot money Fast-moving currency deals, involving exchanges for speculative purposes.

human capital Investment which has taken place in education and training which enhance the productivity of the individual.

income-elastic demand A given change in income will result in a larger percentage change in quantity demanded in the same direction.

income elasticity of demand The percentage change in the quantity demanded divided by the percentage change in money income; the responsiveness of the quantity demanded to changes in income.

income-inelastic demand A given change in income will result in a less than proportionate change in demand in the same direction.

indemnity insurance The protection offered by policy or contract whereby, on the occurrence of the risk insured against, the insurance company concerned will reimburse the financial loss incurred by the insured. For example, a mortgage indemnity policy covers the building society, or bank, in the event of a repossessed property being sold below the value of the mortgage.

index numbers These express the relative change between one period of time and some other period of time, selected as the 'base year'. For example, the base year index number is set at 100 and the related years are expressed above or below 100 according to their percentage deviation from the base.

inferior good A good of which the consumer purchases less as income increases. Goods of this nature are exceptions to the general rule.

inflation A sustained rise in prices, formally measured by the Retail Price Index.

inflationary gap The amount by which aggregate monetary demand exceeds that necessary to achieve full employment.

initial yield The annual net income from the date of purchase expressed as a percentage of the purchase price.

injections Supplementary inputs into the circular flow of income not originating from the domestic sector; can include investment, government purchases and exports.

interest rates These are the payments made as the cost of obtaining credit, or the rewards paid to owners of capital.

intermediate macroeconomic targets As the name suggests these are not the final goals of policy but means of achieving them. For example, targeting a specific measure of money supply may enable the control of inflation.

internal economies *see* **economies of scale**

internal rate of return (IRR) The highest rate of interest at which an investment can be funded if the related cash flow generated is to be sufficient to repay the original outlay.

inverse relationship A relationship that is negative, such that an increase in one variable is associated with a decrease in the other and a decrease in one variable is associated with an increase in the other.

investment The spending by businesses on things like machines and buildings, which can be used to produce goods and services, in the future.

joint-stock bank *see* **commercial bank**

labour The human resource involving productive contributions of persons who work, which involve both thinking and doing.

land The factor of production that is virtually fixed in quantity. In the economic sense it includes natural resources such as coal, oil and water, natural vegetation and climate.

law of demand Quantity demanded and price are inversely related—more is bought at a lower price, less at a higher price (other things being equal). Also known as the *theory of demand*.

law of diminishing (marginal) returns After some point, successive increases in a variable factor of production, such as labour, added to fixed factors of production, will result in less than a proportional increase in output.

law of increasing opportunity costs This law is an economic principle that states that in order to get additional units of a good society must sacrifice ever-increasing amounts of other goods. (It may also be referred to as the law of increasing relative costs.)

law of supply The relationship between price and quantity supplied (other things remaining equal) is a direct one. For example, as price increases so does the quantity supplied.

leakages Those parts of national income not used for consumption. For example net taxes, saving and imports. These used to be called *withdrawals*.

liabilities All the legal claims for payment that can be made on an institution or company. In short, the amount owing to others.

liquidity This describes the ease with which an asset can be used to meet liabilities. Cash is the most liquid asset.

local authority bills *see* **commercial bills**

long run That time-period in which all factors of production can be varied.

long-run average cost curve (LAC) This represents the cheapest way to produce various levels of output given existing technology and current prices. It is derived from a compilation of short–run positions (*see figure 7.4b*).

low inflation A term used to describe a trend of annual price increases below 5 percent.

macroeconomics The study of economy-wide phenomena, such as total consumer expenditure.

macroeconomic objectives Targets relating to the whole economy, such as employment, price stability and the balance of payments.

marginal cost (MC) The change in total costs owing to a one-unit increase in the variable input. The cost of using more of a factor of production.

marginal physical product (MPP) The output that the addition of one more worker produces. The marginal physical product of the worker is equal to the change in total output that can be accounted for by hiring one more worker.

marginal propensity to leak (MPL) The proportion of an increase in national income that is withdrawn from the circular flow. For example, a 0.2 MPL indicates that out of an additional £100 earned £20 will be used on imports, saving and/or tax.

marginal revenue (MR) The change in total revenues resulting from the sale of an additional unit of the product in question.

market An abstract concept concerning all the arrangements that individuals have for exchanging with one another. Thus, we can speak of the labour market, the car market, the commercial property market, the housing market, the building materials market, the credit market and so on.

market-based instruments These involve various incentive systems designed to operate through the price mechanism to encourage environmentally friendly behaviour. For example, carbon tax and deposit refund systems.

market-clearing price *see* **equilibrium price**

market economy An economy in which prices are used to signal firms and households about the value of individual resources.

market failure A situation in which the free forces of supply and demand lead to either an under- or over-allocation of resources to a specific economic activity.

market mechanism *see* **market economy** *and/or* **price mechanism**

market structures The characteristics of a market which determine the behaviour of participating firms such as the number of buyers and sellers, and the ease of entry into (and exit from) a market.

market supply schedule A set of numbers showing the quantity supplied at various prices by the firms comprising the industry. The horizontal summation at each price suggests the market supply. *See figure 5.2.*

maximum price legislation A price ceiling set by a government agency that identifies a level in a specific market beyond which prices must not rise. A common example is the control of rents.

medium of exchange *see* **money**

menu costs The resources used up revising price lists (eg restaurant menu cards and changing slot machines) owing to inflation.

merit good A good that has been deemed socially desirable via the political process, as if left to the private market it may be under–consumed.

microeconomics The branch of study that considers economic behaviour of individual households and firms, and how prices of goods and services are determined.

minimum efficient scale The lowest rate of output at which average costs reach a minimum point.

MIRAS *see* **Mortgage Interest Relief at Source**

mixed economy An economic system in which the decision about how resources should be used is made partly by the private sector and partly by the government.

MMC *See* **Monopolies and Mergers Commission**

mobility of labour The ease with which labour can be transferred from one type of employment to another. Mobility of labour can thus be considered in terms of geographical or occupational mobility. The converse concept *immobility of labour* is often employed by economists.

models Simplified representations of the real world used to make predictions or explanations more accurate.

monetarists Individuals who believe that changes in the money supply are important in the determination of the full employment level of national income.

money This is represented by anything that is generally accepted as a means (medium) of payment for goods and services, or the settlement of debts (ie deferred payments). Ideally it should act as a store of value and unit of account, although during inflation it may become deficient in these respects.

money at call Very short-term lending by commercial banks, ranging from an overnight loan to one that lasts for 14 days. The discount houses are the principal borrowers of these funds.

money supply A generic term used to denote the amount of 'money' in circulation, which has many definitions. For example, see figure 14.1, where a range of assets that may be regarded as money are listed alongside three official definitions of the money supply

Monopolies and Mergers Commission (MMC) This government agency was formally established in 1965 to undertake studies of unfair competition. Its function is to investigate and prohibit mergers that are not in the public interest and break up undesirable monopolies. It is part of the Office of Fair Trading and thereby accountable to the Director General of Fair Trading and the Secretary of State for Trade and Industry.

monopolistic competition A market situation where a large number of firms produce similar but not identical products. There is relatively easy entry into the industry.

monopoly A market structure where a single supplier dominates the market.

Mortgage Interest Relief at Source (MIRAS) This is a subsidy to those who take out a mortgage to buy a home. The mortgage holders get tax relief on the interest paid for the loan, but there is a ceiling on the size of the loan eligible for this subsidy—currently £30,000. Since 1991 the amount of relief is standard regardless of income. The standard rate will fall from 25 per cent to 20 per cent in 1994, and to 15 percent in 1995.

multi-agency The appointment of two or more competing agents to dispose of the same property. Only the successful agent is rewarded with a commission, consequently the risks (from the agents' perspective) and fees are higher.

multiplier The number by which an initial injection into an economy must be multiplied to find the eventual change in national income. Mathematically, it is the reciprocal of the MPL, where MPL is the marginal propensity to leak.

national income A generic term for all that is produced, earned and spent in a country during one year. Strictly speaking it should be GNP minus capital depreciation.

national income accounting A measurement system used to estimate national income and its components. This is one approach to measuring an economy's aggregate performance.

nationalisation The taking into public ownership of some part, or all, of an economic activity previously located in the private sector.

nationalised industries Examples of these vary from time to time and country to country. Basically they involve the government owning and running an industry, the products of which are sold through the market and priced accordingly.

natural monopoly The peculiar characteristics of an industry that is best suited to production through one firm only. Such situations arise when production requires extremely large capital investments.

negative equity This describes a situation in which the value of someone's home has fallen below the value of his or her mortgage, approximately 1 million people were in this position during 1993.

neutral equilibrium A theoretical concept closely associated with a two-sector economy where the established levels of activity persist forever, since there are no pressures for change.

nominal rate of interest The market rate of interest that is expressed in terms of today's pounds.

nominal terms The current prices that we observe in today's market, without any adjustment for inflation.

normal goods Goods for which demand increases as income increases. Most goods that we deal with are normal.

normal profit The minimum rate of profit necessary to ensure that a sufficient number of people will be prepared to undertake risks and organise production. More formally, it is the normal rate of return to investment—which will differ from industry to industry.

normative economics Analysis involving value–judgements about economic policies; relates to whether things are good or bad. A statement of *what ought to be*.

notes and coins The currency of a nation, normally referred to as cash.

novation A term coined during the early 1990s to describe a client-led contractual bonding between an architect and building contractor. *See* **design and build**

occupationally immobile *see* **mobility of labour**
OECD The Organisation for Economic Cooperation and Development. This could be regarded as a club comprising all the capitalist countries as members who discuss together economic issues of mutual interest. In fact the OECD has 24 member countries, including Australia, Europe, Japan, the United States and Canada. The organisation's offices are based in Paris and it produces various economic publications each year, eg environmental indicators.
OFFER *See* **Office of Electricity Generation**
Office of Electricity Generation This office is funded by government to regulate the privatised generators of electricity, eg Powergen and National Power.
Office of Fair Trading This government agency was established in 1973. Since then it has acquired the acronym OFT. Its purpose is to protect consumer interests. *See also* **MMC**
Office of Gas Supply This office is funded by government to regulate the privatised gas industry.
Office of Population, Censuses and Surveys (OPCS) A government agency responsible for processing data on demographic, economic and social issues within the UK. Data has been collected every ten years since 1801. Obviously the nature of the questions has changed as society has evolved. For example, Scotland is now processed separately from England and Wales.
Office of Telecommunications This office is funded by government to regulate the activities of those involved in telecommunications, for example BT and Mercury.
Office of Water Services This government-funded office regulates the privatised water authorities.
official intervention Sales and purchases of currency by central banks.
OFGAS *see* **Office of Gas Supply**
OFTEL *see* **Office of Telecommunications**
OFWAT *see* **Office of Water Services**
oligopolistic *see* **oligopoly**
oligopoly A situation in which a large part of the market is supplied by a small number of firms. The firms may behave as if they are interdependent.
on-demand bond *see* **performance bond**
OPEC *see* **Organisation of Petroleum Exporting Countries**

open market value This is a common basis of valuation as it represents what a willing seller might expect to obtain given a reasonable time to negotiate the sale. The concept specifically excludes consideration of what a buyer with a special interest might pay.

opportunity cost The highest-valued alternative that must be sacrificed to obtain something else.

Organisation of Petroleum Exporting Countries This is a group of 13 petroleum-producing nations. The organisation was formed in 1960, to control supply and prices; it is an example of a cartel.

parent company guarantee *see* **guarantee**
passive solar design The sun can be utilized as an energy source, eg if a building is structured around an atrium or conservatory the fabric of the surrounding area will heat up and release warmth to neighbouring rooms. This is use of 'passive' solar energy, it contrasts with 'active' solar energy which is generated via a technological medium such as a photovoltaic cell.
PD forms These are official instruments used to administer any transfer or sale of land or property. The relevant *'particulars'* of the transaction must be *'delivered'* to the Stamp Office and Land Registry within 30 days of the transfer.
perestroika A Russian word meaning economic reconstruction. Gorbachov introduced such a programme in June 1987 when a transition towards a market-type socialist economy was first envisaged. Concepts such as the price mechanism and private property were employed.
perfect competition A market structure in which the decisions of buyers and sellers have no effect on market price.
perfectly competitive firm A firm that is such a small part of the total industry picture that it cannot affect the price of the product it sells.
perfectly elastic A supply or demand curve characterised by a reduction in quantity to zero when there is the slightest increase or decrease in price, ie producers and consumers respond 100 per cent to any change of price.
perfectly inelastic The characteristic of a supply or demand curve for which quantity supplied remains constant, no matter what happens to price. Producers and consumers are completely unresponsive to price changes.
performance bond A sum of money, guaranteed by a third party, available to be drawn upon if the contractor fails to carry out certain terms of the contract.
planning curve Another name for the long-run average cost curve.
planning gain This involves an agreement between a local authority and developer, permitting a developer to build in return for funding or organising some community benefit(s), eg providing social housing as an integral part of a commercial scheme.
planning horizon Another name for long-run cost curves. All inputs are variable during the planning period.
polluter pays principle A strategy devised during the 1980s where the emphasis to a cleaner environment was deemed to exist via the price mechanism by imposing instruments such as carbon tax. As the Secretary of State for the Environment expressed it in 1987 'The polluter must bear the cost of pollution'.
positive economics Analysis that is strictly limited to making either purely descriptive statements or scientific predictions; for example, if *A, then b*. A statement of *what is*. Positive statements can be checked against the evidence.
post-occupancy survey These involve questioning tenants about experiences relating to their property's performance. The survey is carried out after the tenants have been resident for a short period of time.

present value The value of the future amount expressed in today's pounds; the most that someone would pay today to receive a certain sum at some point in the future.

price-elastic demand When the price change of a good or service results in a more than proportionate change in quantity demanded it is said to be 'elastic'.

price elasticity A measurement of the responsiveness of the quantity demanded/supplied to a change in unit price.

price elasticity of supply A measurement of the responsiveness of the quantity produced for the market due to a change in price.

price index The cost of today's basket of goods expressed as a percentage of the cost of the same basket during a base year.

price-inelastic demand When a change in price results in a less than proportionate change in demand it is said to be inelastic.

price mechanism Prices are used as a signalling system between firms and households concerning the use of resources. Where the price mechanism operates there is a market economy, consequently the terms 'price' and 'market' are interchangeable.

price system An economic system in which (relative) prices are constantly changing to reflect changes in supply and demand for different commodities. The prices of those commodities are signals to everyone within the system about which is relatively expensive and what is relatively cheap.

price-taker A key characteristic of a perfectly competitive firm. A price-taker is a firm that must take the price of its product as given from those that it competes with.

principle of exclusion This simply means that anyone who does not pay will not be allowed to benefit from consuming a particular good or service—they will be left out.

private commercial A category used to consider privately funded commercial developments such as shops, offices and leisure facilities.

private goods Goods that can only be consumed by one individual at a time. Private goods are subject to the principle of exclusion.

private industrial A category used for considering the construction of privately funded developments like factories and warehouses. Since the privatisation of public utilities such as gas, water, electricity, the significance of this category has increased.

privatisation In very general terms this involves the transfer of assets from the public sector to the private sector.

privity of contract A legally binding agreement between landlord and tenant which persists throughout the entire term of the lease (eg 25 years) regardless of sublettings or assignments.

procurement A generic term used by professionals within the built environment to describe the general process of obtaining, acquiring or securing some property or land.

production function The relationship between inputs and output. A production function is a technological, not an economic, relationship.

production possibility curve A curve representing all possible combinations of total output that could be produced assuming (a) a fixed amount of productive resources and (b) efficient use of those resources.

productive efficiency The utilisation of the cheapest production technique for any given output rate; no inputs are wilfully wasted. Also known as 'technical' efficiency.

product markets In this market households are the buyers and businesses are the sellers of consumer goods (see figure 11.1).

profit The income generated by selling something for a higher price than was paid for it. In production, the income generated is the difference between total revenues received from consumers who purchase the goods and the total cost of producing those goods.

progressive income tax A tax system in which, as one earns more income, a higher percentage of the additional pounds is taxed. Put formally, the marginal tax rate exceeds the average tax rate as income rises.

public goods Goods for which the principles of exclusion and rivalry do not apply; they can be jointly consumed by many individuals simultaneously, at no additional cost and with no reduction in the quality or quantity of the provision concerned.

public (non-housing) A category used for considering the construction of roads, prisons and schools etc. In short, public sector works other than housing.

public sector The simplest definition is to include all forms of ownership by central and local government.

public sector borrowing requirement (PSBR) The shortfall between government expenditure and tax revenue. This position needs to be considered each year and financed if necessary. It refers to the combined funding for central and local government and public corporations.

quantity theory of money An age–old theory that changes in the price level are directly related to changes in the money supply. *See also* **Fisher's equation of exchange**

quasi-public goods Goods or services which by their nature could be made available for purchase by individuals, but which the state finds administratively more convenient to provide for all the nation (eg roads).

rate of discount *See* **discounting**

rational expectations hypothesis A theory that suggests that individuals combine all available information to form judgements about the future.

real rate of interest The rate of interest obtained by subtracting the rate of inflation from the nominal rate of interest.

real terms Measurement of economic values after adjustments have been made for changes in prices between years. Also known as real value.

recession A period of time during which the rate of growth of business activity is consistently less than its long-term trend, or is negative. If it is unduly prolonged a recession may become referred to as an economic depression.

regional policy Government grants and incentives made available to firms moving into certain designated areas. For example, up to 20 per cent of a project's cost is available and, on average, £6,000 of grant is made for every job created or protected. *See* figure 15.4 for some of the designated areas.

rent controls A law which imposes a price ceiling on private rented accommodation. Several examples exist since it was first introduced in 1915. The initial intention was to protect the tenant from the unscrupulous landlord; they distorted the market, however, and are no longer popular.

rental-only contracts This restricts customers to rental or lease terms, which can be anticompetitive where there are no alternative methods of acquiring those goods.

rental value The periodic return (monthly/yearly) that a property might reasonably be expected to command in the open market at a given time. For example, some office space during 1993 could be acquired for £10/sq ft.

research and development policy (R & D) These activities are undertaken by a wide range of institutions, in the UK approximately 50 per cent is government funded. In historical terms the UK has been strong in research but less effective in development.

residual method of valuation A method of determining the value of a property or land (site) which has development potential. It is calculated by deducting all the costs of development from the value of the completed project. The resultant figure is then adjusted back to the date of the valuation to give a capital value.

resource allocation The assignment of resources to their various uses. More specifically, it means determining what will be produced, how it will be produced, who will produce it and for whom it will be produced.

resources Inputs used in the production of the goods and services that we desire. Commonly categorised as land, labour, capital and entrepreneur (*see* separate dictionary entries for details). Also called factors of production.

retail money market A financial network based upon the deposits made by individuals and other customers with banks, building societies and other high-street financial intermediaries.

Retail Price Index (RPI) A statistical measure of a weighted average of prices of a representative set of goods and services purchased by the average household.

reverse yield gap This refers to a difference between long-term borrowing rates and the rental yield on property.

RIBA Is the principal professional body in the British Isles concerned with Architecture. It was established in 1834 and its full–blown title is Royal Institute of British Architects. Of the 27,000 members, 6,000 are now registered overseas.

RICS is the principal professional body in the British Isles concerned with surveying in its various guises. It was founded in 1868 and now has over 85,000 members across its seven different divisions. The acronym stands for Royal Institution of Chartered Surveyors.

Right to Buy Act This government legislation was passed in 1980 and gave council tenants of three years' standing (subsequently reduced to two) the legal power to acquire their houses at a discount of the market value.

scarcity A reference to the fact that at any point in time there exists only a finite amount of resources in relation to the infinite amount of 'wants' that people have for goods and services.

services Things purchased by consumers that do not have physical characteristics. Examples of services are those obtained from doctors, lawyers, dentists, educators, retailers, surveyors, wholesalers and welfare staff.

short-run That time-period in which a firm cannot alter its current size of plant.

sick building syndrome is a problem relating to the health of office workers. It is commonly defined by a group of symptoms which people experience while they are in specific buildings. The common symptoms being: irritated eyes, nose or throat; a dry or irritated skin occasionally with a rash or itching; headaches and lethargy. This problem has become widely acknowledged since 1980 and research has taken place in most European countries, the USA, Canada, Japan and Australia. No definite causes have yet been identified—but reference to mechanically ventilated buildings do seem to be prevalent in the literature reporting this syndrome.

site value The value of a developed property attributable to the land. This may be calculated on the assumption that the existing building(s) remain or that they have been cleared away for redevelopment.

social price The total price when *all* costs and benefits have been considered, ie when the private costs and benefits are added to the external costs and benefits.

special deposits Interest-earning accounts that are not active; held at the Bank of England on behalf of the commercial banks. The Bank of England requested these funds when it wished to curb liquidity.

stable equilibrium A situation in which, if there is a shock that disturbs the existing relationship between the forces of supply and demand, there will normally be self-corrective forces that automatically cause the disequilibrium to be remedied. Eventually another equilibrium situation will occur.

standard of deferred payment A quality of an asset that makes it desirable for use as a means of settling debts. *See also* **money**

store of value *see* **money**

structural rigidities These are obstacles within markets which prevent a swift response to changing forces of supply and demand. They are more prevalent in some markets than others, for example commercial leases affect the dynamics of the property market.

subnormal profits A rate of return that is below the rates being earned elsewhere. More commonly these would be referred to as a loss.

substitute goods Two goods are considered substitutes when one can be used in place of the other. A change in the price of one, therefore, causes a shift in demand for the other. For example, if the price of butter goes up, the demand for margarine will rise; if the price of butter goes down, the demand for margarine will decrease.

supernormal profits A rate of return that is greater than the rates being earned elsewhere. Also referred to as abnormal profits.

supply curve The graphic representation of the supply schedule; a line showing the supply schedule, which slopes upwards (has a positive slope).

supply-side economics This generally refers to government attempts at creating incentives for individuals and firms to increase productivity; that is, it is concerned with the level of aggregate supply.

tax bracket A specified interval of income to which a specific and unique marginal tax rate is applied. For example, a tax bracket may exist between £3,500 and £23,000.

tax burden The distribution of tax incidence within society as a whole.

theory of the firm A theory of how suppliers of any good/service should make choices—in the face of changing constraints.

third party These are the persons who are external to negotiations and activities between buyers and sellers. If you agree to buy a car with no brakes and then run me over, I am a third party to the deal struck between you and the seller of the car and my suffering is a negative externality.

time deposits Savings account balances and certificates of deposit held in commercial banks and building societies. The bank or building society can require, say, 30 days' notice of your intent to withdraw from your deposit account, but often this time requirement is waived.

total costs All the costs of a firm combined. For example, rent, payments to workers, interest on borrowed money, rates, material costs etc.

total expenditure The total monetary value of all the final goods and services bought in an economy during the year.

total income The total amount earned by the nation's resources (factors). National income, therefore, includes wages, rent, interest payments and profits that are received, respectively, by workers, landowners, capital owners and entrepreneurs.

total output The total value of all the final goods and services produced in the economy during the year.

total revenues The price per unit times total quantity sold.

trade-off A term relating to opportunity cost. In order to get a desired economic good, it is necessary to trade off some other desired economic good whenever we are in a world of scarcity. A trade-off involves a sacrifice, then, that must be made in order to obtain something.

transaction costs All of the costs associated with exchanging, including the informational costs of finding out price and quality, service record, durability etc, of a product, plus the cost of contracting and enforcing that contract.

transfer payments Money payments made by governments to individuals for which no services or goods are concurrently rendered. Examples are social security payments and student grants.

Treasury bill *see* **commercial bill**

unit–elastic demand If a percentage change in price leads to an identical percentage change in demand, then the product has an elasticity of unity, ie an elasticity of 1.

unit of account A measure by which prices and values are expressed; the common denominator of the price system, hence a central function of money.

upwards–only rent review This is a standard clause of commercial property leases. It permits the landlord to raise the rent at set intervals. A typical lease would run for 25 years with upward reviews every 5 years.

U-value A traditional measurement of heat loss. As the U-value coefficient moves nearer to zero the insulation quality of the material being measured improves. In other words, as the U-value lowers there is less heat lost through the fabric of the building.

variable costs Those costs that vary with the rate of production. They include wages paid to workers, the costs of materials and so on.

vendor A seller—especially one who sells land and/or property.

vertical equity is concerned with achieving 'social justice' by providing different benefits to people with different needs.

VTT (Valtion Teknillinen Tutkimuskeskus) The acronym for one of Finland's government-funded research centres. They maintain over 10 laboratories each with their own library, studying various forms of building technology and community development.

wage councils Bodies set up by the government to determine the pay of those in occupations which were traditionally poorly rewarded. At their peak these government bodies were fixing wages for over 1 million employees in trades such as retailing and agriculture.

wage-price spiral An inflationary process, whereby incomes and retail prices follow each other in an upward direction. *See figure 13.4.*

warehouse Premises used for bulk storage, pending onward transit in reorganised batches.

wholesale money market The financial network of funds derived from banks, pension funds and other institutions. Sometimes referred to as the *inter-bank market*.

years' purchase (YP) This is a valuer's method of expressing the price of an investment to the revenue it earns. It is done by multiplying the rental income by a factor called YP. YP is calculated by the formula $100 \div$ yield. YP is a similar concept to the price-earnings ratio used on the stock market.

Answers

Chapter 5

3.

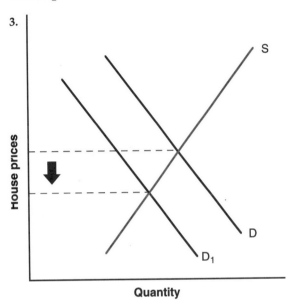

Increased interest rates will cause mortgage rates to rise. Consequently, the demand for houses will decline at each and every price. This is represented by the demand curve shifting to the left.

5.

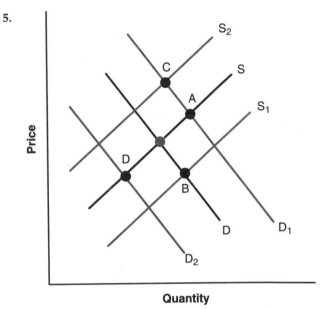

Note: For the answer to D there are two possibilities, as follows:

Point *D*   If investment on the stock exchange is seen as a substitute for speculative development, the demand curve will shift to the left.

Point *A*   If confidence and increased turnover on the stock-exchange is seen as increasing funds and/or expectations, the demand curve will shift to the right.

Chapter 6

1a. See figure 6.2 on p 40.

1c. Income seems to be the more important determinant. But neither price or income seem to be critical; they do not display consistent relationships.

5.

Price	Quantity Demanded	Total Sales Revenue	Elasticity Greater or Less Than One	Elastic Inelastic or Unitary?
13	7	91		
11	9	99	>1	Elastic
9	11	99	1	Unit
7	13	91	<1	Inelastic

Chapter 7

1a. See abbreviated notes in column heads in red in table below.

1c. No. You need information relating to revenue, before it is possible to identify a profit-maximising position.

1b.

Q Output (Col 1)	FC Fixed Costs (Col 2)	VC Variable Costs (Col 3)	TC Total Costs (Col 4) =Col 2+ Col 3	ATC Average Total Costs (Col 5) =Col 4 Col 1	MC Marginal Costs (Col 6) Δ TC Δ Q	AFC Average Fixed Costs (Col 7) =Col 2 Col 1	AVC Average Variable Costs (Col 8) =Col 3+ Col 1
0	100	0	100	-		-	-
10	100	100	200	20	10	10.00	10.00
20	100	180	280	14	8	5.00	9.00
30	100	230	330	11	5	3.30	7.60
40	100	260	360	9	3	2.50	6.50
50	100	350	450	9	9	2.00	7.00
60	100	500	600	10	15	1.60	8.30
70	100	670	770	11	17	1.40	9.50
80	100	860	960	12	19	1.25	10.75
90	100	1160	1260	14	30	1.10	12.80

Chapter 8

1a. In cases where average total cost exceeds the average revenue (ie the price in a perfectly competitive firm) losses are made. This occurs where marginal cost equals marginal revenue. The diagram will look as follows:

1b. Average revenue (AR) line would not be horizontal.

6.

Capital Outlay £	Annual Net Income £	Average Net Return %	Marginal Units of Capital Outlay £	Marginal Net Income £	Marginal Net Return %
200,000	40,000	20			
400,000	76,000	19	200,000	36,000	18
600,000	108,000	18	200,000	32,000	16
800,000	136,000	17	200,000	28,000	14
1,000,000	160,000	16	200,000	24,000	12
1,200,000	180,000	15	200,000	20,000	10
1,400,000	196,000	14	200,000	16,000	8

4.

Type of market	Number of firms	Freedom of entry	Nature of product eg homogeneous or differentiated	Examples from the built environment	Implication for competition policy
Perfect competition	Numerous	Yes	Homogenous		None. Firms price -take. They are fair.
Monopolistic competition	Many	Yes	Differentiated	1. Plumbers 2. Estate Agents	No problem. Firms are competitive.
Oligopoly	Few	Restricted	Differentiated	1. Cement 2. Plasterboard	Prices can be rigged
Monopoly	One	No	Unique		Have considerable control over price and quality.

Chapter 9

2. For some examples see figure 9.3. on p 74

3a.

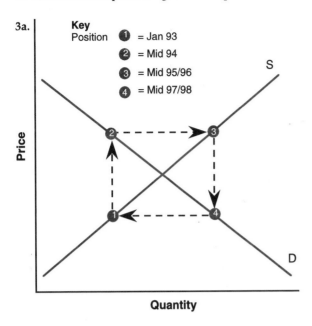

Key
Position ❶ = Jan 93
❷ = Mid 94
❸ = Mid 95/96
❹ = Mid 97/98

Price

Quantity

S

D

3b. i) increased unemployment
ii) higher interest rates

4a. Inconsecutive order: toll gate money, road building cost, reduced travelling time, noise pollution. (These are just examples, other possibilities exist.)

b. A

c. B, 25 million

5a. eg i) global warming due to increased carbon dioxide emissions
ii) the beauty of the English countryside
iii) death of rare animals.

b. eg i) road accidents
ii) reduced travelling times

These would be expressed in money terms on the principle of opportunity cost.

Chapter 10

5. **B** (the level of unemployment falls)

Chapter 11

1. **Figure 11.5: A model of income flows**

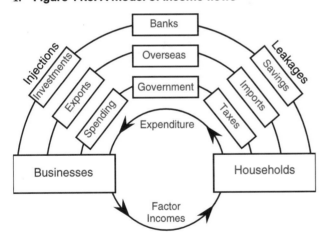

Injections
Investments
Exports
Spending
Banks
Overseas
Government
Expenditure
Leakages
Savings
Imports
Taxes

Businesses

Households

Factor Incomes

2e. Yes

3a. 20 percent
b. New commercial buildings, new dwellings, vehicles and machinery.
c. 10.97 percent (including transfer costs).
10.1 percent (excluding transfer costs).
d. Less than 10 percent
e. 16.5 percent public sector and 83.5 percent private sector.
f. Repairs and maintenance of existing property, commercial lettings, do-it-yourself decorating etc.

4. D

5. B

Chapter 12

1a. Consumer expenditure + government expenditure + investment expenditure + *net export expenditure (ie exports-imports) = aggregate demand*

3. D

4. Calendar:

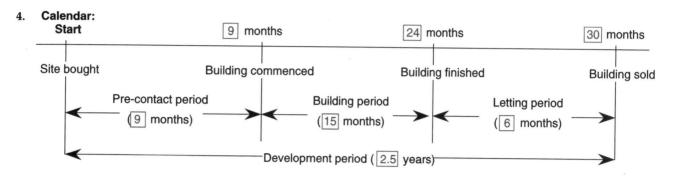

Chapter 13

1. The statement explains a cause, it does not say what inflation is. Definitions should be 'cause'–free.

2.

Cause	Cure
Demand-pull inflation	Money supply control
Cost-push inflation	Price and incomes policy

3b. 1930: Deflation, 1970: Inflation, 1980: Disinflation, 1990: Low inflation.

7a. 60 percent, b) 33.3 percent, c) -25 percent

8a. Building cost (495 percent increase compared to 480 percent).
b. Industrialisation etc.
c. Quality
d. No. Index numbers allow comparisons, without specifying the units to which they refer.

Chapter 14

2. There are many possibilities, according to the textbook one looks in, the following are six examples:

Manages exchange rate

Supervises monetary sector

Acts as lender of last resort

Bankers' bank

Government's Bank

Attempts to control money supply

5. (1) deregulation
(2) house price inflation
(3) equity withdrawal
(4) increased interest rates
(5) negative equity

3.

Liabilities	Assets
Interest-bearing accounts	Banks' balances with Bank of England
Deposit account	Loans to commercial property developers
Share Capital	Bank buildings

Index

absolute terms *see* nominal terms
accounting profits   50
adaptive-expectations hypothesis   103
  also see Dictionary
advanced building information service   38
  also see Dictionary
AFC *see* average fixed costs
aggregate demand   95, 97, 99, 102
  also see Dictionary
aggregate demand curve   96-97
aggregate supply   96-99
  also see Dictionary
aggregate supply curve   96-98
agriculture   46-47, 52
allocative efficiency   12
  also see Dictionary
appreciation   22
  also see Dictionary
architects   16, 38, 59, 79
ARCUK (Architects Registration Council of the UK)   79
assets   110-111
  also see Dictionary
ATC *see* average total costs
AVC *see* average variable costs
average cost curves   53-56
average costs *see* average fixed costs
average fixed costs (AFC)   53-54
  also see Dictionary
average total costs (ATC)   53-54
  also see Dictionary
average variable costs (AVC)   53-54
  also see Dictionary

balance of payments   84
  also see Dictionary
balances with Bank of England   111
  also see Dictionary
bank bills *see* commercial bills
Bank of England   85, 112-113
  intervention in foreign exchange market   22-23
  see also central bank
bankers' bank *see* Bank of England
banks   6, 110-112, 114
  see also Bank of England
barriers to entry   73
  also see Dictionary
base year   101-102
  also see Dictionary
benefits   76
  external *see* externalities
bills *see* commercial bills
Black Wednesday   23
  also see Dictionary
'blue book' *see* United Kingdom National Accounts
booms   71, 81, 83-84
  also see Dictionary
broad measures   109
Building Cost & Information Service (BCIS)   102, 105
  also see Dictionary
building industry *see* construction industry
building regulations   28, 129-130
  also see Dictionary
Building Research Establishment (BRE)   124, 130
  also see Dictionary
  see also VTT

building societies   102, 112-113. 115-116, 118
  also see Dictionary
built environment   6, 65, 104
business cycles   6, 83
  also see Dictionary
business expansion scheme   98
  also see Dictionary
business park   31

capital   1, 2, 49, 89
  also see Dictionary
capital consumption *see* depreciation
capital gains   93
  also see Dictionary
capital goods   4-5
  also see Dictionary
capital values   100, 116-117
  also see Dictionary
capitalist economy   9-10
cartel(s)   69
  also see Dictionary
  cement industry   69
cash, *see* notes and coins
CBA *see* cost-benefit analysis
CBI *see* Confederation of British Industry
CD *see* certificate of deposit
cement industry   69, 130
central bank   23, 111-112
  also see Dictionary
Central Statistical Office *see* CSO
centrally planned (model)   9-11
  also see Dictionary
certificate of deposit (CD)   111
  also see Dictionary
ceteris paribus   18-19, 27, 28
  also see Dictionary
chaos theory   94
  also see Dictionary
church commissioners   119
circular flow model   89-92
  also see Dictionary
cobweb theorem   71-72
  also see Dictionary
Coleman, A.   126
collateral *see* property
  also see Dictionary
collusion   72
  also see Dictionary
command economy   10, 11, 15
'commanding heights' of the economy   121
commercial bank(s)   110-112
  also see Dictionary
commercial bills   111
  also see Dictionary
commercial economies   56
commercial property   81, 98, 100, 107, 112-114, 116
  cycles *see* property cycle leases
competition   34, 72-73, 122
  see also monopolistic competition; perfect competition
competition policy   73
  also see Dictionary
complementary goods   28
  also see Dictionary

Confederation of British Industry (CBI)   113
  also see Dictionary
conservative policy   13, 127
constant returns to scale   56
  also see Dictionary
construction industry   38, 71-72, 91, 100, 121
Construction Industry Council (CIC)   79
  also see Dictionary
consumer expenditure   89, 97, 99
consumer goods   4-5
  also see Dictionary
consumer sovereignty   9
  also see Dictionary
contracting-out   122
  also see Dictionary
cost-benefit analysis   73-74
  also see Dictionary
cost-push inflation   102-103
  also see Dictionary
council housing see local authority
credit multiplier   111
  also see Dictionary
crowding out   121
  also see Dictionary
CSO (Central Statistical Office)   90
  also see Dictionary
current accounts see sight deposits
current prices   72
  see also nominal terms
current-account   84
cycles see business cycles and property

defensible space   126
deficits   23, 88
  balance of payments   84
  see also PSBR
deflation   101
demand   27-29
  elasticity   39
  equation   29
  function   29
  also see Dictionary
  law of   27
  also see Dictionary
  see also effective demand
demand curve   27-29, 67
  see also aggregate demand curve
demand management   91, 95, 97-98
  also see Dictionary
demand-pull inflation   102-103
  also see Dictionary
demand schedule   18
  also see Dictionary
demand-side   95
  also see Dictionary
demographic data   132
depreciated replacement cost (DRC)   131
  also see Dictionary
depreciation   53
  also see Dictionary
depressions see recession
deregulation   11, 73, 79, 98, 115, 128
  also see Dictionary
design and build   59
  also see Dictionary
design warranties   115
  also see Dictionary
developer's profit   68
  also see Dictionary
diminishing marginal returns see law of diminishing (marginal)
  returns
direct relationship   18
  also see Dictionary
discount houses   111
  also see Dictionary
discounted cash flow see discounting
discounting   117
  also see Dictionary
diseconomies of scale   56
  also see Dictionary
disinflation   101
  also see Dictionary

distribution of income   72, 73
do-it-yourself-shared ownership (DIYSO)   127

eaves height   129
  also see Dictionary
economic forecasting   85-86, 88
economic goods   2
  also see Dictionary
economic growth   84, 85, 90
  also see Dictionary
economic indicators   83-84
economic profit(s)   49-50
economic system(s)   9-11, 15, 121
  also see Dictionary
economics   2, 5
  also see Dictionary
economies of scale   55-56
  also see Dictionary
effective demand   30
  also see Dictionary
efficiency   12, 64, 71, 77
  see also allocative and productive efficiency
elasticity   39-47, 72
  demand and supply   39-44
  and total revenue   41
EMF see European Monetary Fund
employment   38, 83, 91, 96, 102
EMS (European Monetary System) see Exchange Rate Mechanism
endogenous variables   85
  also see Dictionary
energy saving initiatives   36, 102, 124, 129
enterprise culture   114
  also see Dictionary
entrepreneurs, entrepreneurship   2, 49-50
  also see Dictionary
environmental policy   123-124
  also see Dictionary
equation of exchange see fisher equation
equilibrium   19, 65, 84, 90-91
  also see Dictionary
equilibrium price   19-20, 35, 65
  also see Dictionary
equity see vertical and horizontal
equity withdrawal   93, 112
  also see Dictionary
ERM see Exchange Rate Mechanism
essay questions   125-126
European MonetaryFund (EMF)   23
  also see Dictionary
Exchange Rate Mechanism (ERM)   22-23
  also see Dictionary
exchange rates   22-23
excludability   74
  see also principle of exclusion
exogenous variables   85
  also see Dictionary
expectations   28, 34, 40, 103-105, 113
  see also adaptive expectations and rational expectations
explicit costs see private costs
exports   90, 95-96
external benefits and costs see externalities
external economies of scale   56
  also see Dictionary
externalities/externality   72-76, 79
  also see Dictionary

factor markets   89
  also see Dictionary
factors of production   1
  also see Dictionary
farming see agriculture
financial economies   56
financial institutions
  financial intermediaries   110-112, 115
  also see Dictionary
fine-tune   95
  also see Dictionary
firm(s) see also theory of the firm
fiscal policies   85
Fisher equation of exchange   110
  also see Dictionary

fixed costs   53
  also see Dictionary
forecasting, economic   85-86, 88
foreign exchange
  intervention by Bank of England   23
foreign exchange market   22-23
  also see Dictionary
free enterprise   9
  also see Dictionary
free good   2
  also see Dictionary
free market model   9-10
  also see Dictionary
free-rider problem   71
Friedman, M.   74, 110
full employment   83, 91, 96-97, 99
full repairing and insuring lease   68, 70
  also see Dictionary

GDP see gross domestic product
geographically immobile labour see mobility of labour
GNP see gross national product
goods
  capital and consumer   4
  economic and free   2
  normal and inferior   27
  substitutes and complimentary   28
government   7, 9-11, 28, 34
  in circular flow model   90
  intervention   73, 77, 98
  role in economy   83-88, 121-122
government expenditures in GDP   95-96
government failure   77, 121
  also see Dictionary
graphic analysis   3, 18
graveyard management   57-58
greenhouse gas   130
gross domestic fixed capital formation   93
  also see Dictionary
gross domestic product (GDP)   84, 90, 93
  also see Dictionary
gross national product (GNP)   90
  also see Dictionary
growth see economic growth
guarantee   115
  also see Dictionary

headline inflation rate   101
  also see Dictionary
high street bank see commercial bank
homogeneous products   61
horizontal equity   12
  also see Dictionary
hot money   22
  also see Dictionary
housing   40, 42, 45-47, 73, 79, 102
  associations   59, 67-68, 127
  Conservative policy   13, 86-87, 98
  energy efficient   129
  equity withdrawal   93, 112
  Government initiatives   86-87, 127
  inner city estates   126
  intermediate macroeconomic target   99
    also see Dictionary
  Labour policy   13-14
  local authority (council)   80, 123
  market   15, 40, 98, 128
  market failure   80
  market iniatives   128
  prices   17, 106, 108, 116
  tenure   127, 128
human capital   1
  also see Dictionary
human resources   1

immobility see mobility of labour
income   30
  circular flow   89
  determinant of demand   27
  see also distribution of income; national income
income elasticity of demand   42
  also see Dictionary

income-elastic demand   42
  also see Dictionary
income-inelastic demand   42
  also see Dictionary
income redistribution see distribution of income
incomes policies see prices and incomes policies
income tax   73, 75, 98
increasing costs, law see law of increasing opportunity costs
indemnity insurance   15, 30
  also see Dictionary
index numbers   101, 106
  also see Dictionary
  commercial property index   102
  HARP index   106
  house price index   102
  tender price index   105
  see also retail price index
indicators
  economic   83-84
industry
  long-run situation   65
inferior good(s)   27
  also see Dictionary
inflation   101-108
  also see Dictionary
  causes   102-103
  cures   103
  definition   101
  disinflation   101
    also see Dictionary
  economic indicator   83
  headline rate   101
    also see Dictionary
  low inflation   101
    also see Dictionary
  measurement   101-102
  menu cost   101
    also see Dictionary
  trend   84, 101
  see also wage-price spiral and expectations
inflationary gap   97
  also see Dictionary
infrastructure   79, 94, 130
initial yield   68
  also see Dictionary
injections   90-92
  also see Dictionary
institutional investor   70
institutional lease   70
interest rate(s)   112-114
  also see Dictionary
  determination of rates   113, 118
  effect on inflation   106, 108
  monetary policy   85, 103, 113
  see also real rate of interest
intermediate macroeconomic target   98, 99
  also see Dictionary
internal costs see private costs
internal economies/diseconomies of scale   56
internal rate of return (IRR)   118
  also see Dictionary
international transactions   22-23, 84, 95
inverse relationship   18
  also see Dictionary
investment
  also see Dictionary
  bank asset   111
  in circular flow   90
  in aggregate demand   95-96

joint-stock banks see commercial bank
Juglar   83

Keynesian economics   91-92, 95-96, 114
  demand management   95-97
  fiscal policy   85
  multiplier   91
  also see Dictionary

labour   1, 49
  also see Dictionary
  see also mobility of labour

_ see long-run average cost curve(s)

_affer curve   75

land   1
  also see Dictionary
  price determination   46

law of demand   27
  also see Dictionary

law of diminishing (marginal) returns   51-53
  also see Dictionary

law of increasing opportunity costs   4, 36
  also see Dictionary

law of supply   33
  also see Dictionary

law of variable proportions   *see* law of diminishing (marginal)
  returns

leakages   90-91
  also see Dictionary

liabilities   110, 111
  also see Dictionary

liquidity   110-111, 113
  also see Dictionary

local authority bills   *see* commercial bills

local authority
  accommodation   80, 123
  tenants   127, 128

long run   50-51
  also see Dictionary

long-run average cost curve(s) (LAC)   55-56
  also see Dictionary

Low inflation   101
  also see Dictionary

M0   109
M2   109
M4   109
M5   109

Macroeconomic objectives   83-85
  also see Dictionary

macroeconomics   5-6, 12, 83-85, 114, 123-124
  also see Dictionary

managerial economies   56

manufactured resources   1

marginal cost(s) (MC)   54, 62-65
  also see Dictionary

marginal physical product   52
  also see Dictionary

marginal propensity to leak (MPL)   91
  also see Dictionary

marginal revenue (MR)   62-64
  also see Dictionary

market(s)   15, 17-25, 112, 113, 118
  also see Dictionary

market-based instruments   75
  also see Dictionary   .

market-clearing price   *see* equilibrium price

market economy   10, 17-18
  also see Dictionary

market failure   20, 71-76, 81
  also see Dictionary

market rate of interest   *see* nominal rate of interest

market mechanism   17

market structures   61, 66
  also see Dictionary
  see also types of competition

market supply schedule   33
  also see Dictionary

maximum price legislation   *see* rent control
  also see Dictionary

MC   *see* marginal cost(s)

medium of exchange   *see* money

menu costs   101
  also see Dictionary

merit good   73
  also see Dictionary

microeconomics   5-6
  also see Dictionary

minimum efficient scale   56
  also see Dictionary

MIRAS   *see* Mortgage Interest Relief at Source

mixed economy   11
  also see Dictionary

MMC   *see* Monopolies and Mergers Commission

mobility of labour   124, 128
  also see Dictionary

models   9-11
  also see Dictionary
  circular flow model   89-90
  Treasury model   85, 99

monetarism, monetarists   103, 109
  also see Dictionary

monetary policy   85, 113

money   109
  also see Dictionary

money at call   111
  also see Dictionary

money multiplier   *see* credit multiplier

money supply   103, 109-110
  also see Dictionary

money values   *see* nominal terms

Monopolies and Mergers Commission (MMC)   73
  also see Dictionary

monopolistic competition   66
  also see Dictionary

monopoly   61
  also see Dictionary

mortgages   30
  change in rates   118-119
  foreign currency   24
  indemnity insurance   15, 30
  mortgage interest relief at source (MIRAS)   86-87
  also see Dictionary

MPL   *see* marginal propensity to leak

MR   *see* marginal revenue

multi-agency   24
  also see Dictionary

multiplier   91
  also see Dictionary
  see also credit multiplier

narrow measures   109

national income   90
  also see Dictionary

national Income accounting   90, 93, 95-96
  also see Dictionary

nationalised industries   121-122
  also see Dictionary

nationalisation   121
  also see Dictionary

natural monopoly   121
  also see Dictionary

near-public goods   *see* quasi public-goods

negative equity   116
  also see Dictionary

negative externalities   72-73, 74, 78

negative income elasticity   42

neutral equilibrium   90
  also see Dictionary

nominal terms   71, 116
  also see Dictionary

nominal rate of interest   108, 118
  also see Dictionary

normal goods   27
  also see Dictionary

normal profit   49
  also see Dictionary

normal rate of return (NROR)   49-50

normative economics   5
  also see Dictionary

notes and coins   109, 111
  also see Dictionary

novation   59
  also see Dictionary

NROR   *see* normal rate of return

occupationally immobile labour   *see* mobility of labour

OECD (Organisation for Economic Cooperation and
  Development)   84
  also see Dictionary

OFFER   123
  also see Dictionary

Office of Fair Trading (OFT)   57-58, 69, 73
  also see Dictionary

official intervention   22
  also see Dictionary

OFGAS   123
  also see Dictionary

OFTEL   123
  also see Dictionary

OFWAT   123
  also see Dictionary
oligopoly/oligopolistic   70
  also see Dictionary
on-demand bonds   115
  also see Dictionary
OPCS (Office of Populations, Censuses and Surveys)   133
  also see Dictionary
OPEC (Organisation of Petroleum Exporting Countries)   102
  also see Dictionary
open-market value   131
  also see Dictionary
opportunity cost(s)   2, 49-50
  also see Dictionary
Organisation for Economic Cooperation and Development *see*
  OECD
Organisation of Petroleum Exporting Countries *see* OPEC
other things being equal *see* ceteris paribus

Paish, F.   97, 114
parent company guarantees   115
particulars delivered *see* PD Forms
passive solar design   102
  also see Dictionary
PD Forms   40
  also see Dictionary
perestroika   11, 121
  also see Dictionary
perfect competition   61-62, 65, 66
  also see Dictionary
perfectly competitive firm   61
  also see Dictionary
perfectly elastic (demand/supply)   43-44
  also see Dictionary
perfectly inelastic   43-44
  also see Dictionary
performance bonds   115
  also see Dictionary
planned economy *see* command economy
planning curve   55
  also see Dictionary
planning gain   79
  also see Dictionary
planning horizon   55
  also see Dictionary
polluter pays principle   75
  also see Dictionary
population census   132-133
positive economics   5
  also see Dictionary
positive externalities   72-73, 78
post-occupancy evaluation/survey   129
  also see Dictionary
potential output   97
present value   117
  also see Dictionary
price changes *see* index numbers
price elastic demand   39
  also see Dictionary
price elasticity   43-44
  also see Dictionary
price elasticity of supply   42-43
  also see Dictionary
Price Index   101
  also see Dictionary
price-inelastic demand   39
  also see Dictionary
price mechanism   9, 17-25
  also see Dictionary
price system   17-25
  also see Dictionary
price taker(s)   61
  also see Dictionary
price-wage spiral *see* wage-price spiral
Prices and Incomes Policies   103
principle of exclusion   74
  also see Dictionary
private commercial   38
  also see Dictionary
private costs   73, 74
private goods   73, 121
  also see Dictionary

private industrial   38
  also see Dictionary
private rented sector   80, 127, 128
private sector   121, 122-124, 127, 133
privatisation   11, 122-123, 130, 131
  also see Dictionary
privity of contract   81, 117
  also see Dictionary
procurement   16, 59
  also see Dictionary
production function   51
  also see Dictionary
production possibility curve   3-4
  also see Dictionary
productive efficiency   12
  also see Dictionary
product markets   17
  also see Dictionary
profit(s)   49-50
  also see Dictionary
profit-maximising   50, 62-64, 68, 78
profit-maximising rate of production   62-64
profitability versus liquidity   110
progressive income tax   73
  also see Dictionary
property   49
  as collateral   112
  cycle   6, 47, 71-72, 81, 83
  finance   112, 116
  international   22-23
  leases   70, 81, 107, 116-117
  valuation   36-37, 68, 108, 131
PSBR see public sector borrowing requirement
public expenditure   91, 94, 122
  see also transfer payments
public goods   74
  also see Dictionary
public (non housing)   38
  also see Dictionary
public ownership see nationalisation
public sector   121, 122-125, 127, 131
  also see Dictionary
public sector borrowing requirement (PSBR)   85, 88, 122
  also see Dictionary
public spending see public expenditure
pubs   70

quantity theory of money   110
  also see Dictionary
quasi-public goods   74
  also see Dictionary

R & D (research and development) policy   124
  also see Dictionary
rate of discount *see* discounting
rational expectations hypothesis   104
  also see Dictionary
real rate of interest   108
  also see Dictionary
real terms   81, 108
  also see Dictionary
recession(s)   83, 84, 90
  also see Dictionary
regional policy   124
  also see Dictionary
regional unemployment   124
regulations   129-130
  see also deregulation
rent control   76, 80
  also see Dictionary
  see also upwards only rent reviews
rent to-mortgage scheme   127
rental value   68, 81, 100, 114
  also see Dictionary
rented housing   43, 80, 123, 127, 128
research and development *see* R & D
residual method (of valuation)   68
  also see Dictionary
resource allocation   9-12
  also see Dictionary
resources   1-2
  also see Dictionary

restrictions on entry *see* barriers to entry
retail money market   118
  also see Dictionary
Retail Price Index (RPI)   83, 102
  also see Dictionary
reverse yield gap   114
  also see Dictionary
RIBA (Royal Institute of British Architects)   16, 79
  also see Dictionary
RICS (Royal Institution of Chartered Surveyors)   36-37, 123
  also see Dictionary
Right to Buy Act (1980)   80, 123, 127
  also see Dictionary
risk-bearing economies   56
road building   78, 94, 130
RPI *see* Retail Price Index

saving(s)   90, 118
scarcity   1, 2, 4-5
  also see Dictionary
services   7, 38, 84
  also see Dictionary
shifts vs. movements   28, 34
short run   43, 50-51
  also see Dictionary
short-run average cost curves   53-55
sick building syndrome   28, 58-59
  also see Dictionary
sight deposits   110
site value   67
  also see Dictionary
Smith, Adam   72, 74
social price   73
  also see Dictionary
special deposits   112
  also see Dictionary
speculation, speculators   22-23, 31, 36
spillovers *see* externalities
stable equilibrium   19
  also see Dictionary
standard of deferred payment   109
  also see Dictionary
standard of value *see* unit of account
store of value *see* money
straight-line production possibilities curve   3
structural rigidities   71, 98
  also see Dictionary
subnormal profits   65
  also see Dictionary
substitute good   28
  also see Dictionary
Sunday trading   133
supernormal profits   64
  also see Dictionary
supply   33-38
  elasticity   42-43
  law of   33
  also see Dictionary
  see also aggregate supply
supply curve   19, 33, 35
  also see Dictionary
  see also aggregate supply curve
supply elasticity *see* price elasticity of supply
supply-side   95-98
  also see Dictionary

taxation, tax(es)   74, 75-76, 85, 86-87
tax bracket   98
  also see Dictionary
tax burden   80
  also see Dictionary
technical economies   56
theories, *see* law of ... models

theory of the firm   49-65
  also see Dictionary
third parties/third party   72-73
  also see Dictionary
tied tenants   70
time deposits   111
  also see Dictionary
time-lags   40, 43, 71-72, 86, 99, 114
total costs   53-54, 64
  also see Dictionary
total expenditure   89, 95
  also see Dictionary
total fixed costs   53
total income   89, 90
  also see Dictionary
total output   89
  also see Dictionary
total revenues   62
  also see Dictionary
  and elasticity   41
total variable costs   53
trade cycle *see* business cycles &/or property
trade-off(s)   3, 4, 79, 85
  also see Dictionary
transaction costs   24
  also see Dictionary
transfer payments   73, 122
  also see Dictionary
Treasury bill(s) *see* commercial bill
Treasury model   85, 99
types of competition   66

UBR *see* Uniform Business Rates
unemployment   83, 84, 91, 95, 124
uniform business rates   87
unit elastic demand   39
  also see Dictionary
units of account   109
  also see Dictionary
United Kingdom National Accounts   90, 93
upward only rent-review   81, 107, 116-117
  also see Dictionary
'u' value   51, 130
  also see Dictionary

valuation   36-37, 68, 104, 108, 131
value added tax (VAT)   34, 74, 75, 129
value-judgements   5, 27
variable costs   53
  also see Dictionary
VAT *see* value added tax
vendor   9
  also see Dictionary
vertical equity   12
  also see Dictionary
VTT   132
  also see Dictionary

Wage Councils   98
  also see Dictionary
wage-price spiral   104
  also see Dictionary
warehouse   129
  also see Dictionary
wealth of nations   7, 18
wholesale money market   118
  also see Dictionary
withdrawals *see* leakages

years purchase   68
  also see Dictionary